# TRIPPING IN AMERICA

# TRIPPING IN AMERICA

## Off the Beaten Track !!

*Who is always love, AM*

BILL THOMAS

*To MA Roach & the Doctor wishing you many special moments throughout your journey. Know always AM is in H.P. and cares deeply for you both !! — call if ever in need of hand or conversation.*

*TKs for the memories we shared.*

## CHILTON BOOK COMPANY

RADNOR, PENNSYLVANIA

Copyright © 1974 by Bill Thomas
First Edition    All Rights Reserved
Published in Radnor, Pa., by Chilton Book Company
and simultaneously in Ontario, Canada,
by Thomas Nelson & Sons, Ltd.
Designed by William E. Lickfield
Manufactured in the United States of America

Library of Congress Cataloging in Publication Data

Thomas, Bill, 1934-
  Tripping in America.

  1. United States—Description and travel—1960-
—Guide-books.  2. United States—Miscellanea.
I. Title.
E169.02.T49 1974      917.3'04'924      74-1076
ISBN 0-8019-5772-9
ISBN 0-8019-5970-5 (pbk.)

# CONTENTS

# INTRODUCTION

In the center of Australia is a sweeping expanse of unforgettable terrain, little known and little explored, called the Outback. A similar area of indefinable boundaries exists in the United States—sometimes described as an intangible quality—that is also little explored and little known. Yet it's the essence and the backbone of a fun-loving nation. I like to call it "Offbeat America."

When I was a fledgling reporter on a small Kentucky newspaper, I became keenly aware of the "offbeat" and was fascinated by the exploration and discovery of such events and places. At first, I felt they were small gems sporadically scattered across the country. But as I began to broaden my own horizons, I found they were more than that; they were an integral part of the American way of life.

At that time, it appeared many such attractions were hardly noticed by the general public. A few local people were interested in their own community events, but 30 or 40 miles down the road scarcely anyone gave them a fleeting thought. Of course, during that period from the early 1950s to the 1970s, more than 75 percent of the American people began to broaden their horizons, to travel more extensively. With a booming economy, finer automobiles and more recreational vehicles plus a major network of multilane superhighways, the average family became more willing to travel great distances.

Thus the pendulum of interest has reversed itself, and many more Americans have become concerned with the details of life, the local color and prevailing atmosphere that gives our nation character. Big name events and places have slipped out of vogue. Travelers realize that a visit to Niagara Falls or New Orleans' French Quarter, or an elevator ride to the top of the Empire State Building or a stroll around San Francisco's Fisherman's Wharf leaves a lot to be desired. One should not turn wholly away from such places, of course, for they have earned a certain tenure that keeps them high on the monumental pedestal of our society. But after one goes there, what does he do for an encore?

The answer to that question lies, of course, in America's outback. Here are the events and the places that define a way of life, events and places that prevent us from becoming a "paper doll" society. Here are the attractions that aesthetically bind together a nation and give it flavor.

Many Americans of considerable means have traveled the world looking in vain for the ingredients of happiness they might have found within their own country. Some of these ingredients are deeply entrenched, dating to the days when this land was first settled, to the westward movement, to ethnic groups that have miraculously retained a bit of their own colorful heritage. The National Basque Festival in Nevada is such an event; Oklahoma's Cow Chip Throwing Contest is strongly bound to the days when that territory was first settled by hardy pioneers.

Every time I travel across America, I become more and more aware that the United States possesses a wealth of material literally unknown to most of its own people. In doing research for this book, I found that even many state travel officials had not heard of some of the events and places mentioned here, despite the fact that some of these attractions have existed for more than a quarter of a century. It's indeed wonderful that, during a time when we pride ourselves on instant electronic and printed communications, areas still exist in this country that one can actually discover for himself and explore at leisure.

There are plenty more events and places, other than those covered in this guide, still unexposed by publicity—and hopefully there always will be. But if you care to look into the heart and soul of America, to explore the backroads and listen and learn and experience, this book has been compiled both as a practical guide to aid you in your travels and as an entertaining compilation of people, places and things that you can enjoy from your armchair.

I don't intend to play down the wonders that are well-known and longstanding travel attractions in America, but instead to add spice to your itinerary, to entice you to look around the corner or down the street, to remove the icing from the cake and see what lies beneath. How many Americans are aware, for instance, that camel races are still held in the desert country of California, that old Ford trimotor airplanes daily serve the islands of Lake Erie, that small boys representing the states along the Mississippi River gather each year at Hannibal, Missouri, to paint Tom Sawyer's fence?

In North Carolina, some of the loudest voices in the nation gather annually for the National Hollerin' Contest; while down Mississippi way, the nation's best spitters congregate for the Tobacco Spitting Championships. In Texas and Louisiana, prison rodeos are held with inmates as performers; in Florida, there's a contest for worm fiddlers; and at Friendship, Indiana, men and women in period dress compete in the National Muzzleloading Rifle Association Championships. In Oregon, you can go underground to visit sea lions in their caves; and at Gaddy's Boarding House for Wild Geese in North Carolina, you can feed Canada honkers from your hand.

It's good to know such places and events still exist.

# TRIPPING IN AMERICA

# Alabama

## Coon Dogs, Old Fiddlers and Anvil Shoots

Coon Dog
Graveyard

In the northern part of the Yellowhammer State, you will find one of the world's most unusual monuments. South of the town of Cherokee, in the mountain lakes region of Alabama, there is a unique burying ground—the National Coon Dog Cemetery. Here are interred the remains of great coon dogs, which ran the woodlands, swamps and hills of the South in hot pursuit of one of the wild kingdom's most intelligent and elusive creatures—the raccoon. Any dog lover would fully appreciate a visit here; but only the owner of a beloved coon dog whose yodels and barks once led his master over many miles of dark terrain would fully understand it.

It all began during the Depression era with a dog named "Old Troope", a dog that continued to live for many years after his death in the memory of coon-hunting sportsmen everywhere. A cross between a birdsong and a red bone, the great red and white spotted hound stood 28 inches tall at the shoulder and weighed 90 pounds. Many great hounds come from this bloodline, but none compare with Old Troope. Bred in Mississippi, he was devoted to two masters during his lifetime; and it's said that, in the backwoods of Alabama, a nobler dog never lived. His second and final owner was Key Undersood, one of Alabama's most noted coon hunters and sportsmen, who on September 4, 1937, buried Old Troope at the head of Sugar Camp Creek where he had spent many hours playing his wit against the wily raccoon.

Since that time, there has existed an unwritten law which specifies this area as sacred ground for the royalty of the coon-hunting world. Before a dog can be eligible for inclusion, he must first of all be a coon dog. Secondly, during his lifetime, he must have acquired an indisputable reputation as a relentless and outstanding hunter and friend to man. Each year, sportsmen who have dogs buried in this tree-shaded cemetery reenact a Labor Day ritual of bringing flowers to decorate the graves. On the cemetery grounds is a replica of a tree snag. A raccoon on top peers down at two coon dogs, the mere sight of which is enough to bring tears to the eyes of dog lovers everywhere. In this secluded cemetery, there are many tangible reminders of man's dedication to his most loyal friend.

Ave Maria
Grotto

A few miles south of Cherokee and just off I-65 at Cullman, there is another man-made shrine—the re-creation in a single miniature city of all the great cathedrals, missions and churches from around the globe. Most of it is the work of one man, Brother Joseph Zoettl, a Benedictine monk, who spent almost half a century meticulously constructing in miniature and to scale a great collection of man's architectural monuments to his deity. Called the Ave Maria Grotto, the 4-acre shrine is located on the campus of Saint Bernard College.

Here the visitor can stand and view all the glory and majesty of past ages brought together in one spot by this patient genius. And since his death in 1961, local artisans have dedicated their efforts to preserving and perpetuating his work. The replicas range from celebrated European and middle Eastern cathedrals, shrines and churches to the California missions. The Grotto is open daily, with a small admission charge, from 7 A.M. to sunset.

Brother Joseph Zoettl, a Benedictine monk, labored nearly a lifetime creating miniature replicas of some of the world's greatest shrines and churches at Cullman, Alabama.

The city of Decatur, Alabama, is located more than 300 miles from the Gulf of Mexico and a great deal farther from any ocean. But that didn't prevent a group of residents from bringing a slice of it to their own backyard—Point Mallard Park. The result may be the only inland ocean created by man in all the western hemisphere.

The concept began when the Department of Interior and the Tennessee Valley Authority turned over to the city an unused 790-acre tract of forest land near the broad waters of Flint Creek and the Tennessee River. About the same time, an Ohio resident, J. Austin Smith, who had seen wave pools in Germany and Japan, visited Decatur and sold park planners on the idea of building a wave pool at Point Mallard.

The "ocean" is a fan-shaped pool, 8-feet deep at the narrow end. Alternating air blasts from high-speed pumps force the deep water upward and outward, resulting in a series of 3-foot waves which race down the pool's 180 feet. As they reach shallow water and flare out to fill the widening pool, breakers form and whitecaps slap against the "beach." Youngsters chase the hissing waves as they retreat, but turn tail as another comes along. And in deeper water, hundreds of swimmers happily battle the waves as they would at Virginia Beach. The park is open to the public. One New York visitor commented, "This is just like Jones Beach used to be, but without the salt water, beer cans and seaweed."

## Point Mallard Park

Heralding the arrival of autumn in the hill country of northern Alabama each year are strains of music as heartwarming as an open fire on a winter day. They come from the annual Tennessee Valley Old Time Fiddler's Association Convention on the campus of Athens College in Athens.

Traditionally held the first Saturday in October, thousands of visitors from all parts of the nation are attracted to this mecca of old-time country fiddlin'. Strangely, the fiddle has always had an uncanny power over people.

Once when Davy Crockett was traveling in the wilds of Arkansas, he heard a fiddle through the wilderness where he believed no one lived. Tracing the sound to a swollen creek, he came to a fiddler in a buggy in midstream. "What in tarnation are ye doin'?" yelled Davy. "Wal," said the fiddler, "here I am stuck in this creek thinking I might drown in the rising waters. I knowed I could holler for help till I got hoarse and nobody'd come. But this fiddle will draw a crowd every time...."

The Old Time Fiddler's Convention is no different. They arrive in Athens from the hills and hollows and cities across America. Hundreds of musicians pit their skills, handed down through generations of rural, front-porch musicians, against one another—fiddle, banjo, dulcimer, jew's harp, old time string band and buck dancing contests. The occasion is launched by the anvil shot—the ringing boom of powder on the iron. Sometimes called "the poor man's cannon," the custom has been handed down from our pioneer past. It's reenacted by placing black gunpowder between two heavy anvils and setting off the charge with a fuse. The blast propels the top anvil high into the air and can be heard for miles.

There's something almost religious about this event; something you sense only when you see and hear it. It provides a magical trip into the past; a path-

## Old Fiddler's Contest and Anvil Shoot

way for a nostalgic stroll into the bygone era of horse collars, kerosene lamps and the pungent odor of wood fires crackling in the fireplace. Nowhere else in America is fiddling music more of a tradition than in the Tennessee Valley.

## Ma Cille's Museum of Miscellania

Just 9 miles northeast of Carrollton, along AL 17, is Ma Cille's Museum of Miscellania, one of the South's most worthwhile free attractions. The museum, owned and operated by Mr. and Mrs. Norman House, is a helter-skelter collection of fascinating odds and ends—the culmination of a family dream.

Crowded with displays of old bottles, dishes and stuffed animals, the museum was begun when Ma Cille started digging up bits of pottery and glassware around old home sites. She traded articles of furniture for antiques that would fill her envisioned showplace of western Alabama's history.

Today it has grown from one small room into a sprawling building containing artifacts up to 150 years old. A renovated log cabin nearby is stocked with furniture reminiscent of the early 1800s, complete with weaving loom and wood piles. Included in the display is a Choctaw Indian skeleton; more than 4,000 bottles of all sizes and description; a replica of a bedroom dating back to pre-Civil War days; and a copy of the *New York Tribune* dated May 31, 1862, with a front-page map and story describing Civil War battles in western Alabama.

Ma Cille began her museum in the days when her own children were young and couldn't afford to go anyplace. It became a family hobby to create something at home which others would want to come and see. No admission is charged, although there is a donation box for those who wish to contribute. "I don't want to charge," Ma Cille explained, "because then there might be children who wouldn't get to come inside and see what we have here." It's open all year, from sunup to sundown.

## Bed Races

At the University of South Alabama, Mobile, an exciting bed-racing competition over a ¼-mile relay track is held each spring. Sponsored by the Sigma Alpha Epsilon Fraternity, the races normally are held in Municipal Park with sororities and fraternities of the university participating. The beds are deco-

Bed races are held each spring at the University of Southern Alabama, Mobile, Alabama. *(Courtesy of University of Southern Alabama)*

rated and built by the students, usually a bicycle frame with either three or four wheels attached to the bed. Along with the races, which usually take place in May, a Miss Bed Bunny is chosen.

On the first Monday of each month, Scottsboro stages its century-old Barter Day. Natives from the surrounding mountains, many of them pure-blooded descendants of British Revolutionary War soldiers, flock to the Court House Square. Coon dogs, antiques and junk are swapped or sold, accompanied by strumming banjos, voices exchanging news and gossip and the occasional thump of a domino. Visitors find fun and bargains.

The Blessing of the Shrimp Fleet is an annual event held in Bayou La Batra. Raffish in gay decorations, shrimp boats parade down the bayou before receiving the blessing of the clergy. The charming and moving custom of blessing boats as they go out to sea is as old as seafaring itself. This event is held the last Sunday in June.

The Chandler Mountain Tomato Festival is held in Horse Pens 40, Steele. Contests involve all manners of cooking and preserving tomatoes, tomato games and tomato tossing. This event is held annually in late October.

The International Possum Show is an annual event held in Chilton County Possum Corral, Clanton. Fiddler's contest, square dancing and possum judging, with entries from the United States, Mexico and Canada, is traditionally held the third week in September.

The National Slingshot Shooting Contest, Horse Pens 40, Steele, is held annually in early July. Prizes are awarded for the best slingshot shooters at designated targets.

For additional information, contact the Bureau of Publicity and Information, State Highway Building, Montgomery, Alabama 36104.

# Alaska

## Furthest Off the Beaten Track

Klondike Safari

Much of the way was paved for civilization in this great land to the north by the Klondike Gold Rush of 1898. Adventurous men, with the glint of gold in their eyes, came to Skagway and began a hike through the Chilkoot Pass that would lead them to the gold fields.

Today, one of the most offbeat happenings in Alaska is the annual retracing of that adventure on a backpack safari along the Klondike Trail. The trek, re-created by an Alaskan named Skip Burns, provides an insight into and an association with the hardships of the 20,000 or so men and women who came north to the riches of the Klondike.

All along the way, beginning at the ruins of Canyon City, you witness history—the remains left by the gold prospectors themselves: old stoves, decaying cabins with peat floors, boots, solder-top tin cans, broken lanterns. You can still see remnants of the tripod-shaped tramway supports, stretches of broken telegraph wire and an occasional weathered shoe. At night as you camp along the trail, you can almost hear the tromp of feet—ghost feet of weary travelers, men cursing and women crying. You soon discover it's just the wind moaning, or the clatter of a rock dislodged by a chipmunk. At Sheep Camp shelter is an old gambling table left over from the roaring days of the Klondike.

As you proceed along the trail, you climb gradually higher until you ultimately are above timberline, transgressing a snowfield, even in summer. You pass the Scales, where packers reweigh their loads before tackling the last steep climb on the 35-degree scree made so famous by E. A. Hogg's photos of the classic gold rush scene. Altogether, it's a 5-day hike, skirting Crater Lake, Long Lake and finally reaching Lake Bennett where the trail becomes waterborne all the way to Dawson.

The Chilkoot is still indelibly marked after all these years by the packing of the stampeders, still monumented by the grave markers of those who did not make it, still as dangerous and challenging as the day the first adventurers passed this way. The Chilkoot is a little over 30 miles long and climbs to approximately 3,500 feet above sea level. You must be physically prepared for the trek and be sure to make your reservations early; it's a very popular event which runs from mid-June to late September.

Another Klondike safari is operated via the White Pass & Yukon Railroad out of Skagway to the Yukon River, then by boat to Dawson in the Klondike—all in country immortalized by author Jack London.

For additional information, contact Klondike Safaris, P.O. Box 1898, Skagway, Alaska.

## World's Smallest National Forest

Much of Alaska is covered by two great national forests heavily populated by timber. But near the top of North America, far beyond the Arctic Circle, is what many term Alaska's most unusual travel attraction—the nation's smallest national forest. It isn't much to see, unless you know something of the background that established it.

Here, firmly rooted in the tundra where no trees grow, is a single, shaggy-looking black spruce; its limbs withered by severe elements, neatly enclosed by a white picket fence. Beside it is a sign on which is imprinted a healthier-looking tree and the words "Kotzebue National Forest." In 1958 the tree was planted there by Sam Lauser and other members of the 748th Aircraft Control and Warning Squadron of the Kotzebue Air Force Base. Returning from a fishing trip in lower Alaska, they decided to bring back the seedling and see if it would survive the vigorous climate of the Arctic tundra. Lauser felt it would add a touch of beauty to a drab landscape. Now 12-feet tall, the spruce somehow continues not only to thrive, but to grow, even though the permafrost of the tundra in this area extends to a depth of 40 feet with only 2 to 3 feet of the surface melting in the summer. The tree is the pride of the Air Force Base and is not under the jurisdiction of the U.S. Forest Service. The aviators at Kotzebue, which is really an Eskimo village, have designated honorary forest rangers whose job it is to look after the welfare of the Kotzebue National Forest. Charter tours to Kotzebue in the summer always pause for visitors to take a good look at America's smallest national forest and the biological wonder of the tree that survives there.

Alaska, which is roughly 2½ times larger than Texas, is filled with geographical phenomena, among them Little Diomede Island. Located far out in the Bering Sea, Little Diomede is just 1½ miles from the International Date Line and 3 miles from its sister island—Big Diomede, which is in the Soviet Union. In the winter, you can walk out on the ice pack and actually pass into the future or the past, depending on the direction you're traveling. This can't be done anyplace else in the world.

**Little Diomede**

The Inguklimiut Eskimo village of Diomede on Little Diomede Island is for those who are world weary and desire a place to get away. This rocky, 1,300-foot mountain island sticking out of the foggy narrows is one of the most isolated spots in the world; yet it definitely provides a link to the history of western civilization.

Archeologists worked for years on the problem of when the Diomede Islands were settled by their present occupants, unquestionably Siberian Eskimos from the Chukotski Peninsula. Most of the old people living on Little Diomede at this writing actually are Soviet citizens; for the main village was on Big Diomede and they came to Little Diomede only to hunt, gather bird eggs and pick the wild greens which grow profusely. It was their destiny to be on Little Diomede at the precise moment when the Iron Curtain fell in 1949 and, thus, to have no alternative but to stay.

On three sides of Little Diomede are sheer cliffs, towering almost a thousand feet above the water. During the summer months, thousands of sea birds swoop down from the ledges of these cliffs to search for food in the frigid waters of the Bering Sea. On the western side, the island drops less steeply into the water; and here thousands of auklets nest, making the island slopes above the village appear like a honeycomb. Ornithologists who regularly come here to study the birdlife estimate there are more than a million auklets, kittiwakes, murres and other northern sea birds on the island.

From February to spring thaw in late May, one may catch the mail plane to the island or charter a bush pilot plane to land on the ice. But in summer months, travel is by Eskimo skin boat, a trip that takes some 3 hours from the mainland at Wales.

Each July in the "land of the midnight sun," the Eskimo Olympic Games are held at Fairbanks. They are claimed to be the most flamboyant gathering of Eskimos at one time anyplace in Alaska. The sporting occasion includes games unique to the Eskimos—contests in seal-skinning, harpooning a seal, walking a greased pole, blanket tossing, a tug of war and the traditional knuckle hop for men. Competing with the Eskimos are their cousins—the Athabaskan Indians of the interior sections of Alaska.

**Eskimo Olympics**

For example, it takes an Eskimo woman only 60 seconds to skin a seal. As for the blanket toss, called nalukatuk, the jumper must maintain a vertical position while he is tossed from a blanket high into the air. The job of those tossing the blanket is to keep the hide under the jumper; a miss can be very discouraging.

The most rugged game is the knuckle hop. A contestant stretches out on the ground as though he were going to do push-ups; but instead of resting his weight on the palms of his hands, he makes a fist, putting his weight on his

The Kodiak Crab Races are a main feature of the Kodiak Crab Festival, Alaska. *(Courtesy of Alaska Travel Division)*

knuckles. The idea then is to hop along on his knuckles, dragging his body on the toes of his shoes. Hopping like this for 60 or more feet across the field leaves knuckles cut and bleeding. The most persistent contestant is the winner.

Ear weight lifting is another strenuous category; tie 17 pounds to one of your ears and walk 860 feet without touching the weight. Another game of the Eskimo Olympics involves two men sitting back to back, attempting to push each other out of a drawn circle which represents the perimeter of an igloo. The one who succeeds in a set number of minutes is declared the winner. Other events include authentic Eskimo dances and folkways, and preserving these is the real purpose of the games.

Instead of a runner bearing a torch as in the world-wide Olympics, the Eskimo Olympics are symbolized by a Stone Age whale-oil lamp with a wick made of moss, the likes of which were being used in these northern lands long before the Greeks held their first games. The color of the occasion, the chants and dances of these people, from such far-flung places as Nome, Barrow, Kotzebue, Hooper Bay, Bethel and King Island, are among the most primitive on earth today. Spectators are reminded of the day when a natural land bridge connected Asia's Siberia by way of Big and Little Diomede to the mainland of Alaska and thus North America.

## Mount Marathon Race

At Seward is another annual sporting event, but one not limited to Eskimos. Dating back to the turn of the century, this foot race is one of the most grueling in North America. Each Fourth of July, many spectators gather to watch.

The event supposedly started when two sourdoughs had an argument about whether it was possible to climb and descend the 3,022-foot mountain in less than one hour. To settle the argument and the resulting wager, it was decided that the two should hold a race and the loser would buy drinks for the crowd. At the same time, enterprising merchants put up a suit of clothes and other prizes; today the purse amounts to more than $2,500. The optimistic sourdough lost his wager, for it took them just 2 minutes over one hour to finish the course. That time has been bettered many times since to 44 minutes and a few seconds.

The rugged course, which attracts runners from all parts of the world, starts in downtown Seward, goes up the mountain over rock-strewn gullies, craggy bluffs, loose shale slides and often snow and ice fields. The racers must circle around a judge at the top of the mountain at a flag pole and then start their descent. The descent is often the most exciting part of the race, as many of the runners take tumbles of more than a hundred feet. In 1964, a junior race division was created and called the Dennis Hitt Memorial Trophy Race in memory of a local boy killed while training on Mount Alice in 1963 for the Mount Marathon Race. This special contest covers only half the distance of the adult race.

## Other Points of Interest

Sitka Alaska Days features the reenactment of the transfer of Alaska from Russia, held each October.

The Kodiak King Crab Festival features crab races, seal-skinning contests, Pillar Mountain climb foot races, traditional blessing of the 500 fishing boat fleet plus parades, carnivals, beauty contests.

A trip out of Skagway, Alaska, via narrow-gauge White Pass & Yukon Railroad, passes through some of the nation's most spectacular scenery. You can take your car aboard the same train on this day-long trip.

The Annual Ice Worm Festival is held at Cordova, Alaska. *(Courtesy of Alaska Travel Division)*

Japanese glass fishing floats and agates can be collected along the shores of the Aleutian Islands.

The annual Iceworm Festival at Cordova, normally held in early February, features the Iceworm's emergence from hibernation—an art show, skeet shoot, teen rodeo, Queen's pageant, airboat races, ski events, crab-shaking contests, dances.

World Championship snowshoe baseball tour is held during the Kenay Zemeny Karnival at Kenai in early February. It also features junior snowmobile and snowshoe races.

Old Man's Sled Dog Race, Fairbanks, is usually held in mid-March; participants are over 50 years of age.

Midnight Sun Festival, Nome, held in mid-June, features midnight raft races down the Nome River, midnight baseball games and a parade.

For additional information, contact the Alaska Travel Division, Pouch E, Juneau, Alaska 99801.

# Arizona

### Phantom Indians, a Slide Down a Stream and a Grand Canyon Raft Trip

**Grand Canyon's Phantom Indians**

Each year thousands of American tourists stand along the rim of Grand Canyon without ever realizing that within those gaping depths actually lives a people—Indians sometimes called the phantom tribe of the Grand Canyon. More appropriately, they're the Havasupai (people of the blue green water). Using water from a tributary of the Colorado for irrigation and tending small patches of corn, beans, squash and melons, as well as peach, apricot and fig trees, the Havasupai settlement is indeed an improbable oasis in the midst of a walled-in desert.

In a small Indian town called Supai, on the floor of a secluded side canyon, some 200 Havasupai live; and the least of their problems is smog. In fact, Supai is claimed to be the most smog-free town in America. The only way to get to Supai is by helicopter or horseback; the latter down a narrow winding trail that takes at least 3 hours to negotiate from the canyon rim. When you get to Supai, you find Main Street is a narrow, tree-shaded trail with none of the stores and shops you find in most towns. There is, however, a post office, the Havasu River where Indian children spend hours swimming, primitive steam baths beside the river and a rodeo arena built of willow logs, where the younger men engage in the grueling sport of bronc busting. Much of the cooking is done over outdoor fires; you can wander down the street in the late evening and watch the various evening meals being prepared—an unusual study in itself.

The Havasupai are friendly and hospitable, and visitors are welcome. The journey down the side of the canyon is a hair-raising one. To get to Supai, make arrangements at Grand Canyon Village or at Hilltop, both on the south rim of the canyon. Lodging is available on the reservation for a modest fee; but reservations are needed 3 to 4 months in advance. Contact Havasupai Tourist Enterprise, Supai, Arizona 86435.

You can see parts of Navajo land in your own automobile, of course, but you'll get a more educational tour and far greater insight into the life-style of the Navajo people if you take one of the tribal tours offered. Among other things, these 5 and 6-day tours include a visit to the tribal museum at Window Rock, overnight stays in tribal lodges where you'll get the opportunity to meet some of the Navajo Indians, a tour of the south rim of Canyon de Chelly, a boat tour on scenic Lake Powell plus visits to Hopi Indian villages, Coalmine Canyon and the Navajo National Monument. The Navajos will show you some of their industry, too; perhaps, if you're there at the right time, you'll be able to see some sand painting and basket weaving or some tribal dances.

Navajo Land

For additional information, contact Navajo Scenic Tours, P.O. Box 418, Window Rock, Arizona 86515. Window Rock is near the New Mexico border on AZ 264.

It's doubtful you'll find greater industry and enthusiasm of an Indian people anywhere other than among the Apaches of eastern Arizona. A visit to the Fort Apache Reservation is one of the most unusual outdoor vacations you could hope to find. The scenery is superb; the air is crystal clear, as are the mountain blue lakes. There are campgrounds along the banks of trout streams where you may angle for fighting rainbows. You can boat on the lakes and hike on the trails. And if you want to meet some Indians, just drive or walk down the road. They'll be happy to talk to you.

Apache Country

The reservation, which contains more than 1.6-million acres, is the largest privately owned recreation area in the west, open to the public at little expense. If you look carefully, you'll see plenty of wildlife; for this is natural habitat for deer, elk, antelope, bear, jabalina, mountain lion, wild turkey, beaver, grouse, dove, wild pigeon, bobcat, coyote and fox.

Indian rodeos, tribal fairs and Apache ceremonial dances are held on the reservation at various times throughout the year, and visitors as well as photographers are welcome to attend. You'll also find many ruins and historical sites on the Fort Apache Reservation; but no digging or removal of artifacts is permitted.

For further information, contact the White Mountain Recreation Enterprise at Whiteriver, Arizona 85941.

With all the thrill and excitement of a roller coaster, you can ride through the Grand Canyon in a jet helicopter. Up and down the side walls, the craft descends and climbs so close you can practically reach out to touch them. Swooping low, you have a bird's-eye view of the Colorado River raging torrentially. Depending on the tour, you may set down at Phantom Ranch on the canyon floor; the view upward is unbelievable.

Roller Coaster Through Grand Canyon

A helicopter ride through the canyon has to be, beyond all doubt, one of the most thrilling and colorful experiences you will ever encounter. Wind and weather conditions must be right for the trip, for up and downdrafts in the canyon can cause severe turbulence under certain conditions. If you're interested in this seat-gripping experience, inquire about the helicopter tours at Canyon City.

Floatdown    One of the most carefree annual events in Arizona is the Floatdown and World Inner Tube Race on the Colorado River. Traditionally held in late June or early July, more than 2,000 participants and thousands of spectators gather for the floatdown. Among the participants are many families—Mom, Dad and all the little ones.

The race always includes a number of entries from out-of-state, some from as far away as Minnesota. Held in the Yuma section of the Colorado, the floatdown is under the auspices of the Yuma Chamber of Commerce. Additional races are held on the Colorado to coincide with the floatdown—a Pyrawa

World Inner Tube Racers gather for one of Arizona's biggest fun events. *(Courtesy of U.S. Army, Yuma Proving Ground)*

inflatable canoe race and a kayak competition. The racers run over a 7-mile course which normally takes in excess of 3 hours. Inflatable canoes run a longer race, but in shorter time, of course. Along with other related events, a race queen is selected each year. Yuma is located on U.S. 95 and U.S. 80 in the southwestern part of the state.

At the edge of Arizona's Verde Valley is Jerome, once a billion dollar copper camp with a population of more than 15,000. Today it has less than 300 residents and is acclaimed as America's largest ghost city.

**America's Largest Ghost City**

Each year in late May—with the starting point at Ghost Crossing—a guided tour is offered through this romantic old ghost town. Until recent years, a sign at the outskirts of Jerome declared the camp to be the "most unique city in America." Unique it was—and still is. Perched at the base of Cleopatra Hill, the ruins climb up the steep slope. Behind them are the ramparts of Arizona's Black Hills.

In an earlier day, Jerome had multistoried buildings and fine homes, although—like many mining boom towns—it also had its share of clapboard shacks, dark dens and perfumed cribs. Today crumbling masonry and foundations show where stores, saloons, restaurants and theaters once provided thousands with food, clothing, refreshment and amusement. The city began in the second half of the nineteenth century and flourished for many years. But when the mine was shut down in 1938, Jerome became a ghost town; its population suddenly dropped to 200 people. Those who remained organized the Jerome Historical Society and established a museum which tells the romantic story of mining in the Verde district.

Since then an art colony and gallery have been established. Today a visit to Jerome remains one of the most rewarding experiences in Arizona. It's located between Prescott and Flagstaff on U.S. 89A.

Fifteen miles out of Tucson is the Mission San Xavier del Bac, sometimes called the White Dove of the Desert. Labeled a National Historic Landmark in 1963, there are few missions as impressive as this one. To this day, the mission has never been fully completed; although construction actually began in 1783, it still continues.

**White Dove of the Desert**

The mission serves the 71,000-acre San Xavier Papago Indian Reservation, including 11,000 Papagos. It is the base for 60 chapels and missions as well as schools serving 600 Papago children. Three times since 1797, the present structure was relinquished to a state of near ruin, and three times it's been pulled from its own grave. It has survived three political jurisdictions, two explosions, one major earthquake, countless lightning strikes and decades of poverty and indifference. Yet today, the White Dove of the Desert stands a timeless monument, serene and proud and certainly most functional. Open to the public 8 A.M. to 6 P.M. daily, it's located off U.S. 89, south of Tucson.

Have you ever eaten a wild burro? Well, you probably won't either—at least not at the annual Wild Burro Barbecue at Bullhead City. However, this wasn't always the way. Until 1970, when the Arizona Livestock Sanitary Board put a stop to it, wild burro was the entrée at the annual event; now there's beef substitute. But the burros are raced and lots of people come just to watch; others are fascinated by the past history of the occasion.

**Wild Burro Barbecue**

The race is held on AZ 95 for a distance of 4 miles. Although the highway is jammed with onlookers cheering for their favorite team, traffic is blocked off and detoured during that time. Many of the courageous burro drivers are dragged the entire route, while others have to drag, carry or push their burros to get them to move. As an additional feature, a burro baseball game is held, and there are races for the children. The outdoor beef barbecue over mesquite fire is unusual, too, and many come just to eat. The event usually is held in late May; to get there take AZ 95, north of Needles, California.

## Oak Creek Slide

In a section of colorful Oak Creek Canyon, there is a slide rock...and that doesn't mean a slide of rocks. It means you can ride down a spillway of water rushing over some of the slipperiest rocks to be found in Arizona. It all adds up to great fun; and if you wear some old clothes, you'll find the Oak Creek Canyon slide rock provides a great experience.

On any summer day, you'll find U.S. 89A lined with cars at certain stretches; and if you wonder why, park your car and take the well-worn path by the creek (you cannot see the slide from this point)...or just follow the sounds of frolicking, shouting, screaming youngsters. The slide rock is not just for children; it's for all ages. You'll even find senior citizens sliding along the water, propelled by its current. It's a cool refreshing ride over rock so slippery that you cannot stand still. The slide rock is located just upstream from Oak Creek Falls.

## Colored Canyon Moon Trip

In the Smoky Mountain territory of Arizona, there is an area truly "out of this world." As you approach the area, imagine yourself an astronaut. The terrain has become a moonscape; there are moon craters, corona-like rings and the feeling of desolation. Then you arrive at Colored Rock Canyon where the display of color (ever changing with the sun) will leave you absolutely breathless. The visit to Colored Rock Canyon is an organized tour offered by Canyon Tours, starting in Page, Arizona. Page is located on U.S. 89, near the Utah border.

## Wickenburg Christmas

For a truly old Western Christmas, there's none to compare with that at Wickenburg. The first hint of Christmas appears in mid-December when the final details of the children's party are made and wreaths are hung on authentic old West storefronts. The sounds of Christmas carols emerge from the supermarket, and guest ranches are all spruced up in holiday finery.

Families in four-wheel-drive vehicles trek across the desert and into woodlands to cut their own piñon, fir or pine trees. The week before Christmas, Santa arrives by stagecoach escorted by youthful horsemen decked out in spurs and sleigh bells. On Christmas Eve, the guest ranches and private homes present a festive scene. All are outlined by the mellow light of luminaries—candles glowing inside paper bags filled with just enough sand to hold them steady. Christmas is unique at Wickenburg, located on U.S. 60 and U.S. 89.

## Other Points of Interest

Mystery Castle, near Phoenix, is an unusual edifice built of native rock at the foot of South Mountain.

The Sun Worshipper Statue is a 1,600-pound welded steel giant constructed by physician Walter Emory. Standing 19-feet tall, it greets visitors to the Park Central Shopping Center off North Central Avenue, Phoenix.

The world's largest fountain is located at Fountain Hills near Fort McDowell and Salt River Indian Reservation. The Swiss-engineered nozzle and pumps maintain a column of water in the air weighing more than 8 tons. At full force, the water jets skyward 560 feet, three times higher than Old Faithful in Yellowstone Park.

The world's tallest fountain, spraying a column of water 560 feet into the air, is the thematic centerpiece of Fountain Hills, Arizona. *(Courtesy of Joanne Patton Ralston and Associates, Inc.)*

The Hall of Flame, an antique fire museum, is located in Scottsdale at Civic Center Plaza.

The Barringer Crater, located near Winslow, gives one a close-up study of what a moonscape might be like. The crater is one of the most remarkable phenomena on Earth.

For additional information, contact the Visitor Development Section, Department of Economic Planning, 3003 North Central Avenue, Phoenix, Arizona 85012.

# Arkansas

## Diamond Fields, Turkey Callers and Ozark Folk Songs

**Diamond Fields**

There are few other places in the world where you can go into the fields and woodland and prospect for your own raw diamonds. Over the years, some mighty important finds have been made at the Crater of Diamonds in Arkansas's Pike County. The crater includes a 78-acre diamond-bearing volcanic pipe, the only known diamond-producing area in North America.

Diamonds were first discovered in the Murfreesboro area in August 1906. When the discovery became known to the public, the news started a diamond rush that for a short period threatened to take the path of the California gold rush of 1849. For nearly 40 years, numerous attempts were made to mine the crater commercially, but all attempts were shrouded in mystery and bedeviled by abuse.

Then in 1952, the crater was opened as a tourist attraction. For a small fee, you could spend a day mining—or looking for—diamonds. The two most famous stones found at the site are the "Uncle Sam" and the "Star of Arkansas." The former weighed 40.23 carats; the latter 15.31 carats. As late as 1972, a Missouri resident found a stone that weighed in excess of 6 carats in the rough. More than 60,000 diamonds have been taken from the crater, which in 1972 became a state park. To get there, take U.S. 70 out of Little Rock to AR 27 which runs through the town.

**Quigley's Castle**

One spring morning in 1943, as Albert Quigley headed for work, Mrs. Quigley rounded up their five children and ordered: "We're going to tear down the house." By the time Quigley returned home that night, the house was flattened and his belongings sheltered in a chicken house. "I knew he'd never build a new house as long as the old one was standing," said Mrs. Quigley.

So Quigley *had* to build a new house. The handiest thing available was a mountain-size pile of fossils and rocks that Mrs. Quigley had been gathering since she was nine years old. Working diligently, Quigley fashioned the rocks into 4 two-story walls. The rocks used were selected for their beauty of shape and color, their resemblance to familiar objects or their place in history.

On the north wall are a piece of petrified wood, a fossilized turtle shell, a prehistoric imprint of a deer's hoof, an Indian grist stone, a rock shaped like a Prussian helmet and ordinary American marbles the Quigley children had played with through childhood. To achieve an earthy effect, Mrs. Quigley had her husband leave the soil bare between the edges of the floors and three walls inside the house. Here she planted subtropical shrubs, trees and flowering plants, along with southwestern cactuses. Year-round, the sun beamed through twelve 4-by-6-foot windows, stirring the plants into lush growth until they now reach the second-story ceiling.

For 7 months, the family slaved at the building. Their own trees were sawed and planed into lumber at nearby mills where Quigley worked. Only $2,000 was spent on the house, and that money was earned from raising turkeys. Today the house is a stopping place for travelers and has been appraised at more than $60,000. Quigley's Castle is located 4½ miles south of Eureka Springs on AR 23.

## Wild Turkey Calling Contest

In Yellville, Arkansas, each autumn, the National Wild Turkey Calling Contest is held, with entries from many parts of the nation. Callers use anything and everything from their vocal chords to a cedar stick inserted in a corncob and rubbed against a slate.

At various times during the Arkansas Turkey Trot Festival, wild turkeys are dropped from a low-flying plane, and anyone on the ground who can catch one takes it home. The result is a melee of people climbing trees, chasing turkeys across fields and up telephone poles.

Other events include a Miss Drumstick beauty pageant in which the girls

Musicians perform at the Arkansas Folk Festival, Arkansas. *(Courtesy of Arkansas Department of Parks and Tourism)*

Log splitting is demonstrated at the Arkansas Folk Festival at Mountain View, Arkansas. *(Courtesy of Arkansas Department of Parks and Tourism)*

are chosen only by the looks of their legs (their bodies being shielded from the public and the judges), a turkey auction and a turkey target shoot. Yellville was named after a man named Yell...and that's certainly appropriate during this once-a-year event. Yellville is located on U.S. 62 in northern Arkansas.

**World Duck Calling Contest**

The turkey callers do not attain top billing alone; for at Stuttgart, the World Championship Duck Calling Contest is held each autumn (usually in November). The contest is held in conjunction with an agricultural festival when a wide variety of agriculture exhibits is on display on the streets downtown. The contest is held in three divisions—a Junior World Championship for youngsters under 12, a Women's World Championship and one for the men. Other events include the choosing of a Miss Queen Mallard, a beauty contest. Stuttgart is located on U.S. 79, just 66 miles northeast of Pine Bluff.

**Ozark Folk Center**

The Ozark Folk Center, located on 80 beautiful woodland acres one mile out of Mountain View, has one of the finest displays of Ozark folk life. Since the center opened in 1973, it has served as a showcase for the arts, crafts, music and lore of the Ozarks. Live demonstrations of such crafts as shuckery, rail splitting, doll making, quilting and blacksmithing are held. The center consists of 59 buildings constructed of native stone, western cedar and lots of glass. The Rackensack Folklore Society also play their old-time instruments and old-time songs at the center on a regular basis.

There are antique shows and antique fairs, but seldom does one encompass the flavor of the War Eagle Fair in Arkansas. It's held every spring on the War Eagle Farm located in the Ozark backwoods in a beautiful valley almost entirely surrounded by a bending, twisting river. Upon arriving at the 250-acre farm, you will find a primitive building with a sawdust floor in the middle of a cow pasture. Nearly 50 booths are set up each year by collectors from the area, offering antique glassware, china pieces, guns and knives, old and rare coins, wooden tools, old-fashioned toys including china dolls, handmade quilts and coverlets, clocks, brass and copper objects and old paintings. There are also furniture, rare books, bottles and jewelry. If you tire of shopping or looking at antiques, you can take your fishing pole across the meadow to War Eagle River in quest of bream, crappie or channel cat. War Eagle Farm can be reached by taking AR 68 from Springdale until it intersects with AR 303. From there, follow the signs along the gravel road.

**War Eagle Antique Fair**

For additional information, contact the Department of Parks and Tourism, 149 State Capitol, Little Rock, Arkansas 72201.

# California

## Land of Diversity

In the extreme southern part of the state, only one hour's drive from the Mexican border, you will see America's dying sea. Located 232 feet below sea level, it's more commonly known as Salton Sea, with a saline content several times greater than that of any ocean. Yet it supports one of the most fantastic fisheries in all the nation—the orangemouth corvina which grows to more than 30 pounds and is one of the fish kingdom's greatest delicacies. Born in this century when the waters of the flooding Colorado River rampaged over the desert into a giant salt sink, the Salton Sea is expected by scientists to completely dry up before the year 2,000 unless the results of a study now underway by federal and state authorities can save it.

**Lakes of Fantasy**

Only 14 miles at its widest point and some 33 miles long, the sea offers a unique vacation spot where temperatures in the summer sometimes reach 130 degrees. But there's camping at Salton Sea State Park, trail riding, charter boat fishing, boat rentals, hiking, golfing, boating, swimming and water skiing.

Far to the north, just 15 miles from the east entrance of Yosemite National Park, you will see another of California's unusual bodies of water—Mono Lake. Sprouting out of its shoreline are some of the most spectacular formations ever sculptured by nature. Known as the Tufa Towers, the shapes were formed by freshwater springs beneath the inland sea, blending with the heavy mineral waters of the lake to precipitate limestone deposits. Chemical action forms the tubular geysers around the bubbling stream of water. A drop in the lake level has exposed the towers.

Located along CA 395, flanking the eastern Sierras, the lake is 15 miles long and 9 miles wide, resting in a volcanic depression at an elevation of 6,409 feet. The formations—some of which have exotic names such as King's Chalice, the Queen's Chessman, Dinosaur Bones, Forgotten City and Dragon's Mouth—give the lake a unique and unearthly appearance.

## Whiskeytown Lake

North of San Francisco in the midst of the Whiskeytown-Shasta-Trinity National Recreation Area is another unique adventure. When the water is clear and the sun hits at just the right angle, you can look to the bottom of the lake and see the remains of a ghost town. At one time, this was a rip-roaring mining town called, appropriately enough, Whiskeytown. It was drowned by the rising waters of the reservoir back in 1962. Each year the visible remains dwindle; but for some time to come, perhaps even past the turn of the next century, boaters will be able to ride over the tops of the buildings of this old California ghost town. The only thing you'll see moving around are the fish and perhaps a scuba diver or two probing through the ruins.

## Eagle Lake

The natives say many mysterious things happen on Eagle Lake, near the Nevada border. The place is haunted by bizarre wildlife and unnatural phenomena that even scientists can't explain. As you look out on Eagle Lake, waves and surface disturbances sooner or later begin to form, without any apparent reason.

The Eagle Lake species of trout can be found no place else in the world. The tui chub which everywhere else is just a minnow grows to 3 pounds here. Birds that nest on the ground elsewhere, nest 40 feet up in the trees. If you enter one of the lava caves, you'll find crickets that have survived unchanged since the Ice Age.

Indeed, it would not be surprising to see California's own breed of Loch Ness monster emerge from these waters. Scientists and study groups from various universities keep camps on the shores of Eagle Lake at all times, hoping to unscramble its mysteries. It's a fascinating place to visit and to exercise your imagination. Eagle Lake is located 18 miles northwest of Susanville, just off CA 139.

## Whale Parade

Speaking of monsters, you can witness one of nature's most breathtaking traditions—the migration of the giant gray whales, usually single file, as they travel southward from the Bering Sea along the Alaska Coast to their breeding grounds in Baja, California. From mid-December through March, visitors may watch these mighty whales through high-powered binoculars. The best place to view the parade is from Cabrillo National Monument on Point Loma near San Diego; the monument is open daily from 9 A.M. to 5:30 P.M.

Hollywood certainly is not unknown, but many of the things connected with moviemaking are. For example, take Anderson's Animal Park. Here young and old have the rare opportunity to meet and play with the animal stars of television and movies.

**Glitter of the Stars**

This is the home of many of the trained animals seen across America, including "Neena," the elephant; "Sweet William," a 600-pound bear who spends most of his time in the bathtub; "Joe," a 550-pound African lion; "Rijo," a 700-pound Siberian tiger; "Clyde," a 300-pound jaguar; and "Spot," an African leopard. Here, too, is a children's pet playground and a sanctuary for orphaned animals. Open year-round, an admission is charged; it is located on U.S. 101 at Buellton.

At the Orange County Airport, not far from Disneyland, you'll find an incomparable collection of historical aircraft. The aircraft have been restored by Frank Tallman and Paul Mantz. Planes used in famous Hollywood films are displayed in movie-set backgrounds; examples include the Fokker D7 replica, Sopwith Tripe, Fokker Tripe Jenny and the Nieuport 28. Rides in an open-cockpit biplane are part of the attraction. It's open year-round with a small admission charge.

**Hollywood Planes**

Not far away, in Buena Park, you'll find another collection—Movie World Cars of the Stars and Planes of Fame. Claimed to be the world's largest collection of celebrity automobiles, it has over 100 vehicles on permanent display from an inventory of more than 700 antique, classic and motion-picture automobiles. Included are Ma Barker's 1930 Cadillac, Al Jolson's 1929 custom-built Mercedes-Benz and Nevada Smith's 1930 V-16 Cadillac; as well as historic motion-picture props, movie miniatures and sets, a famous sword collection and automobile and motorcycle memorabilia (since 1909). Planes include aircraft from the Wright era, the wood and wire planes of World War I, the fighters of the forties, jets and space vehicles. Among the collection are many one-of-a-kind aircraft such as the World War I Hanriot Scout flown by French Ace Charles Nungesser.

**Movie World Cars and Planes**

One hour's drive away is Hollywood's all-purpose Albertson Ranch, located in the Canejo Valley. Before driving to the location, it's best to call and find out if it is open to visitors at that time. Probably more movies are shot here than at any other place in the world. It can serve as the Sahara Desert or a Texas cattle ranch. Rommel's Afrika Korps fought over its rolling hills; it was also the setting for a Japanese prison camp in the movie "King Rat." Included in its 11,200 sprawling acres are rugged mountains, flatlands, woods and underbrush, as well as farm buildings and frontier-style streets. Even cattle and sheep are available as extras.

**Albertson's Ranch**

Where on Earth this side of Saudi Arabia would you find camel and ostrich races? In California's Coachella Valley. Each year in mid-February at the National Date Festival at Indio a scene emerges right out of Arabian Nights. Al-

**Burros, Camels and Ostriches**

though the festival hosts a great many events, no activity is more "offbeat" than the camel and ostrich races. Camels were once used extensively in this part of the country; as late as the Civil War, they were experimented with in arid parts of Arizona, New Mexico and Texas as beasts of burden. It's only natural that this part of America's heritage should be kept alive by this annual event. Indio is located on I-10.

### National Burro Derby

At Big Bear Lake each year in August, a 3-day, 40-mile National Burro Derby is held. It's difficult to describe 85 to 100 wild jackasses being held back by anxious wranglers, awaiting the starting gun. The animals are intent upon one

Burro slips pack over his head at the National Burro Derby, Big Bear Lake, California.

thing—gaining their freedom. The wranglers are intent upon another—pulling, dragging and cajoling their burros to a point some 40 miles away so that they may win a substantial cash prize. The conflicts of interest between man and beast provide one of the most hilarious sporting events in all North America. This derby is part of an event called Old Miners' Day. Big Bear Lake is located on CA 18, east of San Bernardino.

Camel and ostrich races are held at the National Date Festival, California. *(Courtesy of National Date Festival)*

**Tevis Cup Trail Ride**

Another grueling annual event is the Tevis Cup Trail Ride, usually held in July. Before dawn, more than 150 horsemen canter out of Tahoe, California, toward the Sierra Nevadas. They will ride by the light of the "riding moon," the last full moon of late summer, so named by the Indians because it lighted the trail for their migrations. It permits the earliest possible start for what may be the toughest endurance event of all equestrian sports—the 24-hour, 100-mile Tevis Cup Trail Ride.

The first rider to reach the trail's end at Auburn, with his horse still in good condition, is awarded the Lloyd Tevis Cup, named for the president of Wells Fargo during its heyday. The ride is through mountain passes; up and down canyons; past azure lakes, fish-filled streams and meadows ablaze with wildflowers. It draws the best horsemen around the nation, as well as numerous riders who come primarily to enjoy some of the most rugged and beautiful scenery in the world.

**Horse and Mule Roundup**

Each autumn near Yosemite National Park, the last great horse and mule drive in the West is reenacted. In the frosty chill of a November dawn, down 3,000 feet in altitude and across 85 miles of rolling ranch country, more than 300 horses and mules are brought out of the Sierra Nevadas to winter pastures in the upper San Joaquin Valley. The route is through the gold Mother Lode country in the heart of Mariposa County to a 6,000-acre ranch outside the snow belt.

The drive, which began in 1866, has not changed since that time. Hundreds of spectators gather along the route to watch and to gain a feeling of association with the Old West and to relive the days of the great cattle, horse and mule drives. In summer the animals are used for pack trips in the Sierras; the drive back into the mountains is held again sometime in the spring, depending on weather and seasonal conditions.

**Tule Elk**

West of Bakersfield just off I-5 is the Tule Elk State Park wherein the last of this species is preserved from extinction. These magnificent creatures are considered some of the world's rarest animals. Visitors are allowed in the viewing area of this 350-acre range to watch the elk; but the remainder of the park is closed to the public. Admission is free and the best viewing time is 3 P.M.—feeding time.

**Oakland's Wildlife Refuge**

Lake Merritt Park, in the heart of Oakland's business district, may look like any other large city playground built around a sparkling blue saltwater lagoon. But it's different than any other city park in the nation: this park is for birds. It's the oldest official wildlife refuge ever established.

Since 1926, the lake has been an official duck banding station, one of the oldest in the country, for which it has been designated a National Historical Landmark. Established by the state legislature in 1870 under the persuasion of then Mayor Samuel Merritt, the 150-acre lake provides a habitat for more than 4,000 wildfowl. Considering its location, this "refuge" provides visitors an interlude of quiet in an otherwise bustling city.

**Soaring Sailors**

At no other place in America will spectators see greater soaring activity than along the 300-foot sea cliffs of San Diego's Torrey Pines Mesa. In February or March each year, the Pacific Coast Mid-Winter Soaring Championships are held. Al-

Sailplaning is demonstrated at Torrey Pines, California.

most any weekend, when weather conditions are right, you'll see scores of sail-planes riding the thermals from the sea. During the championships, pilots fascinate spectators by demonstrating their skills in events of altitude, duration, distance, spot landing and "bomb" dropping. A special sailplane aerobatic dis-play—featuring series of loops, spins and stalls—takes place during the 2-day event. The cliff tops provide unusually good vantage points for visitors.

**Kite Sailors**

At various times of the year, a growing breed of daredevil sportsmen gather to sky surf. You'll find them wherever there are cliffs or hills, including greater San Francisco and Fremont. Using giant kites, they leap from the cliffs and soar about like birds, manipulating controls slung under the kite. It's an excit-ing, breathtaking adventure for the spectator as well as the sky surfer.

**Kiteflying and Sailboats**

Off the tip of Harbor Island in San Diego, the annual Go-Fly-a-Kite-and-Sail Race is held; it's the only event of its kind in the world. Usually held in Au-gust, this nautical contest demands not only sailboat racing skills, but also the ability to maintain a flying kite from each boat during the entire competition. More than 50 boats usually enter the contest. Spectators can watch the event from vantage points along the western tip of Harbor Island, where there are restaurant facilities and ample free parking.

## Kiteflying Competition

While some kite enthusiasts prefer the above mentioned competition, others prefer to fly their kites without the bother of a sailboat. One of the oldest kiteflying competitions in America is held at Ocean Beach, a suburb of San Diego. Usually held in March, the huge flying contest attracts around 1,000 youngsters. Each kite is constructed by the youngster who flies it.

Events get underway in the early afternoon with a colorful parade of kids and kites led by bands and majorettes. Upon arrival at the beach area, everyone is on his own; each contestant tries to get his or her kite into the air first and guide it skillfully higher than all the rest. Even with the acres upon acres of beach, kites collide and tails and strings become hopelessly entangled. Kites in the hands of too eager pilots crash to the sand and must be taken to the "kite hospital" manned by parents and friends. Fancy designs and unusual kite shapes adorn the skies; prizes are awarded on design and construction as well as performance.

## Rough Water Swim

At LaJolla Cove, usually in September, the annual Rough Water Swim is held. The classic race, dating back to 1916, is sponsored by the LaJolla Town Council and normally draws more than 700 ocean swimmers and thousands of spectators. A 150-yard triangular swim course is set up for 10 to 12-year-old boys and girls, while older entrants undergo a grueling one-mile swim over a similar ocean course. The event is free to visitors who sit along the sea cliffs to watch the activity.

## Sand Castles and the Sea

Also in the San Diego area, one of America's greatest events for all ages is held—the Mission Bay Sand Castle Contest. Held in July, more than 200 sand slappers, ranging from preschoolers to granddads, serve as architects for a day. Although castles dominate, any sand sculpture is eligible to compete for contest awards. Traditional entries have included dragons, whales, turtles, mermaids and flying fish. Judging is based on design, originality and overall effort. No reinforcing material can be used in the sand structures and nothing can be added to change the consistency of the sand; however, any type of material can be used to decorate the exterior.

## Jumping Frog Jamboree

Perhaps no contest in California is more heartwarming or forms a greater link with tradition than the annual Jumping Frog Jamboree in Del Mar, a suburb of San Diego. The contest, sponsored by the San Diego Jaycees to raise funds for cancer research, is held at the Del Mar fairgrounds. California bullfrogs, rounded up by the Jaycees in a massive night search along Spook Canyon Creek near Encinitas, are available at a "rent-a-frog" booth, or you can bring your own. Admission is free. Each frog has 30 seconds to take its first jump. Competition distance is measured from the middle of the launch pad to where the frog lands on his first jump.

## World Gold Panning Meet

Meanwhile, upstate at the Tropico Gold Mine near Rosamond there is another contest linked with California's history—the World Championship Gold Panning Meet. Normally held the first weekend in March, several hundred compete to see who can pan, from an artificial stream filled with gold dust, the most gold in the allotted time. Visitors are also guided through what was once California's largest and richest gold mine, including a view of the 900-foot shaft that drops into the vast "glory hole" which produced thousands of dollars in gold bullion. Mine tours are available June through September, with a small admission charge.

In a place where least expected, you will find one of California's most "off-beat" tidbits of culture—opera in Death Valley. At a spot called Death Valley Junction, Marta and Tom Williams reopened and refurbished a ghost-like theater into a dazzling center for the arts.

Death Valley Opera

On Fridays, Saturdays and Mondays, Marta (who was a professional New York ballerina) dances, while her husband emcees and handles the curtains, props and lights. Soon after their opening in this near ghost town (population less than 50), they played to audiences of only one or two people; but more recently, the theater is packed with busloads of fans from Las Vegas, 100 miles to the east, and Los Angeles, 300 miles southwest. No admission is charged, but a minimum contribution of $1.50 from each adult is requested. Death Valley Junction, sometimes called Amargosa, is at the intersection of CA 127 and CA 190.

In the mountains east of San Diego is the picturesque town of Julian, where each May is held the Julian Wildflower Show. Thousands of wildflower blossoms, from San Diego County mountain and desert areas, paintings and other art objects are exhibited. The show, which lasts a couple of weeks, attracts visitors from virtually every state as well as many foreign countries. Some of the wildflowers on exhibit include wild lilac, wild flowering currant, flowering gooseberry, wild strawberry blossoms and baby blue eyes.

Julian Wildflower Show

Each year in November, the state holds a most unique attraction for little children—a Mother Goose Parade. Featuring the characters of Mother Goose and fairyland, the parade often exceeds 3 miles in length, with more than 50 bands and 25 floats. The parade is held on I-8 at the city of El Cajon.

Mother Goose Parade

Fortune cookies are not made by some strange magic, they are made by human hands. You can verify this fact by a visit to the Lotus Fortune Cookie Co., in the heart of San Francisco's Chinatown. You're welcome to watch how modern techniques and ancient Chinese customs combine to produce this prognosticating dessert. Located at 436 Pacific Avenue, the bakery is open for tours 10 A.M. to 5 P.M. weekdays.

Fortune Cookie Bakery

Also located in San Francisco is the largest Buddhist temple in America. Free guided tours are offered. Highlights of the four-story building include a 6-foot mosaic of Buddha, the Monastery of the Bamboo Grove, a chapel model of the place where Buddha lectured 2,500 years ago and a unique rooftop garden with Bodhi trees and lotus pond.

Buddhist Temple

On the outskirts of San Jose is Mrs. Winchester's Mystery House. The 160 chambers of this Victorian mansion have fascinated guests and passers-by since the turn of the century.

Winchester Mystery House

A spiritualist once advised Mrs. Winchester she would never be bothered by ghosts if she kept building on her house. Being a rich widow from the East, Mrs. Winchester hired a crew of 50 carpenters and kept them working round the clock for 38 years. The result is a bizarre, weathered mansion which ultimately cost her $5 million and includes 160 rooms, 2,000 doors, 13 bathrooms,

10,000 windows, 47 fireplaces, dozens of fake closets, 50 stairways with steps that vary from 2½ to 18 inches in height, an elaborate system of peek-holes, passages which double back to where they began, corridors that dead end and a dozen fake chimneys not connected to flues or ducts. All this was designed to "fool" any would-be ghost intruders. Today the house is open to the public year-round for a small fee.

## Shunpiking à-la-Carte

A great shunpiking motor trip in the San Francisco area includes a drive north through Mill Valley, past the home of John Muir, to Point Reyes National Seashore. There you'll find an interesting lighthouse and some of the most severe winds on the entire Pacific Coast.

Perhaps the most picturesque of shunpiking tours anywhere is a drive down the Big Sur Highway past Monterey where you might pause to visit John Steinbeck's Cannery Row or take a small sidetrip on the 17-mile Del Monte Drive along the coast of the Monterey Peninsula. Heading south, you'll pass Carmel, a fashionable artist's colony, and then Big Sur, home of writer Henry Miller and the oldest hippie commune in America. As the road wends its way precariously alongside the Pacific, you'll also see some of the most breathtaking vistas in North America.

## Bird Egg Museum

In the town of Bloomington near San Bernardino is what is known as the Bird Egg Museum. Actually named the San Bernardino County Museum, it offers an invitation to view the world's largest scientific collection of bird eggs. Also on exhibit are numerous specimens and, in particular, the condor (an endangered species). Other points of interest include a research center on early man, a prehistoric Indian exhibit, cactus gardens and historic murals.

## Little Tokyo

If you want to visit Japan without leaving the United States, Little Tokyo is located in the center of Los Angeles. Exotic Oriental shops and restaurants make Little Tokyo a good walking tour for imported ceramics, fabrics, tailor-made kimonos and garden accessories. While there, you can sample the food at Japanese restaurants and authentic teahouses. During Nisei Week, which traditionally comes in August, there are displays in bonsai and doll making and such cultural entertainment as the traditional Ondo parade, featuring costumed dancers who snake through the streets of Little Tokyo. The area is bounded by Central Avenue, First and Second Streets and Los Angeles Street.

## Forest Lawn Art

While most people do not enjoy visiting cemeteries, Forest Lawn offers an unusual walking tour which includes some of the graves of stars who still live on screen and television and some of the finest religious art treasures in the world.

There is actually more than one Forest Lawn cemetery. The one in Glendale Park is the most famous and has the largest collection of art treasures. Among them is *The Last Supper Window*, a stained-glass re-creation of Leonardo da Vinci's painting; the *Crucifixion* by Jan Styka, the largest religious painting in the world, measuring 195 by 45 feet; and the *Resurrection*, painted by American artist Robert Clark. Similar art treasures are displayed at Forest Lawn-Hollywood Hills and Forest Lawn-Covina Hills in Los Angeles County and Forest Lawn-Cypress in Orange County. The cemeteries are open daily 8:30 A.M. to 5:30 P.M. year-round.

Located in the 1,400-acre Balboa Park in San Diego is a model railroad exhibit claimed as the largest scaled model operation in the nation. Admission is free and it's open daily year-round.

The Halls of Desert Glass, located at National City, features the history of America in sun-colored glass. Nearly 5,000 glass pieces, ranging from a wealthy financier's table setting to a desert rat's pack, tell the story of Americana. Massive jars and delicate vases, ornate figurines, squatty ink wells and paper weights are displayed here. Vases reflect hues of purple and gold from the California sun. Located at 1315 E. 4th Street, this exhibit is open daily.

Also located near National City is Wilbur Bradley's Gourd Farm, one of the most visited farms in the state. Thousands of persons come annually to gaze at the variety of gourds raised by Bradley.

Bradley got into the gourd business in 1955 and that year sold 2,000 gourds. Now he sells upwards of 50,000 gourds annually but raises only a small portion of them. He contracts other growers but has one of the most amazing displays to be seen anywhere. The Gourd Farm is located at 170 East 31st Street.

At Big Bear Lake, a rock-skipping contest is held each October.

Brookside Wineries, the largest direct-to-the-consumer wine sales operation in the United States, opens its cellars to the public free, 7 days a week, year-round (with 28 locations throughout California).

At Santa Monica, the International Underwater Film Festival is held each February.

Annually in September, the Rural Olympics are held in Lancaster.

At Long Beach, royal tours are offered aboard the world's most beloved ship, the Queen Mary, which is permanently stationed in the harbor.

In Los Angeles, a tiny train takes visitors on a free journey through the world's largest camellia garden, a 150-acre estate which also abounds in roses, begonias, lilacs and lilies and 150 species of birds. The address is Descanso Gardens, 1418 Descanso Dr., La Canada.

Every December in Long Beach, the Naples Christmas Parade of Lighted Boats is held on Alamitos Bay.

In Palm Springs, the Mounted Police Rodeo and Parade is held each January.

During winter, the Palomar Observatory offers an opportunity to see the world's largest telescope, which enables scientists to explore an area one billion light-years away. It is located 65 miles north of San Diego.

In San Francisco is the world's largest producer of hybrid orchids. The Rod McLellan Company, 1450 El Camino Real, offers visitors a guided tour of the 37-acre blooming indoor garden. You will see some 500 orchid species plus a novel "boarding house" for plants whose owners are on vacation.

For additional information, contact the California State Office of Tourism, Department of Commerce, 1400 Tenth Street, Sacramento, California 95814 or the Southern California Visitors Council, 705 W. Seventh Street, Los Angeles, California 90017.

# Colorado

Pikes Peak Marathon, the World's Most Unusual Music Festival
and a Fishing Worm Contest

**Pikes Peak Marathon**
Perhaps no other sport event is more grueling and challenging than the annual Pikes Peak Marathon. To run up and then down this 14,110-foot mountain is one of man's most remarkable sporting feats. Normally held in August, the race extends over a 26.8-mile course. The starting line forms early in the morning at the Manitou Springs Cog Railway Depot, which happens to be at 6,600 feet above sea level. From that point, the incline is steep all the way to the summit.

Track teams and individual runners from across the nation compete in this marathon; there are men, women and teenagers of all ages. It's a big challenge to reach the top and descend again in record time. For this reason, the race is a great spectator event. All along the way, there's room for spectators to gather and watch. Most of them assemble at the summit and at the finish line. After completing the marathon for the second year in a row, one runner commented: "If you can run up Pikes Peak and down again, you can do anything."

**Pikes Peak Hill Climb**
The marathon is not the only competitive event held on Pikes Peak each year; there's also the Pikes Peak Hill Climb which normally takes place the last Sunday in June. It comprises three divisions—stock cars, four-wheel-drive vehicles and motorcycles. The motorcycle competition is on-the-road competition, while the others are timed events with cars starting at 3-minute intervals. The course is approximately 12-miles long, finishing at the summit of the 14,110-foot peak.

**Colorado's Sahara**
It's ironic indeed that nature could pile up gigantic sand dunes a thousand miles from any ocean. But, here in the midst of Colorado are dunes rising as much as 600 feet above the valley floor and extending for some 10 miles along the foot of the Sangre de Cristo mountains. Geologists theorize that prevailing southwesterly winds collected sand from an old ocean bed and dropped it at the base of the mountain barrier over a period of thousands of years. Today the Sahara of Colorado has been labeled the Great Sand Dunes National Monument. To get there, take CO 150 out of the tiny village of Mosca, which is 13 miles north of Alamosa.

**Leadville's Bur-Rodeo**
One of Colorado's leading "offbeat" tourist attractions is the annual Leadville Boom Days celebration, traditionally held the first weekend in August. The feature attraction of this celebration is the burro race. The race is run over a 21-mile trail and there is a first prize of $1,000.

The racer can neither ride nor do anything other than the usual methods of pulling, pushing or carrying his burro over the trail to the finish, even though the balky burro may have other ideas. Contestants and their cantankerous burros circle the monument to the renowned Father Dyer, the snowshoe itinerant. The race then proceeds down East Seventh Street, following the route taken for so many years by Baby Doe Tabor before her tragic death and thence to the rodeo grounds and the finish. Both men's and women's divisions are held. Leadville is located on U.S. 26, southwest of Denver.

**Fishworm Judging**

The feature attraction of the Logan County Fair, in Sterling, is the annual Fishworm Judging Contest. Each showman may enter six worms in each of the two classes: red worms and night crawlers. Although the well-groomed critters display their qualities well on paper plates, they do become extremely active. Care must be taken not to tilt the plate, lest an entry be squashed under tramping feet. Worm tenders are present to make sure these worms stay on their plates until judged.

Judges rate the worms on vigor, color, strength and other "wormly" characteristics, such as toughness when placed on a fish hook. How do you do that? "You can tell by feeling the worm," said a Colorado State University wildlife specialist, the head judge of the event. Sterling is located just off I-80S in northeast Colorado.

**Denver's Mountain Parks**

Around Denver there is a host of unusual mountain parks comprising some 20,000 acres. One is Bergen Park where the main attraction is Clock Manor, an unusual museum of odd and wonderful timepieces collected by horologist Orville Hagans. Approximately 4 miles away, via U.S. 40, is Genessee Park where lookout points permit you to watch buffalo and elk herds grazing at the edge of the timber. Two miles farther, take a left turn on CO 68 to 7,500-foot Lookout Mountain where there's a free museum displaying Buffalo Bill Cody's

The Sahara of Colorado has been labeled the Great Sand Dunes National Monument, Colorado.

Annually, a public hike is held through the Arapaho Glacier area, Boulder, Colorado.

guns, clothing and mementos of his career. Buffalo Bill's tomb is also located here. If you're at the museum in the late afternoon, it might be worthwhile to pause and watch Denver's lights flicker on as darkness creeps across the Plains.

**Train to Silverton**

For an experience in the Colorado wilderness only accessible by rail, you must ride the narrow-gauge Silverton train. It's one of the few trains in America that can take you back to an 1882 adventure. Not far out of the station, rolling through the majestic wilderness of the San Juan National Forest, you may see a multitude of wildlife, including deer, elk, bear and even a mountain lion. Naturalists have counted more than 140 species of wild grass along the route and 300 different flowering plants, including the glacier blue columbine, Colorado's state flower.

The tracks of this narrow-gauge railroad were laid in 1882. When you reach Silverton, there's time for shopping, strolling around town and dining before the trip back to Durango. The railroad has been established as a National Historical Landmark. Because of the popularity of this attraction, it's wise to make reservations early. The train operates from late May until October 1, weather permitting. To get to Durango, take U.S. 550 or U.S. 160.

**Arapaho Glacier Hike**

Twenty-eight miles west of Boulder is Arapaho Glacier, the largest glacier in the state and the only city-owned glacier in North America—used as an urban water supply. On the second Sunday in August, a public hike to the glacier is held. Over

Dog sled tours are offered at Ashcroft, Colorado.

a steep trail wending 3½ miles from the base camp, the annual hike has been held each summer since 1939. Breakfast is served before the start and dinner awaits their return. The Boulder Chamber of Commerce sponsors the event.

The scenery is fantastic; the glacier is one mile in length and 3/4 mile wide. By actual measurements, the glacier is moving from 11 to 27 feet per year. The ice is estimated to be from 100 to 500-feet thick. The hike leads to the saddle of the glacier, where a rock-climbing and rescue-mission exhibition is given. Boulder is located on U.S. 36, northwest of Denver.

## Mountain Rescue Team

For a thrilling demonstration of rock climbing and military mountaineering, the Fort Carson Leadership School holds open house each Tuesday and Thursday from early June through late August. The one-hour show is staged in North Cheyenne Canyon, southwest of Colorado Springs, and features the Army's mountain rescue troops in some hair-raising episodes. Although there's no parking at the climb site, shuttle bus service is provided and there's no admission charge.

## Sled Dog Tours

Between the first of December and mid-April, at Ashcroft near Aspen, one and two-day adventures crosscountry by dog sled are offered. Headquarters for the winter safari is the Stuart Mace ranch which has a kennel for 90 huskies. The trip, with a team of 13 to 21 barking huskies, is unlike any other you've ever taken.

The scenery is memorable in every way—from magnificent mountains shining in the distance to the tracks of a snowshoe rabbit at trailside. Two can ride the sleds with a third trailing behind. If you have chosen a one-day trip, you stop at Montezuma Chalet for lunch. Otherwise, you spend the night there and leave after lunch the next day. To make reservations, write to Maces of Toklat, Aspen, Colorado.

For additional information on Colorado attractions, contact the Travel Development Section, Division of Commerce and Development, 600 State Services Building, Denver, Colorado 80203.

The Red Rocks Theatre seats 10,000 at Colorado Mountain Park, Denver, Colorado.

# Connecticut

Dinosaur Tracking, Sail Sewing and Clock Watching

In 1966, the first dinosaur track near Rocky Hill was discovered. Ultimately others were uncovered, and the scientific worlds at Harvard and Yale became as enthusiastic as a child with a new toy. The result is one of the nation's newest and most exciting public parks—Dinosaur State Park—which allows one to inspect more than 1,000 dinosaur footprints.

A geodesic dome, constructed over parts of the area, protects footprints exposed to the elements and allows visitors daily from 10 A.M. to 5 P.M., with the exception of Christmas. The prints, according to the State Natural History and Geologic Survey, were made from 180- to 225-million years ago by at least three different types of creatures. Most of them measure about twice the size of a man's hand. At no other spot on the globe have the prints of dinosaurs been uncovered in such profusion.

Dinosaur Park is situated on West Street not far from the Veterans' Hospital. Rocky Hill, 10 miles south of Hartford, is approximately 100 miles from New York City via the Connecticut Turnpike (I-95) and I-91. Admission is free.

**Dinosaurs at Rocky Hill**

An event bound to fill you with pride is the annual muster of Revolutionary War musicians reenacted at Deep River. Approximately 2,000 fifers and drummers, garbed in uniforms of Revolutionary and pre-Civil War eras, participate during July in the largest muster in the United States.

First formed when settlers organized militia units for protection, the muster has continued down through the years in commemoration of our heritage. During the middle of the eighteenth century, British regulars taking part in the French and Indian Wars introduced fifing to the colonists. With a traditional British style of drumming added, the muster was and still is exciting to watch and hear. A parade is held and awards are made for best authenticity. The annual muster is held on Devitt Field in Deep River, located on CT 9, just 3 miles north of I-95.

**Muster Day at Deep River**

All along Connecticut's seacoast, you'll find crafts closely connected with life at sea. In a small secluded shop in Old Mystic, you'll find the most exquisite maker of sails in the nation—Van Zandt's Sail Shop. Once you reach Mystic, you'll have to ask directions to Van Zandt's, for he doesn't cater to visitors, although he doesn't turn them away.

His small shop is dedicated to the making of fine sails (some of the greatest sailboat races are won on Van Zandt sails). Here, from January to early fall, you can see workers design, cut and sew sails. A family-operated business, it's one which few people actually see or experience. Old Mystic is located on I-95, southeast of Norwich.

**Sail Sewing at Old Mystic**

The annual muster of Revolutionary War musicians at Deep River, Connecticut. *(Courtesy of Connecticut Development Commission)*

**Clock Watching**

Connecticut is the birthplace of the once great American clock industry and, particularly, the so-called "Dollar Watch." In Plymouth and at Bristol, mass production of the American clock industry had its origin. Hundreds of millions of clocks and watches were made in this locale.

It is only natural that the Museum of American Horology or, more specifically, the Clock and Watch Museum should be established in Bristol. On exhibit are brass and wooden movements in tall, tower and shelf clocks and examples of eighteenth and nineteenth-century craftsmanship by skilled cabinetmakers, country carpenters or joiners. The history of time-making devices in this nation can be traced in its entirety in this one museum. The museum, open to the public daily, except Mondays from April to October, is located on Maple Street in Bristol, just off U.S. 6.

**Line Meeting House**

Collectors of odd and irrelevant pieces of information will want to visit the Line Meeting House on the Connecticut-Rhode Island border between Ekonk and Sterling off CT 49. A bride and groom cannot be married facing the pulpit in this building because the line between the two states runs through the house in such a way as to legally cast them asunder. However, many couples enjoy the novelty of being married in this building. If the bride and groom are united on the Connecticut side, the marriage is legal. However, couples who take their vows on the Rhode Island side of the room must then find a nearby church in order to be legally wed in Connecticut.

A short distance from Bristol is the Lock Museum, consisting of thousands of locks. Many of the lock manufacturers of America originated in Connecticut. The birthplace of the cabinet and truck lock industry was at Terryville, the location of the museum. The collection includes the entire 5,000-lock inventory of the Eagle Lock Company, including cabinet, trunk, padlock, post office, safe combinations, safety deposit and many other type locks. It's open to the public May through October, except Monday afternoons. Terryville is located on U.S. 6, only 6 miles east of Bristol, at 114 Main Street.

**Locks of the Nation**

One of Connecticut's most garish attractions is the Hartford home of Mark Twain, an opulent Victorian showplace. Completed in 1877 at a cost of $130,000, the house has stenciled brick on the exterior with Tiffany doors and paneling inside. Its estimated value today is in excess of $1 million. Throughout the house are peacock green walls, imported Italian marble floors, Tiffany lampshades, carved mahogany desks, cathedral doors of heart-of-pine, a bed imported from Venice and a fireplace from a Scottish castle. Here, too, are several of Twain's smoking pipes, several of his inventions and a room built with carved star-shaped beams to give a riverboat cabin effect. Twain's famous Rube Goldberg-type printing press is in the basement. Among the works produced in this house were *Huck Finn, Tom Sawyer* and *The Prince and the Pauper.*

**The Abode of Mark Twain**

New-Gate Prison was once the San Quentin of the Colonies. Named after the notorious Newgate in London, it was first used as a prison in 1773. Designated as a place of confinement for burglars, horse thieves and counterfeiters, it was later used as a Revolutionary prison for Tories. Despite several uprisings which resulted in the escape of a number of inmates and the destruction of its buildings three times by fire, New-Gate gained a reputation for great strength and security. In 1790 Connecticut made New-Gate and its subterranean cells a permanent state prison; it was abandoned in 1827.

**New-Gate Prison and Copper Mine**

Before New-Gate became a prison, however, it had already gained a reputation as a copper mine. From 1707 until 1773, it was extensively worked and the ore was shipped to England for smelting. A lack of mining knowledge and machinery, plus some financial disasters, brought about the close of this operation just before the prison was founded on the site. Today the grounds and buildings have been partially restored by the Connecticut Historical Commission, and visitors are welcome Tuesday to Sunday from Memorial Day through October. New-Gate Prison and Copper Mine is located on Newgate Road, just off CT 20, east of Granby.

Among Connecticut's unusual museums is the Nut Museum. The nut exhibit, displayed in one room of a nineteenth-century mansion in Old Lyme, offers visitors an unusual display of all types of edible and nonedible nuts, paintings of nuts, nut trees and a variety of nutcrackers. Admission is one nut, regardless of variety. An 8-foot nutcracker hangs from one of the many nut-bearing trees which appropriately shade the museum. Tours of the Nut Museum are personally guided by its owner and founder—Miss Elizabeth Tashjian, an Armenian

**Nut Museum**

who claims nuts originated in old Armenia. The Nut Museum is located on Ferry Road at Old Lyme, on CT 156, just off I-95.

## Post Card Museum

A unique Post Card Museum—probably the only one of its kind in North America—is situated in Canaan, Connecticut. Located in an 80-year-old red barn, one-half block from the town's post office, the museum displays more than 6,000 richly colored picture post cards. Operated by Mr. and Mrs. George MacCallum, a retired couple who began collecting post cards years ago, the museum offers more than 300 themes.

Among the categories are get-well cards; bon voyage; wedding congratulations; bereavement messages; tourist attractions in Europe, Australia and the United States; Biblical texts; Bible Land scenes; and patriotic motifs; as well as paintings of the masters. The museum is located in Canaan, just off U.S. 7 and U.S. 44.

## Trolley Rides

At the Branford Trolley Museum at East Haven, one may ride on an old-time trolley along shoreline salt marshes, woods, hillsides and cliffs, trestles and rivers. It's a step back to a time when trolleys were a major means of trans-

Trolley cars click down the rails through yesteryear at Branford Trolley Museum, East Haven, Connecticut. *(Courtesy of Connecticut Development Commission)*

portation. Also at the museum, you'll see more than 60 trolleys left over from that era in the United States and Canada; every kind from horse car to streamliner, open cars, interurbans, a parlor car, convertibles, a snow plow, elevated cars, gay nineties trolleys and many others. The museum, operated by the Branford Electric Railway Association, is open April through November and is located near the green in East Haven, just off the Connecticut Turnpike.

For additional information, contact Vacation Travel Promotion, Development Commission, State Office Building, Hartford, Connecticut 06115.

# Delaware

## Little State of Surprises

The Great Cypress Swamp encompasses thousands of acres of hauntingly beautiful territory, wherein numerous legends and folklore have been born. Tiny hamlets like Shaft Ox Corner and Pepperbox are located in the maze of small untraveled byways that twist and wind themselves through dense pine

The outstanding natural beauty of the Great Cypress Swamp at Trap Pond State Park, Delaware. *(Courtesy of Delaware State News)*

forests, stretches of native American holly (Delaware's state tree) and the northernmost stands of bald cypress in North America. Also found in the swamp are three ponds of outstanding natural beauty—Trap Pond, Raccoon Pond and Trussum Pond.

History is inherent to the Great Cypress; for here is a marker left by two intrepid eighteenth-century surveyors—Mason and Dixon. Delaware is the only state that lies north, south and east of the Mason-Dixon Line. Just west of Delmar, a small shelter covers one of the stones that mark the transpeninsular line and the southern point of the state's western border. Positioned one per mile in 1763 to 1767 by Mason and Dixon, these marker stones were quarried near Portland, England, and engraved with the arms of the Penns on one side and those of the Calverts on the other.

Rustic Christ Church at Laurel and several old water-powered grist mills in the area are also of historical interest. Antique buffs should visit Ocean View, where three large barns are stuffed to the rafters with everything from period furnishings to inspiring "new antiques" of the Victorian era.

The Great Cypress Swamp is bounded by U.S. 13 and U.S. 113 on the east and west, DE 24 on the north and the Delaware-Maryland boundary on the south.

**Walking Dune**    Delaware's beaches have been "walking" for centuries; but at no place is the movement more pronounced than at the Great Walking Dune of Cape Henlopen. Because it "walks" a few feet every year, the dune has figured in many strange and swashbuckling stories of the Delaware coast.

Scientific facts show that prevalent northwesterly winds along Delaware's 30-mile Atlantic coast cause the sands to shift, resulting in traveling dunes over a period of time. The same wind action has caused the Delaware coast near the cape to recede and to noticeably flatten and arch closer to neighboring Lewes,

The Great Walking Dune of Cape Henlopen, Delaware. *(Courtesy of Delaware State Highway Department)*

which lies to the west, sheltered on the inner curve of Lewes Bay. The entire jutting peninsula is part of Cape Henlopen State Park. Lewes, gateway to the peninsula and the park, is located at the end of DE 16, off U.S. 113.

For nearly a century, Big Thursday has been a tradition in lower Delaware. Held annually on Slaughter and Broadkill beaches, it amounts to an old-fashioned get-together on the second Thursday of August each year.

Big Thursday started in 1852 when a ban prohibiting the taking of oysters between May 1 and August 10 was lifted. So happy were the oyster-loving residents of the coastal areas of Kent and Sussex counties that they rushed to the beaches to get their fill of Delaware Bay oysters. Later, they joined together in singing, dancing, eating and talking. So enjoyable was the event they agreed to return each year for a day of celebration on the beach.

Visitors from Wilmington and Philadelphia started coming by boat and were rowed ashore in smaller boats. During election years, candidates for political offices found it "good business" to be seen, and heard, at Big Thursday observances; old-fashioned oratory became an established part of the program.

With the advent of World War II, better roads and faster automobiles, people turned their attention to other things, however, and Big Thursday died. In the 1960s, it was revived, much as it was in the old days. No longer held on the beach, Big Thursday is now centered on the banks of the Broadkill River in Milton, where people congregate to watch an old-fashioned bathing beauty contest (vintage 1800s), a parade of decorated bicycles, a fire and water curtain exhibition and other events. Milton, the center of activity for this event, is located on DE 16.

## Big Thursday

Before wealth and bustling business led to its present name, Odessa was once known as Appoquinimink and later as Cantwell's Bridge. About the time it was named after the great Russian seaport, the new Delaware Railroad sounded Odessa's economic death by running its line to nearby Middletown. Odessa virtually became a ghost town.

Today traffic on U.S. 13 zooms through its sleepy crossroads where the traffic light is about the only sign of life. But here, one may still find some of the finest architecture in the state, including the Corbit-Sharp House, a handsome Georgian-Chippendale mansion. Cited a National Historic Landmark, it is filled to the brim with priceless antiques and possessions. Along with the neighboring Wilson-Warner House, the Brick Hotel and the John Janvier Stable, it is one of four properties administered by the world famous Henry Francis du Pont Winterthur Foundation.

At Christmastime, these four homes, plus many private, colonial and federal era buildings, are open to the public, decked out in their eighteenth-century Christmas finery. Odessa, located about halfway between Dover and Wilmington on U.S. 13, is open to the public on a year-round schedule.

## Odessa—
## Monument to the
## Past

For additional information, contact the Travel Development Bureau, Division of Economic Development, 45 The Green, Dover, Delaware 19901.

# District of Columbia

Home of the Presidents' Church, an Underground Railroad and a National Kite Flying Contest

**Presidents' Church**

The day after President Kennedy's assassination, the late President Lyndon Johnson walked head bowed into "The Presidents' Church" and became the thirty-fourth head of state to have prayed there. Only 2 minutes from the White House, across Lafayette Park, Saint John's Episcopal Church has welcomed every president since James Madison.

Designed by Benjamin Henry Latrobe, famous Washington architect, Saint John's has changed little since it first opened its doors in 1816. Latrobe was the church's first organist and choirmaster. Built in the shape of a cross and featuring a glazed cupola, the small church contained only 86 high-backed pews. Pew 28 was set aside as the Presidents' pew, free of rental. A re-design in 1883 gave the President pew 64, but its approximate location is the same as the original pew 28. The old bronze bell that still summons members to Sunday worship was installed in 1822 and was cast in Boston, by the son of Paul Revere, from a British cannon captured in the War of 1812. It was presented to the church by President Madison. During the Civil War, President Lincoln suggested the church hold special vesper services for men in uniform, a rite that continues to this day.

**National Jousting Tournament**

Under the shadows of the picturesque Washington Monument, each year in October is held the National Jousting Tournament—a ritual laid down during the days of King Arthur's court and continued to this day in several parts of the United States. (Jousting has become the official state sport of Maryland, and numerous jousting events are held there throughout the summer months.)

Riders from several states, including the Carolinas, the Virginias, Maryland and sometimes Louisiana, gather to compete in the day-long event. The official Capitol Parks Band comes to play as the kings and queens, the princes and princesses, the court jesters and the page boys and girls gather in costume to mark this momentous occasion. A parade is held around the grounds, the knights are charged by the king of kings and there are humorous skits on horseback.

But the real challenge is a tough competition as rider after rider charges through the arches from which are suspended small white rings to be speared by the knight's lance. If he gets all of them and is able to keep them on the lance, he scores a perfect record; there are few perfect records. Both men and women compete in this event which has retained much of the pomp and splendor of the medieval ages.

The national jousting tourney is held each October near the Washington Monument in Washington, D.C.

**Kiteflying Competition**

Each spring on the Washington Monument grounds, a kiteflying competition is held. Here you'll see kites of every description and size, each trying to outdo the other.

This event was first held several years ago despite district laws against it. The laws have since been rewritten to allow kiteflying within the District of Columbia.

Sponsored by the Smithsonian Institution, the event is designed to encourage experimental kiteflying and constructing. Demonstrations are given by expert kiteflyers in both flying and making kites. The throng of participants and spectators increases each year.

**Underground Railroad**

If kite-making and flying are not your particular cup of tea, perhaps you'd enjoy a ride on the underground railroad that passes from the Capitol to the Senate and House office buildings. However, you can't just walk in and expect a ride; first you must call your Congressman or Senator and have him give you a permit to do so. It's an enjoyable ride and a relatively unknown attraction.

**America's Famous Bean Soup**

Another unique adventure for anyone visiting the Capitol (again you must get permission from your lawmaker to do this) is to eat lunch in one of the Capitol restaurants. For here, bean soup has been a specialty for many years. It's made and served every day by special order of Congress!

For additional information, contact the Washington Convention and Visitors Bureau, 1129 20th St., N.W., Washington, D.C. 20036.

# Florida

## River Drifters, Swamp Buggies and Worm Fiddlers

**Snakes Alive!**

In a small, palm-shaded courtyard, a group of spectators await the appearance of one of Florida's most talked about acts. Suddenly a door opens, an 8-foot, hooded king cobra races toward the crowd, its head erect; close behind is a tall, dark gentleman dressed in white. Just before the snake reaches the gasping crowd, the man reaches out with a metal hook, sweeps the reptile round and grabs it by the neck with his free hand. The man's name is Bill Haast; the place—Miami Serpentarium.

To Haast this is routine. He is only part showman, for now it's milking time. He forces the snake to strike, to sink its teeth into the rubber cap of a glass vial. The audience can see the venom running down inside. Then he force feeds the snake as spectators stand spellbound.

Daily, Haast and his wife stage shows for spectators; but to Haast, it's more than a show. He milks the venom from up to 200 snakes a day. The venom is then shipped to medical research centers and to the Walter Reed Hospital in Washington, D.C., for research and to be used in helping save the lives of those bitten by poisonous snakes.

In the course of his work, Haast has been bitten a number of times and has survived bites by the king cobra, the tiger snake and the blue krait, not to mention the rattler and the copperhead. Visitors can watch as he works with other snakes, collecting ounce after ounce of venom for shipping to distant points. The Miami Serpentarium is located on U.S. 1, south of Miami.

**Rattlesnake Hunt**

Another snake spectacular is held upstate each year: the San Antonio Rattlesnake Festival. Sponsored by the Jaycees, the festival features not only demonstrations of rattlesnake milking and snake handling, but also international gopher races, Seminole Indians and a chicken barbecue. This event is usually held in October. San Antonio is located 5 miles west of Dade City, 3 miles east of I-75 on FL 52.

If you prefer something more subtle than king cobras and squirming rattle-snakes, you should make plans to visit the International Worm Fiddling Contest held annually at Caryville. Traditionally held in summer, usually in July, the contest draws participants from all parts of the nation, as well as some Latin countries and Canada.

Worm fiddling is a very old method of securing earthworms (or fishing worms) for fish bait. The method is also known as "snoring" or "grunting." It consists of driving a wooden stake into the ground to a depth of 6 to 18 inches and rubbing it with some object to cause it to vibrate. These vibrations radiating into the soil around the stake cause the earthworms to come out of the

## Worm Fiddling Contest

The International Worm Fiddling Contest is held annually in Caryville, Florida. *(Courtesy of Florida News Bureau, Department of Commerce)*

ground. Whoever procures the most earthworms within his allotted area in a given amount of time is declared the winner.

The contest offers two divisions—one for those under 14 years of age and one for those over 14. The contestants work in teams of two in an allotted space of 20 square feet. The juniors are allotted 10 minutes; the seniors 20 minutes. A trophy is also awarded for the contestant producing the longest worm. Caryville is located on U.S. 90, east of Pensacola.

Inner tube floating is relaxing on the Ichetucknee River, Florida. *(Courtesy of Florida Department of Commerce)*

**Drifter's Dream**  Florida is full of unusual activities, but probably none match the carefree experience of drifting upon the Ichetucknee River. Along the highways of this section of Florida, you're likely to see pickup trucks, cars and even motorcycles carrying inflated inner tubes, rubber rafts and air mattresses, all headed for the Ichetucknee.

The Florida News Bureau recommends a 3-hour trip along this crystal clear stream which flows over a white sand bed through a heavy forest. Masks and snorkels reveal an underwater panorama. Waving grasses, darting fish, bits of shells, dating from the era when much of the Florida peninsula was under the sea, and occasional Indian artifacts are clearly visible.

Large boats and motors are banned, and the floater moves along with the current at the rate of about 1 mile an hour. This portion of the river, which stretches for 3 miles, is owned by the state and open to the public. The river is patrolled, and a roadside park allows visitors' parking. The trip appeals to families and people of all ages, yet rarely is the river overcrowded with drifters. This section of the Ichetucknee is located near Fort White on U.S. 27.

## Canoeing with the 'Gators

A dozen sleek canoes glide silently through the saw grass, past dormant alligators, within close range of thousands of birds and among some of the most unusual plantlife in America.

Such an experience is offered by the several canoe trails leading out of Flamingo in the Florida Everglades. Occasionally, organized "canoe-a-cades" are held with a National Park Service naturalist interpreting the trail along the way. Most of the trips are one-day long, but they can be lengthened. For a schedule of organized canoe trips, contact the Superintendent, Everglades National Park, P.O. Box 279, Homestead, Florida 33030.

You can either bring your own canoe or rent one by making reservations in advance at Everglades Park Company, General Delivery, Flamingo, Florida 33030. Canoeists are advised to bring their own equipment, including lunches, raingear, water supply for the day, suntan lotion, insect repellent and swimming suits.

## Shelling on Sanibel

Along Florida's west coast, off Fort Myers, are two islands known as the top shelling spots in North America. Surrounded by broad, white sand beaches, Sanibel and Captiva Islands offer hour upon hour of pleasure to those who seek and collect seashells. Occasionally other treasures, including Spanish pieces of eight, have been found.

Public beaches on the islands are easily accessible, and the J. N. "Ding" Darling National Wildlife Refuge offers extensive waterfront lands to be explored. The roads are narrow and the islands have somehow maintained a pristine, uncommercialized atmosphere despite their popularity. They also provide opportunity for bird-watching, swimming and sunbathing. A $3 charge per automobile, collected at the causeway leading to the islands, has helped to control the huge number of people who flock to the islands. To reach Sanibel and Captiva, take FL 867 west out of Fort Myers.

## Sponge Divers

Off the Gulf Coast, in the Greek community of Tarpon Springs, one may take a boat ride to watch all types of sponges being collected by divers in deep-sea diving suits. Back on shore you can purchase those same sponges of various shapes and types at sidewalk markets. Perhaps the greatest event of the year here is the Epiphany ceremony, as ancient as medieval times, held each January. The bishop leads a procession to the waterfront along the sponge docks, raises a gold cross and tosses it into the chilly waters. A holy dove is released by the dove bearer; dozens of the town's young men plunge in after the cross. The one bringing it to the surface is blessed by the bishop in Greek Orthodox fashion.

Afterward, there are the sounds of Greek music and the enchanting smell of Greek cooking. A large party is held for all. In the Sponge Marketplace, the cross retriever and other friends and divers make their rounds singing the traditional Epiphany song. Children dressed in authentic Greek costumes dance in the streets for hours. Tarpon Springs is located just off U.S. 19, 30 miles north of Tampa on the Gulf.

## Keys to Serenity

If you tire of commercialized Florida and wish to do some shunpiking, an island upstate along Florida's Gulf Coast awaits your inspection—Way Key. The town on the island is called Cedar Key; its population is 1,000. The entire area of Way Key is about 1 mile long and no wider than ½ mile. It served as a shipping point during the Civil War, but there's been little activity other than fishing since.

Many of those who visit the island do so not to catch fish but merely to eat them. The Island Hotel offers a superb home-cooked, fresh fish dinner. A menu offering stone crab, green turtle steaks, pompano, shrimp and oysters makes deciding what to order the most difficult part of the meal.

Almost anyone on the island will take you fishing, if you desire to try your own luck. Way Key is a delightful, peaceful shunpiking adventure. To get there, travel 22 miles southwest of Otter Creek (halfway between Tallahassee and Tampa on U.S. 19) and take FL 24.

## Swamp Buggy Races

In southwest Florida, the nation's most unusual races are held semi-annually. Appearing like moon monsters, these strange contraptions called swamp buggies compete on a 40-acre tract of flooded marshland on the edge of the Florida Everglades. Here, these home-fashioned conveyances are a way of life, with their high wheels and ability to get through mud and water under almost any conditions.

Twice a year, usually in November and February, they race for honors and a trophy. Speeding around a figure eight track, three abreast, at rates up to 60 miles per hour, the buggies and their drivers traverse holes which all but inundate them, leaving little to mark their spot but air bubbles and the gurgle of drowning engines. Somehow, most of them manage to pull out of the holes

Swamp buggies compete on marshlands in the Everglades at Naples, Florida.

and finish the race. An added attraction is a Powder Puff Derby for the lady drivers, held at the end of the day's events. To reach the Swamp Buggy races, drive to Naples, turn east on the Tamiami Trail and ask directions at one of several service stations in the area.

Until you've eaten swamp cabbage, you cannot consider yourself a swamp rat, or so it's claimed in south Florida. What better opportunity is there to sample this delectable treat than at the annual Swamp Cabbage Festival at La Belle? The event, usually held in February, is designed by the people of Hendry County in appreciation of that area's prize product—the Sabal Palm, or Cabbage Tree, from which the swamp cabbage is processed. The festival includes an acrobatic competition, a parade, a beard-growing contest, a steak and swamp cabbage dinner, a rodeo, a gospel sing, a country and western music show and a square dance, not to mention a gigantic swamp cabbage exhibit.

Swamp Cabbage Festival

La Belle is located at the intersections of FL 80 and FL 29, about halfway between Lake Okeechobee and the Gulf of Mexico, in the heart of swamp cabbage country.

As you travel south along U.S. 1 through the Florida Keys, you come to one of the most unusual state parks in the nation—Pennecamp is all underwater. Established to preserve a unique coral sea, the park provides visitors the opportunity to explore underwater by using scuba gear, snorkel outfits or, if you prefer to stay dry, a tour in glass-bottom boats. It's one of the greatest opportunities in the nation to observe sea life on a coral reef.

Underwater Park

Motorists wandering south on U.S. 1 near Homestead, Florida, just south of Miami, shouldn't miss visiting the Coral Castle, one man's monument of his devotion to a lost sweetheart. Few visitors fail to be impressed by his undying love. The two-story castle is Edward Leedskalnin's monument to a 16-year-old girl who jilted him on the eve of their wedding, years ago in Latvia. Leedskalnin labored a lifetime and died in 1951, leaving his memorial to romance—a tower house containing 235 tons of coral, not counting the stairway.

Coral Castle

In the garden, he created a complete bedroom suite of coral, including twin beds, children's beds and a baby's cradle. He also built a children's patio, furnished with coral duplicates of the furniture described in *The Three Bears*. He carved rocking chairs weighing thousands of pounds but so delicately balanced they move at the slightest touch. The collection of couches, beds, chairs, fountains and tables includes one 3-ton table shaped like the state of Florida, complete with a waterhole marking the location of Lake Okeechobee.

Leedskalnin was such an expert at determining the balance point of his heavy creations that many a visiting engineer is baffled. A 3-ton stone serves as the garden entrance and moves easily on a single pivot. Equally delicate is the balance of the 9-ton gate in the rear wall. A lifelong bachelor, Leedskalnin was self-educated and worked alone; he did not lack the motivation from a far more powerful source—his lost love—to create this most unusual monument.

Just north of Miami, located on U.S. 1, is the small community of Dania containing 43 most unusual shops. Each shop specializes in a particular kind of antique. One shopkeeper has telephone pole insulators, another English silver; others have early-American wall plaques, Tiffany domes, doll houses, old-country French furniture, eighteenth-century Chinese rare export porcelain or

Florida's Antique City

French jardinieres. Even the ice cream parlor has an old antique look with cedar shingles, marble counters and coffee grinders. Its jukebox is antique, too—a one-cylinder Edison phonograph cranks out the dated music. Functional uses are made of many old antiques. For instance, spittoons are used for flower pots, glass insulators for serving soft-boiled eggs and milkpails for holding umbrellas. The "antique town" idea came into being after the Florida Turnpike took much of the tourist traffic off U.S. 1 and Dania's business district began withering away.

## Sunken Treasure

Besides astronauts and space rockets, Cape Kennedy is noted for at least one other thing—the Museum of Sunken Treasure. Among the items displayed is more than $1 million in gold and silver salvaged from the wreck of the Spanish Plate Fleet in 1715. Visitors carry shoulder strap tape recorders past dioramas depicting the sinking of the fleet and the discovering and salvaging of the wrecks. It is open daily 10 A.M. to 8 P.M.

## Crawler Races

Each year in April, a call goes out for "mamas of crawlers." The crawlers are children under the age of one year—or those who have not taken their first step. The reason for the call is that Mother's Day is drawing near, and that's when the annual Baby Race is held at Jacksonville Beach. Nearly 100 babies are entered each year, making it necessary to run the race in five or six heats.

The crawlers are placed in the center of a large circle drawn in the sand on Jacksonville Beach. The starter shouts "Go!" and the mamas rush to the outside of the circle to coax their offspring, using any persuasive method they think will do the job. The first baby to cross the line is declared the winner. But with separate heats there must be runoffs and, consequently, the race takes most of the day. Spectators love it and so do the babies.

## Other Points of Interest

Shrimp Boat Races at Fernandina Beach are usually held in May and admission is free. This event includes shrimp boat rides at the city docks, bottle shows, bank contests, landing of the pirates at city docks, model shrimp boat contests, parades and, of course, the shrimp boat races. Fernandina Beach is located on Highway A1A, north of Jacksonville.

The Calf and Pig Scrambles are each held in October at Starke. Fifteen registered purebred calves are given away to boys who successfully catch a calf. Two entrants at a time scramble for five calves. The boys must chase a calf, bring it to the ground, place a halter over its head and lead it out of the arena to the pen. A greased pig scramble for girls is also held. Girls must catch and place the pig in a gunny sack. Starke is located on U.S. 301 and FL 230, southwest of Jacksonville.

At Rainbow Springs, visitors can experience a ride on a huge floating leaf. Although the leaf is mounted on a monorail, it actually gives one the impression of drifting through the air on a leaf falling from a tree. The leaf rises to a height of 40 feet and dips almost to ground level. To get there take U.S. 41 to Dunnellon and follow the signs.

Organized turtle watches are formed at Jensen Beach at the height of the egg laying season for giant loggerhead sea turtles weighing up to 500 pounds. Groups gather at beach pavilions after dark and search for turtles flipping out their nests in the sand. The season extends from May 15 to August 15. Jensen Beach is located between Fort Pierce and Stuart, off Florida Turnpike on A1A Highway.

Visitors watch a sea turtle laying eggs at Jensen Beach, Florida.

Held annually, usually in March, at Fort Lauderdale, the Sand Castle Carnival features young participants who compete to build the best sand castle on the beach during an allotted time.

On the edge of the Everglades, shanty boat cruises are offered to the public as one of America's most unusual vacation treats. The 6-day cruise takes passengers through the land of the Seminole, the alligator and some of the greatest fishing areas in all Florida. Shanty boat cruises are operated on the Orange River, 7 miles east of Fort Myers.

Florida is full of cypress, but never will you see a greater collection of cypress knees than at Tom Gaskins Cypress Kneeland, which includes a Cypress Knee Museum, factory and 2,000-foot catwalk in beautiful Cypress Swamp. It's located on U.S. 27, one mile south of Palmdale.

For additional information, contact the Florida News Bureau, Department of Commerce, Collins Building, Tallahassee, Florida 32304.

# Georgia

### Gold, Moonshine and Little Grand Canyon

**Grand Canyon of Georgia**

The Little Grand Canyon of Georgia is one of the natural wonders of the East. More specifically, it's named Providence Canyon, where nature opened a gash 400-feet deep stretching through a pine forest. A trip to Providence Canyon affords a look at this majestic variety of colors created by 43 different types of soil. Believed to be more than 150 years old, the canyon covers several thousand acres. It's filled with oddly shaped limestone towers and minarets. According to legend, the canyon was begun by rain dropping unchecked from a farmer's barn and trickling down ageless Indian paths; it now has become one of Georgia's most popular state parks. Georgia's Little Grand Canyon is located near Lumpkin, on U.S. 27 in southwest Georgia.

**Town Reincarnated**

Enter Westville, Georgia, and you've entered a world of reincarnation; for this town sends you back to the nineteenth century for a closeup look at a bustling farm village. Here today's craftsmen demonstrate the skills of yesterday, i.e., one person still transforms raw materials into a finished product. In a reconstruction of original settings, one can watch the making of quilts, pottery, bricks, baskets and shingles as well as demonstrations of community services such as carpentry and blacksmithing. In the farmhouse kitchens of Westville, fireplace cooking is still an art not only to be watched, but to be savored with the aroma from the cookstove. Open Wednesday through Saturday from 11 A.M. to 5 P.M., Westville is located just ½ mile south of Lumpkin.

**Gold Rush in Georgia**

In 1828, America's first gold rush occurred near the town of Dahlonega, Georgia. Today Dahlonega has taken steps to preserve its historic past with the establishment of the Dahlonega Courthouse Gold Museum. Visitors can now see the graphic mementos of the gold rush days, including samples of Dahlonega gold, old furniture and mining equipment, ancient newspapers and historic photos. Not only that, visitors can still pan for gold in Dahlonega. Warning: it's not a paying proposition—but it's fun and you can keep what you find. To get there, take U.S. 19 north out of Atlanta approximately 60 miles.

**Moonshine Museum**

Some communities or states don't like to admit they have or have ever had moonshine whisky produced within their boundaries; but in Dawsonville, Georgia, they've erected a Moonshine Museum. It's only appropriate it should be located here, for Dawson County was considered, not many years ago, the capital of Georgia's moonshine whisky belt. Located a block west of the town square, the museum is housed in a 30 by 90-foot building covered with log slabs. Out front stands a huge figure familiar to Atlanta Braves baseball fans—Chief White Lightning. Braves' fans call him Big Victor. Inside the museum are four stills—each depicting an era in moonshine history. On duty to help describe the stills and answer questions is a bonafide ex-moonshiner. The stills are so authentic and the rumors so numerous that the Internal Revenue occasionally comes to check the rumors that actual moonshine whisky still is being made. Dawsonville is located in Georgia's Appalachian region on U.S. 19 and GA 53, northeast of Atlanta.

## Rattlesnakes in Winter

When the rattlesnake problem became acute in southwest Georgia a few years ago and several people were bitten, the Community Club of Whigham decided to do something about it—hold a winter rattlesnake roundup. The first one was staged in 1960. That year members of the club and other hunters caught 140 big eastern diamondback rattlers and probably left that many dead in gopher holes. Since that time, the winter rattlesnake roundup has become a tradition; and some years, hunters have taken nearly 500 rattlers. Prizes are awarded for the largest rattler and the greatest number of rattlers caught. Other activities at the event, usually held in January, include a beauty contest and a fish fry. Whigham is located on U.S. 34, 6 miles east of Bainbridge.

## The Enchanting Swamp

One of the most enchanting swamps in America is located in southwest Georgia. The Okefenokee Swamp is one of the nation's largest, most secluded and unspoiled swamps; and you can visit it either through the Okefenokee Na-

The Okefenokee Swamp can be seen at the Okefenokee Swamp Park or the Okefenokee National Wildlife Refuge, Georgia.

tional Wildlife Refuge or through the Okefenokee Swamp Park, a privately operated establishment out of Waycross. In the park, you can take a catwalk through the swamp, climb an enclosed observation tower for an eagle-eye view of the surrounding territory, see a collection of animal and plantlife on Cow Island or take a short guided boat tour of this jungle. If you desire, private guides will take you for an exploratory or fishing tour of the Okefenokee where you'll meet some of its permanent residents—giant alligators, osprey, eagles and hundreds of other species of wildlife. You may fish for jack pickerel, large-mouth bass, bream or crappie and camp in shelters on stilts. Two great rivers have their headwaters here—the Suwannee which flows into the Gulf of Mexico and the Saint Marys which flows to the Atlantic. The Okefenokee can be reached off U.S. 1 and 23 or U.S. 441.

Sawing board trees with cross-cut saw at Georgia Mountain Fair at Hiawassee, Georgia. *(Courtesy of Tourist Division, Georgia Department of Industry and Trade)*

For additional information, contact the Tourist Division, Department of Industry and Trade, P.O. Box 38097, Atlanta, Georgia 30334.

# Hawaii

Sleep in a Volcanic Crater, Slide Down a Waterfall and
Visit America's Only Royal Palace

**Trail Ride into a Volcanic Crater**

Haleakala, known as the House of the Sun, is a volcanic crater which may erupt again someday. This fact makes a horseback ride into the midst of this awesome crater one of the greatest adventures in the nation. Haleakala is the center of a national park which covers some 26,000 acres; and when you reach the rim, you realize most of it is contained within the crater. It's 21 miles around the rim. The floor of the crater—the heart of the park—is sprinkled with richly colored cinder cones and lies 3,000 feet below the summit. It's into this chasm that 30 miles of well-marked trail rides are offered by special arrangement.

The Park Service recommends a 2-day trip with an overnight stay in one of the cabins it provides within the crater; this affords a greater opportunity to observe the native birdlife and scenery. There are no roads within the crater; but you'll find plenty of wildlife, including some rare species such as the Hawaiian goose or nene. Plants are strange, too, but the one most characteristic of the crater is the very rare silversword, which grows as a mass of silvery, saber-like leaves. Its stalk grows to the size of a man and produces hundreds of vivid purplish blooms. Once the seeds mature, the plant dies. This is the only place on American soil and perhaps in the entire world where you can take such a trail ride and sleep in a cabin on a crater floor.

**Slides on Ti Leaves**

On Tantalus, near Kaneohe on the island of Oahu, there are slides where you can experience a unique, thrilling adventure. You sit on gigantic ti leaves and slide down a steep, wet and often muddy bank; you may end abruptly in a clump of trees or a steep drop-off, depending on your ability to control your direction. But that's only half the fun. Getting back up the slippery slope to begin the next run is another memorable experience, particularly when you slide back down as many as a dozen times before reaching the top.

The best time to go, of course, is during the rainy months, December to February, or just after a rain or during a light drizzle. Each New Year's Day on Tantalus, the Hawaiian Trail and Mountain Club (Box 2238, Honolulu) holds a ti leaf sliding party. This same club can give you directions to other slides which you can use whenever they're wet.

**Spirits of Ka Lae**

Located at Ka Lae, which happens to be the southernmost point in the United States, are the ruins of Kalalea Heiau, now designated a National Historic Landmark. Apart from the designated area are the free spirits that roam through the ruins. No visitors have reported seeing them, but the natives have; and even modern fishermen consider the shrine so potent with mana, or ghosts, that they bring offerings of food and drink and advise you not to go inside. The ruins here are part of the oldest known Hawaiian settlement (750 A.D.); strange green sand covers the beaches. On the grounds of an automated light tower where the pavement stops are salt pans (these are actually lava boulders with depressions in which sea water was evaporated over the centuries). Ka Lae is located on the isle of Hawaii.

**Iolani Palace**

In Honolulu stands the Iolani Palace, the only royal palace in the United States. Built in 1879-1880, the first public festivity was a Masonic banquet in 1882 when the king of Hawaii, which was then a monarchy, took up residence. The palace is open to the public today, and it's a showplace that should not be overlooked. The woodwork in the palace is Oregon white cedar, American walnut and Hawaiian koa, kou, ohia and kamani. Exterior walls are cement facing over brick with concrete block trimming. The ground floor is 100 by 140 feet with main towers that reach 76 feet above ground level. Nowhere else can one find such elaborate furnishings and distinctive decor. The palace is located on the grounds of the state capitol.

America's only royal palace is the Iolani Palace in Honolulu, Hawaii. *(Courtesy of Hawaii Visitors Bureau)*

**Beachcombing for Crystal Balls**

Although one may find Japanese glass fishing balls on many of America's beaches, at no other place will one find them in such great numbers. Beachcombing in Hawaii, therefore, takes on a special dimension.

In years past, before so many eager searchers joined the hunt, enough glass balls could be found on the beaches to pile carelessly in the corner of an open lanai or hang in hand-tied nets from the eaves. Now beachcombers are advised to do their searching early in the morning. Many of them do it prior to

Waipahee Slide is a natural waterfall near Kapaa, Hawaii. *(Courtesy of Hawaii Visitors Bureau)*

daylight with strong-beamed flashlights that easily pick up the reflections of the glass in the darkness.

The balls vary in size from that of a small orange to the rare half-bushel giant. Colors range from sea green through shades of aqua to a soft light blue, much like the hues obtained by early colonial glass blowers. Of course, these balls can be purchased in Japan, but that spoils all the fun of it. The excitement is finding these treasures that have actually drifted with the ocean currents all the way from Japanese fishing waters to the islands. Many of those who take beachcombing for crystal balls seriously keep close tabs on weather in Japan; for an ocean storm there is likely to set the balls free to drift. Computing the amount of time it will take for them to arrive in Hawaii is another part of the sport. Some beachcombers have been able to estimate the time of arrival almost to the hour. The best place to hunt for the balls, of course, is on the windward side of the islands.

## Riding Down a Waterfall

Near Kapaa, one of the oldest settlements on the island of Hawaii, is a waterfall called Waipahee Slide. The rocks of the fall are so smooth and the incline so gentle you can actually ride down the falls, letting the force of the water carry you along. However, don't try to get there during the rainy months. The roads are dirt with no pavement or gravel, and you'd be inviting an unexpected and unplanned stay by getting stuck in the mud.

For additional information on Hawaii's unique attractions, contact the Hawaii Visitors Bureau, 2270 Kalakaua Avenue, Honolulu, Hawaii 96815.

# Idaho

## Soda Springs, Ice Caves and Craters of the Moon

## Soda Springs— Town with a Geyser

If you're looking for a town with a fizz-water show, then Soda Springs is your kind of place. Set neatly in a mountain-rimmed valley of fields and horse corrals, Soda Springs has its own geyser located (you might expect) in back of the drugstore. It strikes you subtly at first as you gaze at this natural wonder and watch the surge of water splutter in impatient gasps; but nothing more happens. Then a passerby explains you must go to City Hall to get the geyser turned on.

The townspeople long ago capped the geyser when its erratic behavior caused flooding problems. By turning a valve, the geyser is allowed to shoot skyward as beautiful as Old Faithful. For nearly half a century, it has been a meek servant, responding to the opened valve when its pressure builds too high or when tourists want to see it. If you drive this way, be sure to bring a big bottle to carry home some pure soda water—and be sure to stop by City Hall and ask them to turn on the geyser for you. Soda Springs is located just south-west of Yellowstone National Park on U.S. 30N.

Talmaks—The Indian's Festival

On the mountain at the prairie's edge, under great pines, generation after generation of the Nez Perce gather to ponder on the White Man's religion, to muse upon their own traditions, to retell and relive their Indian legends. In mid-summer, since 1897, in late June and early July, they've come and erected their tents and tepees.

Today, Talmaks is a study workshop, an attempt of a people to retain their fine traditions while practicing devotion to Christianity and accepting the need for growth and understanding of the modern world and its many problems. The first Talmaks was a far cry from a religious camp, however. It was a 2-week celebration, a time for drinking, gambling, horse racing and exchanging wives. Today, it features crafts, an Indian auction and a study of Indian tradition and culture. Visitors are welcome. Talmaks is held near Kamiah off U.S. 12. Ask for directions locally to reach the Kamiah Valley site at Mason Butte.

Craters of the Moon

For 83 square miles, the barren black lava of Craters of the Moon establishes one of the most astonishing landscapes in America. It's a storyland of cinder cones, lava flows, tubes, craters and rifts—as unbelievable as anything this side of the lunar surface. That's why many of the "moon mission" astronauts first were given field training at Craters of the Moon in Idaho. Now a national monument, Craters of the Moon is remote; the small town of Arco is the closest place to purchase food, gasoline and supplies. You may camp at the monument, however, and enjoy some of the greatest drinking water to be found in North America.

Typical examples of the eerie landforms can be seen and visited from a 7-mile drive which circles the northwest corner of the monument. Or you can hike into its interior or take guided nature walks provided by a park naturalist. This unreal and inhospitable black lava sea provides a most unique experience for one or two days or a week. Craters of the Moon is located in Idaho's harsh southeast desert, some 150 miles west of Yellowstone and Grand Tetons National Parks on U.S. 20 and U.S. 26, between Carey and Arco.

Crystal Ice Caves

One place in Idaho which escapes the summer heat is a natural phenomenon located in the central part of the Snake River Lava Plain. Underneath this 20,000 square miles of desert is an incredible array of crystal ice caves. Discovered in 1956 by two amateur spelunkers, the largest of the caves is called simply Crystal Ice Cave. The dazzling beauty of the gigantic ice deposits are now shared with the public.

The cave has several rooms, their floors covered with a mass of rocks and snow and a roof of milky white ice. One room has deep rust red walls studded with diamond-like crystals that reflect in the light. At the foot of the snow in this room lies a lake of pure white ice, and rising to a height of approximately 16 feet are majestic stalagmites. Geologically these are known as "rift" caves, and they're the only ones in the world, at this writing, open to the public. Crystal Ice Cave is located near American Falls, off I-15W.

Idaho's Mammoth Cave

Idaho also has other caves, among them its own Mammoth Cave. One-half mile underground, one finds gigantic rooms many feet high. Visitors may still see the rifts made by escaping gas during the volcanic action that created this cave and may study the many colors in the igneous rock. Shortly after the cave

The dazzling beauty of the Crystal Ice Caves in Idaho. *(Courtesy of Idaho Department of Commerce and Development)*

was formed and cooled, the first large prairie bear came upon the mouth and made this its home and place of hibernation. Skeletons of these huge bears have been found here and are on display in the Cave Museum. Indians later moved into the area, leaving their tools and discarded implements. Many types of arrowheads, knives, maos and mios are also on display at the museum. Artifacts have been found in every direction around the cave and inside it. There is a broken pot in one place and a burial site in another with a mummified Indian wrapped in a twisted rabbit skin blanket. To reach Idaho's Mammoth Cave, drive 7 miles north of Shoshone on ID 93 and 2 miles west on a gravel road. It's open May 15 to October 1 daily.

## Fiddling and Banjo Picking

When a good old-time fiddler tunes up and draws an eager bow over his favorite fiddle, pulses quicken, people beat time with their feet and eyes brighten with happiness and appreciation. That's what happens every year in Idaho when it is time for the Singin' Strings—the National Oldtime Fiddlers Contest and Festival at Weiser.

Usually held in late June, the 4-day festival also includes a pioneer parade, old-time style show, barbecue, all-you-can-eat breakfasts, genuine old-fashioned melodrama, street dancing and about the finest array of old-time musical talent anywhere. To spice up the occasion, there's always a roving band of vigilantes—master clowns and hijinks specialists running on the loose; and no one knows where they'll pop up next.

The array of events at Weiser is unending. Children hardly weaned from the bottle bow a fiddle. No one thinks twice when a six-year-old competes with a master of 70. Fiddling fever bites every age, and the result is usually spontaneous and uninhibited fiddling from street corner to street corner, day and night, anytime, anywhere. People make their own fun with sing-alongs or the traditional snake parade of fiddlers and banjo pluckers weaving in and out of buildings all over town—at 1 A.M. in the morning. Fiddlers and other musicians come from everywhere to participate in the National Contest held at Weiser, and plenty of other folks come just to watch and listen and have fun. Weiser is located on U.S. 95, near the Oregon border.

## Silent City of Rocks

In the Minidoka Division of the Sawtooth National Forest lies a grotesque area known as the Silent City of Rocks, so named because of the close physiographic resemblance to a metropolis, with stone pinnacles reaching some 60 or more stories skyward. The highest tower within the limits of the city, which covers some 10 square miles, is Granite Peak on the northeast edge, rising 7,690 feet above sea level. On the south edge, Twin Sisters climbs 6,838 feet above sea level, or 62 stories above the street below.

Names of immigrants, applied with axle grease, are visible just as they were the day they were painted by the pioneers who came this way on the California Trail. You can still see the rutted wagon tracks across this arid section of Idaho. Other rock formations in the Silent City include Andy Gump, Kaiser's Helmet, Devil's Bedstead, Two Rock Turtles, Elephant Head, Monkey's Head, King on the Throne, Rabbit Rock, Clam Shell, Giant Toadstool, Squaw and Papoose, Saddle Rock, Skeleton Head, Needle Rock and China-

Located on ID 28 on Birch Creek, these kilns were used for charcoal for a smelter which was active from 1883 to 1889 across the valley at Nicholia, Idaho. *(Courtesy of Idaho Department of Commerce and Development)*

man's Head...all so named because of their profile appearance. The Silent City of Rocks is located near Almo off ID 77 in south central Idaho.

## Sahara of the West

Some people call it the Sahara of the West, others the Bruneau Sand Dunes. Located in southwestern Idaho, this small, but most unique, area carries the distinction of having the highest sand dunes in the world. Some of the dunes rise 452 feet, surpassing even the Sahara's highest by more than 150 feet. Now a state park, the area also includes a lake covering 160 acres and a beach for swimming.

Around the lake, the dunes form a high serpentine range 2 miles long, and their height forms a wind crater or natural amphitheater that could hold 10,000 people. On windy days, the great dunes come alive, and long streamers of flying sand float from the peaks like smoke from a volcano. The sides of the larger dunes are quite steep, so much so it may take up to 30 minutes to climb one. But the view from the top is fabulous—the blue green lake lies directly below, the white dunes roll away to the brown desert floor and 20 miles to the south lie the snow-capped peaks of the Owyhees, rising to almost 9,000 feet. The Sahara of the West is located 5 miles northeast of Bruneau just off ID 51.

For additional information, contact the Tourism Division, Department of Commerce and Development, State House, Boise, Idaho 83707.

# Illinois

### Piasa Birds, Garden of the Gods and a Hound Dog Named Boomer

## Theater-on-the-Square

While Sullivan is a good distance from Broadway, the little Theater-on-the-Square regularly lures stars from Hollywood, Broadway and television land. It's not unusual at this small Illinois town to sit next to June Allyson at the soda fountain in Hulbert's Drug Store or be greeted by Eddy Albert at Jibby's Tavern.

At one time, Sullivan's claim to fame was the lush corn and soybean fields which grow around it; but now it boasts a highly successful Equity summer stock theater, perhaps the only one in the country not near a large metropolitan or resort area. It operates a moderately priced 24-week season of top musicals and legitimate plays.

The theater was begun by Guy S. Little, Jr., when he was 21—the result of a childhood dream. The theater remains a family operation in order to help talented youngsters everywhere begin their professional stage careers. Many of those who are alumni of the Little Theater apprentice program in Sullivan are today successful actors and actresses on the national theater circuit. Sullivan is located in east central Illinois, 26 miles from Decatur on IL 121.

Horse ranches inherently belong in the far western United States; but increasingly through the years, ranch life is finding its way East. Such is the Hulling Ranch, quarter horse capital of the world, located in the unlikely spot near Smithton, Illinois. This work ranch includes indoor and outdoor show arenas, horse barns, horseshoe and barber shops, holding stalls, cattle pens and training areas.

One may visit here free of charge and watch cowboys training a quarter horse, cutting a yearling calf from a herd of cattle, roping, bulldogging and demonstrating many other facets of the training picture. More than 500 horses roam on this ranch; among them are the top cutting horses to be found anywhere. The quarter horse, so named because he is able to run a lightning-fast quarter-mile, is bred and trained to work. These horses must be kept in top condition and are so highly responsive to the rider that they are able to literally turn or stop on a dime. You can talk with cowhands at the Hulling Ranch, and they'll be happy to answer any questions you may have pertaining to quarter horses. Refreshments and rest rooms are provided for the public year-round. Hulling Ranch is located a few miles southwest of Smithton on IL 159.

Near the sprawling Mississippi River, within view of the city of Saint Louis, is a most unusual shrine called Our Lady of the Snows. Established by the Oblate Fathers in 1858, the shrine has attracted world-wide renown for its unique landscape, inspiring gardens and devotional sites such as the Lourdes Grotto, the Annunciation Garden and a most unusual outdoor altar made of black marble.

Thousands of pilgrims come to the shrine annually as part of their religious ritual, but hundreds of thousands of others come merely to visit the grounds, to marvel at the architecture and to study the mosaics and other artistic creations. It's open every day of the year and offers a most impressive Easter sunrise service outdoors. It's claimed to be the largest outdoor devotional site in North America. The shrine is located between Belleville and East Saint Louis, Illinois, on Route 460.

In southern Illinois' Shawnee National Forest is another shrine—one carved from the wilderness by Mother Nature. They call this strange array of limestone rock formations the Garden of the Gods. Claimed to be more intricately carved than those of the same name in Colorado, Illinois' Garden of the Gods includes some breathtaking formations. Among them are Anvil Rock, which couldn't have been formed more perfectly by machine; Noah's Ark with its animals; and Rose Rock, made by the weathering of soft grain in a rock. The gardens also include various types of balance rocks, a table rock, a needle's eye and one shaped exactly like an "H." And there's one which creates the image of a sleeping camel. A picnic site is nearby. Garden of the Gods is located on a gravel road off IL 34, near the town of Herod. For specific directions, contact the Headquarters, Shawnee National Forest, Harrisburg, Illinois.

Across the state in southern Illinois is Crab Orchard National Wildlife Refuge, one of the most unique wildlife refuges in the nation. It encompasses many aspects of human endeavor and proves beyond doubt that industry, recreation

## Quarter Horse Capital

## Lady of the Snows

## Garden of the Gods

## Home of the Wild Goose

and wildlife can coexist. More than 2,000 workers are employed at some 27 companies with factories or business establishments on the grounds of the wildlife refuge. It's an unusual sight to see deer and wild Canada and snow geese grazing in the yards of the factories with people walking close by.

Crab Orchard also provides three well-stocked lakes for some of the state's best fishing, boating and swimming; and there're camping and picnicking facilities, too. More than 100,000 wild geese and nearly that many wild ducks make Crab Orchard a stopping place each year on their migratory route south. More than 50,000 winter here each year, providing visitors with close-up views of their neighbors of the wild kingdom. Crab Orchard is located near Marion, just off I-57.

## White Squirrels of Olney

Upstate from Crab Orchard is a small town in east central Illinois called Olney, place of the white squirrels. Other towns and cities may have occasional white squirrels; but since before the turn of the century, Olney has had them by the hundreds. The present squirrel population is estimated at more than 1,000. Consequently, Olney has become known as the "Mecca of White Squirrels." In 1902, a law was passed protecting the white squirrels; and today, running over or molesting one almost automatically results in a $25 fine. The patches on the sleeves of every policeman and fireman in Olney bear the white squirrel insignia. The parks and trees are full of them. Motorists drive out of their way to come through Olney, to park along the streets and to feed the white squirrels. Olney is located on U.S. 50.

## Beall Woods

Southeast of Olney near Mount Carmel is a tract of virgin forest with giant trees the likes of which stood all across America during the days of Boone, Crockett, Clark, Marquette and Jolliet. They call it Beall Woods, which now has been made into a state park and National Historic Landmark. Hiking trails leading from the red barn museum and headquarters of the park pass through the dense stands of timber. Over 70 species of trees grow here, and more than 250 of them exceed 30 inches in diameter with heights up to 150 feet. The largest Shumard oak in the United States dominates one corner of the forest. Poison ivy and wild grape vines as large as a blacksmith's arm snake around the trees, while from high above come myriad bird calls. Occasionally, one may see a pileated woodpecker or a barred owl. Over the years, noted ornithologist Robert Ridgway spent many hours in this forest. Beall Woods is located off IL 1 just south of Mount Carmel.

## Horse Farming Days

Right in the heart of Illinois' Douglas County is a place called Rockome Gardens where each autumn the pages of history are turned back a hundred years. The horse farming days, complete with demonstrations and contests, are staged, allowing visitors an opportunity to watch six-horse hitches with a big gang plow, a six-horse hitch with a 7-foot tandem disc or four horses walking around in a circle supplying power to a huge threshing machine. Visitors also may take train rides or buggy rides down to the Kaskaskia River; they can visit an old Indian trading post and museum or a rock shop located at the gardens. If you're hungry, you can taste Amish shoo-fly pie from the kitchens on the grounds. Rockome Gardens are located just off IL 133, near Arcola.

## The Piasa Bird

In Alton, on the eastern banks of Old Man River, may be found the only known replica of the mysterious monster of the Mississippi—the Piasa Bird. For hundreds of years, on an inaccessible cliff-face of a Mississippi palisade

Demonstrations of horse farming days at Rockome Gardens, Illinois.

above Alton, loomed the ancient portrait of an ominous calf-size creature. It shocked explorers Marquette and Jolliet and their five French Canadian voyageurs when they passed this way in 1673. The description given by them was the first given by white men, but even then the painting was old and deteriorating. It has since been duplicated by residents of Alton, but what it denotes or who was its artist is still baffling.

Near Makanda is a plaque in memory of Boomer, a most unusual hound dog. It reads: "In Memory of Boomer, the hound dog tradition says dashed his life out against the iron abutment of the railroad bridge 300 feet south of this point on September 2, 1859, while running along on three legs trying to put out the flame in a hotbox on the speeding train of his beloved fireman-master."

**Boomer, the Hound Dog**

Boomer belonged to a fireman on the Illinois Central Railroad, and he would run alongside the slow-moving freight train on which his master worked. At first, Boomer's master was on a local freight that stopped at every town, and the dog could easily keep up with him. But soon word got around that the Illinois Central had a dog that could outrun their trains. Railroad officials decided they had to either fire the fireman or outrun the dog.

So they put the fireman on a fast freight that stopped only at water tanks. But Boomer still managed to keep up. Railroad officials were now determined. They sent down their fastest engine—old 1034—from Centralia. They instructed section crews to jack up the worst low joints and smooth up the track. Then they set a day for the big race and instructed employees to guard the crossings.

Hooking ten boxcars behind their engine to hold it onto the tracks, they sent down their craziest and most reckless engineer. Word got out, and people came for miles to see the big race; some even camped overnight along the track. The engineer gave it full throttle, and the fireman was ordered to heave on the coal. The engine vibrated and shook so much they were afraid it was going to leave the tracks; and Boomer still ran alongside.

When they came to the village of Makanda on Drury Creek, the trainmaster looked back and there was no Boomer. "We've left him behind!" he shouted. "But there are four hotboxes blazing back there." (This happens when the bearings get so hot they catch on fire.) Then the trainmaster got another look; and there was Boomer, running along on three legs, trying to put the blaze out on one of the hot boxes. That's when they came to the iron bridge across Drury Creek. The story goes that since Boomer was directing his attention to the fire, he didn't see the iron abutment and smacked fatally into it. That was the end of Boomer, of course, but the legend lives on in these parts. Makanda is located on U.S. 50, south of Carbondale.

**Fort de Chartres Rendezvous**

The spirit of the French in America is rekindled each fall at an ancient pioneer fort on the Mississippi. Dressed in costume, men, women and children of Prairie du Rocher and nearby towns stage demonstrations and activities associ-

The annual French rendezvous at Fort de Chartres, Illinois.

ated with their past, including a flintlock rifle competition, tomahawk throw, tug of war, knife throwing, cannon firing, carpentry and blacksmithing. There's also woodcarving, basketmaking, French cooking, candlemaking and ox cart rides for the children. On the second day of the rendezvous a war canoe race is held on the Mississippi with more than a half dozen of these giant canoes, some of which will carry 25 men, competing over a wicked course. Spectators watch from the banks. The entire rendezvous is admission-free. Fort de Chartres is located off IL 3.

**Carriage Museum**

Virtually in the shadow of the statuary of Abe Lincoln is the New Salem Carriage Museum. Here a most interesting and educational collection of early American horse-drawn vehicles from the United States and several foreign countries is displayed. Also on display are harnesses and saddles used in this era, harness and buggy-making tools, an early post office and a huge array of country store items. New Salem is located on IL 97, approximately 20 miles northwest of Springfield, the state capital.

**Purple Martin Town**

Ever hear of a town that's for the birds? There is one in west central Illinois; they call it Griggsville—"Purple Martin Capital of the World." Behind the program is a single man, J. L. Wade, president of Trio Manufacturing Company, the town's only industry. Wade has installed purple martin houses all over town, including in the park and along virtually every street. Along the median strip of the main thoroughfare, a 70-foot purple martin tower supporting 562 martin apartments is the town's main attraction.

Wade employs a crew during the summer months just to maintain the purple martin houses, to keep other birds from building in them. As a conse-

Purple martin boxes line the streets of Griggsville, Illinois.

quence, Griggsville and the surrounding area in this agriculturally rich land between the Illinois and Mississippi Rivers is virtually without mosquitoes or other pesty flying insects. Also open to the public at Griggsville is a Purple Martin Museum with paintings by wildlife artist Richard Sloan. There are displays of many other bird specimens as well as various other types of wildlife common to the area. Griggsville may be reached by taking U.S. 36 west of Springfield.

**Presley's Cross**

Back in 1937, a rural mail carrier named Wayman Presley spoke with his minister about a need for a place where people of all faiths could worship. They decided a nearby place—Bald Knob—would be an ideal location for such a meeting. Over the months that followed, Presley surveyed for donations to build what he envisioned as a fitting monument for this central gathering place for people of all denominations. At first, a crude cross fashioned from railroad ties marked the spot atop Bald Knob. But Presley wanted more than that; he decided he would work to have a giant cross built that could be seen for miles and miles, a beacon by which people would be guided to this spot.

Meanwhile, services continued at Bald Knob. Easter sunrise services drew hundreds of people and the number increased each year. Word of Presley's campaign spread far and wide. Publicity in national magazines brought donations from many parts of the nation and even from foreign lands. Ultimately, the great cross was constructed; it stands tall and white against the southern Illinois sky and is lighted at night so it can be spotted 50 miles away. Presley's Peace Memorial has become a reality. Bald Knob is located at Alto Pass in southern Illinois.

For additional information, contact the Division of Tourism, Department of Business and Economic Development, 222 South College, Springfield, Illinois 62706.

# Indiana

## Muzzleloaders, Circus Clowns, Sandhill Cranes and Turkey Trots

**Bang Bangs!** At the little hamlet of Friendship nestled in southeastern Indiana's hill country, the National Muzzleloading Rifle matches are held semi-annually in May and August. Thousands of hobbyists and gun enthusiasts, as well as spectators, gather along beautiful and historic Laughery Creek to join in one of the nation's most unusual events. They last for nearly a week and it's as though a page of history were ripped from the books and imposed anew upon the valley of Friendship.

Most of the shooters dress in costume of the era their guns represent. They pit their skills against one another in remarkable tests of dexterity and craftsmanship. Indians compete with mountain men and plainsmen as participants from all walks of life shoot at still targets, run the Seneca course, swap stories and knives, throw tomahawks and play music.

Most of those who come here camp on the extensive grounds of the National Muzzleloading Rifle Association headquarters. Others stay in motels at nearby Indiana towns. When they come to the Walter Cline Range, they are frontiersmen—the Daniel Boones and Davy Crocketts reincarnated in a modern era. Friendship is located in Ripley County some 80 miles southeast of Indianapolis on IN 62, off U.S. 50.

**Courthouse Tree** Not far west of Friendship is Greensburg, the town with a tree growing from the clocktower on the Courthouse roof. The fact that a tree grows from the roof of a building may not be so uncommon, but the fact that *this* tree is a Colorado aspen, a species totally foreign to the Indiana region, remains an unusual mystery. The community is known for the tree, discovered originally in 1866; and

Contestants dress in period costumes for the National Muzzleloading Rifle Association matches in southeastern Indiana.

the little 20-foot aspen has even been authenticated by the Smithsonian Institution in Washington, D.C. There have been eleven such trees to date. Each time one has died, a new one has sprouted, unaided in its growth by human hands except for an annual pruning. Greensburg is located just ½ mile off I-74, between Indianapolis and the Ohio border.

**Santa Claus**

If you're traveling in Indiana, you may visit Santa Claus anytime of the year. For Santa Claus is the name of a town in the southern hill country where many of Santa's letters are answered each year by volunteer townspeople. The post office in Santa Claus is one of the busiest in the nation during the period from Thanksgiving to Christmas, with mail coming from all parts of the nation and even from children in foreign countries. The remainder of the year, Santa Claus is relatively quiet, although there is an amusement park here as well as a giant, most impressive statue of old St. Nick himself, erected by the Curtiss Candy Company, and dedicated years ago to "Children Around the World." Santa Claus is located on IN 245, northwest of Tell City.

**Athens of the Prairie**

At Columbus in the heart of Indiana's agricultural belt, some of the nation's most outstanding architecture can be found. This small city has come to be known as the "Athens of the Prairie," a name first given it by the old *Saturday Evening Post* in an article about the town published just after World War II.

Over the years, through the efforts of one of its founding families, Columbus has attracted the world's leading architects to design all public buildings. As a result, it has become a showplace for unusual building designs, and most members of the architectural world consider the opportunity to design a building at Columbus much akin to that of a musician who is asked to perform in Carnegie Hall. More than 40 buildings are part of the marked architectural tour which begins at the Cleo Rodgers Public Library. Columbus is located on IN 46 and I-65, some 38 miles south of Indianapolis.

## Bluegrass Jamboree

In adjoining Brown County, which features split rail fences and rough-hewn log cabins, one of the world's most unique music spectacles is held each year— the Bean Blossom Bluegrass Jamboree. Bluegrass guitar and banjo pickers from around the country gather here, usually in June, and the picking and singing goes on day and night for a week. The Bean Blossom Festival, one of the largest of its kind in the United States, attracts some 20,000 people. A large percentage of those who attend the festival camp on the grounds. Others stay at nearby Brown County State Park. Bean Blossom is located on IN 135, 6 miles north of Nashville and approximately 35 miles south of Indianapolis.

## Turkey Trot

The first turkey races staged in the United States were held, according to the National Turkey Foundation, in Daviess County in southwestern Indiana. Held each September, the turkey races are a tongue-in-cheek affair, of course; for no one can predict which way the turkeys will go once they're released. But they do provide a lot of chuckles and fun for spectators. Prior to the legitimate race, a mock race is held along with a seminar for sponsors and trainers on the rules of turkey racing. Other events related to the turkey trot include a country music jamboree, rock dance and carnival rides. The turkey trot is moved from community to community in the county on successive years. Daviess County is located east of Vincennes and is dissected by U.S. 50.

## New Harmony

In the flat bottomlands of the Wabash is New Harmony, a study in communal living, home of the Roofless Church, the golden raintree and the Red Geranium. The original communal colony here was carved out of the wilderness by the German followers of George Rapp, a rugged religious zealot. Back in Wurtenberg, Rapp had led the organization of the Harmonie Society, whose members split off from the German Lutheran Church because of their literal belief in the imminent second coming of Christ for a thousand-year reign on Earth. The Harmonists in 1924, for obscure reasons, decided to transfer their operations to Economy, Pennsylvania, and sold Harmony to a Robert Owen, a wealthy Scottish industrialist, and William Maclure.

Owen and Maclure, leaders in a new social movement, gathered educators, scientists and workingmen from Europe and brought them to the town which they had renamed New Harmony. Although this social experiment was to be short-lived, it laid claim to having started America's first kindergarten, first free public school system, first women's club and first free library. The town was also the seat of the nation's first geological survey.

Today you can visit the homes and buildings associated with these movements. Other sights here include the Roofless Church, designed by architect Philip Johnson and shaped like an inverted rosebud, casting the shadow of a full blown rose.

For one of the finest meals in Indiana, visit the Red Geranium Restaurant; and before leaving town, ask one of the natives to show you a golden raintree, imported from the Orient. The best time to see one is in June, during the Raintree Hey Days festival, when the tree is in bloom, or in the fall when the golden leaves sprinkle to the ground like rain. New Harmony is located on IN 66 and IN 68, just 8 miles southwest of I-64.

## Maple Syrup and Covered Bridges

In west central Indiana is Parke County, land of maple syrup and covered bridges—a little bit of Vermont in the Hoosier State. Each year in February and early March, the Parke County Maple Fair is held, with open house at the many sugar camps. In the autumn during the peak of fall color—usually the first part of October—the traditional covered bridge festival is held.

Parke County claims to have the largest number of covered bridges of any county in the United States—more than 36 of them are in top condition and are intricately preserved. As a result, many artists year-round flock to Parke County to paint; the county has an art colony in residence. Billie Creek Village, a restored turn-of-the-century Indiana town, is open to the public 7 days a week from noon until 6 P.M. Activities, however, take place on a scheduled basis (check with the Rockville Chamber of Commerce). Craftsmen working in old-fashioned ways with outmoded tools make this a "living museum" experience. The center of activity is Rockville, the county seat, located on U.S. 41 and U.S. 36, some 50 miles west of Indianapolis.

## Gondolas on the Wabash

No place in America will one find a prouder people than among the residents of Clinton along the Wabash River. This small town, which boasts a high percentage of Italian descendants, annually stages a Little Italy Festival in September. During that time, visitors are afforded a gondola ride upon the Wabash and some of the best Italian food and wine to be found in the Hoosier State. Other features of the festival include the crowning of a Grape Queen, competition in boccie ball (an old Italian game dating back to Caesar's time) and Italian folk dances. Each year as the festival grows larger, it also improves. Clinton is located on IN 63 and IN 163, just 12 miles north of Terre Haute.

## Place of the Amish

Speaking of ethnic groups, you'll also find Indiana's Amish country of great interest. Located primarily in the northeastern part of the state, two Amish attractions are open to the public—Amishville near Berne and Amish Acres near

One of the Amish attractions open to the public at Amishville, Indiana.

Nappanee. At Amishville, horse-drawn sleigh rides and buggy rides are offered along with hiking, swimming, camping and touring of an Amish homestead.

As the traveler drives through this section of the state, he may notice many curiosities that are no longer consistent with today's life-styles. Windmills blow the smell of fresh hay over the grassy farms as horses and buggies clomp along country roads bearing men with bushy beards and women in cornflower blue dresses. The only indication that time has touched this spot is the large, fluorescent safety decal that decorates the rear of each buggy.

It's much the same at Amish Acres, where a major feature is a 45-minute guided tour of the home and barn. Nearing the main house, one passes an Amish garden, complete with vegetables, herbs and spices. Peach and apple trees line the path leading toward the drying house and bake oven. Nearby is a tripod where apple butter is made during the fall and winter months. A smoke house, butcher's block and root cellar complete the outdoor kitchen. By visiting either of these two places, you are given the opportunity of a better understanding and appreciation of the "Plain People of America." Berne is located a few miles south of Fort Wayne on U.S. 27; Nappanee is on U.S. 6, south of Elkhart.

## Sandhill Cranes

Among the visitors to the Hoosier State are thousands of sandhill cranes; they converge, for some unexplainable reason, twice annually at the Jasper-Pulaski State Fish and Wildlife Area north of Lafayette. In late September and early October, depending upon weather, they come by the thousands and may stay as long as mid-November before darkening the skies with their massive flight south.

Again in late March and April, they're on their way back to nesting grounds in Michigan and Canada. Visitors to Jasper-Pulaski can get close to the sandhills by use of massive blinds. They may also watch thousands of migrating Canada geese and wild ducks. Here also are whitetail deer roaming free and, in a wildlife display, elk, deer and buffalo. The admission is free and the refuge offers camping grounds. Jasper-Pulaski Refuge is at Medarville on U.S. 421.

## Peru Circus Festival

At one time, Peru was headquarters for five great American circuses. Today it's the location of the annual Peru Circus Festival with a parade and a big-top show featuring child stars. Normally held in July, the performance is highly recommended.

The performers, chosen at random from the schools of Peru, have an air of professionalism as they stage shows comparable to anything ever seen in the Midwest. Six-year-olds perform on a flying trapeze, ten-year-olds perform as clowns and ride trick horses. A teen-age girl parades with an elephant. They have all been trained by the old pros who have chosen Peru as their home. The training sessions often begin in May; and within two months, the children are ready for their performance. Many of them perform year after year and some have gone from Peru High School to the big circuses to become professionals. Two circus museums offer visitors a look at Peru's heritage. Peru is located on U.S. 31, one hour's drive north of Indianapolis.

## Other Points of Interest

The Round Barn Festival held each July at Rochester in Fulton County includes tours of 15 round barns in the area.

A Pioneer Fourth of July Festival is held at Conner Prairie, a pioneer settlement operated by Earlham College at Richmond.

A canal boat ride on the Whitewater Canal, Metamora, is offered to visitors.

The annual parade of the Peru Circus Festival, Peru, Indiana.

The annual Labor Day auction of antique cars is held at Auburn.

Chesterfield, center of spiritualism in the Midwest, has an open house during the month of August.

For additional information, contact the Division of Tourism, Room 336, State House, Indianapolis, Indiana 46204.

# Iowa

## Amana Colonies, Hoboes and a
## Little Church in the Wildwood

**Amana Colonies**   The Amana Colonies of Iowa represent one of the oldest communes in America; it is a way of life that has withstood the test of time, for the colonies are now more than 100 years old. Some 1,800 persons live in or near the seven Amana villages, which were founded between 1855 and 1862 by a band of German members of the Society of True Inspiration.

The Inspirationists came to Iowa from Ebenezer, New York, in 1855; but they had their beginning in Germany in 1714 when a group separated from their church and eventually emigrated to America in the years following 1842. About 25,000 acres of fertile prairie land in Iowa was acquired in 1855 when

Furniture-making shop at Amana Colonies, Iowa.

The annual Hobo Convention honors the vanishing breed at Britt, Iowa.

"Amana" (a Biblical name meaning "Remain Faithful") was laid out. Later five other villages were established within a 20-mile perimeter—South Amana, West Amana, East Amana, High Amana and Middle Amana. A seventh village, Homestead—a small community 3 miles south of Amana—was bought and added to the holdings in 1861. It is at Homestead that the old Amana Home is located, just one block from U.S. 6.

The home provides visitors with a delightful opportunity to view authentic and original furnishings in an old Amana setting of years ago (open daily 10 A.M. to 5 P.M., 12 noon to 5 P.M. on Sundays).

Amana freezers and refrigerators come from these villages, as do Amana wines, woolens, breads, cured meats and walnut and maple furniture. Their restaurants offer plain German food—and plenty of it. The new Amana Society embodies the features of a joint stock corporation, each member receiving one share of nontransferable stock valued at $40 in 1932. Today the land and factories owned by the corporation are valued at more than $3 million, and "real" value of the stock is $6,000 per share. The retail stores and wineries are closed on Sundays; the restaurants are open every day. The Amana Colonies are located on U.S. 6, some 20 miles west of Iowa City.

## Hobo Convention

The hobo today has slipped to the brink of extinction, his ranks barely reaching into the hundreds. Those still plying the trade of riding the rails and cooking Mulligan stew are indeed a vanishing breed. But once a year—at the town of Britt, Iowa—they come out of hiding to gather in what amounts to the glory and royal dreams of the most imaginative hobo mind. Many of the old hobos who traipsed the rails across America for years are there—The Hardrock Kid, Bud Filer, Slow Motion Short, Connecticut Slim and Steamtrain Graham.

For years, the annual Hobo Convention has been held at this small town in northern Iowa, and events include the election of a hobo king and queen, the serving of Mulligan stew and, in general, a good time. It is usually held in August or September. Britt is located off U.S. 18, west of Mason City.

## Little Brown Church

Perhaps you remember these words from your childhood: "There's a church in the valley by the wildwood, no lovelier spot in the dale; No place is so dear to my childhood, as the little brown church in the vale...." These words, penned by an Iowa schoolteacher over a century ago, make up a verse of one of the world's most beloved hymns. The Bible Belt church they describe, tucked away in the Chickasaw County valley, has become one of America's favorite shrines.

The church, in what once was Bradford, Iowa, isn't big, for it barely seats 150, and it isn't glamorous—the old-fashioned box pews smack of Puritan starkness. It is outdated, from the old hand-operated water pump in the churchyard to a church bell which must be rung by hand. Yet bridal couples and sightseers from all over the nation flock to its altar. Summer Sunday mornings find crowds of people waiting at the door as early as 6 A.M.

Every August, the church stages a celebration of marriage, and hundreds of couples from across the country come for a nostalgic visit. In the church and in the quiet 4-acre grounds landscaped with evergreens, they sing the lively old hymn, renew their marriage vows and make scores of new friends. The Little Brown Church is located just 2 miles northeast of Nashua on IA 346.

## Riverboat Museum

Now you can visit an authentic showboat museum...on a real showboat. The ship was originally launched as the *Steamboat Omar* in 1935 and later rechristened the *Rhododendron* in West Virginia. Various college and university theater groups present plays on summer weekends in the Riverboat Era Theater. The Showboat is located in Clinton on U.S. 67.

## Bily Clock Exhibit

In an old brick-front residence at Spillville is a remarkable collection of hand-carved clocks—the handiwork of Frank and Joseph Bily. Among the artistic works is the elaborate American History Clock which stands nearly 10-feet tall and features 57 bas-relief panels depicting pioneer life. The exhibit is open May to November, 8:30 A.M. to 5:30 P.M.; it's located on IA 325 in Spillville.

For further information, contact the Tourism and Travel Division, 250 Jewett Building, Des Moines, Iowa 50309.

A reenactment of the days of traveling by wagon train is offered by Wagons Ho! at Quinter, Kansas.

# Kansas

### Rolling Prairie Wagons, House of Telephones and a Rose Garden

"Wagons Ho!" came the robust command of the wagon master, and once again history repeats itself. The long wagon train moved out slowly across the High Plain's Smoky Hill Trail in western Kansas. The mules plodded on, raising little clouds of dust with each step; and away to the south, the skies banked in rain clouds. Little has changed in this country since the days when anxious pioneers came this way, plotting their route to the promised land farther west.

Today many city slickers come to take a most unique covered wagon train across the Plains to reenact the spirit of a hundred or more years ago. They call it Wagons Ho, an adventure allowing one to ride saddle horse or shotgun on the stagecoach or in a covered wagon.

The trail offers much the same experience the pioneers endured—except it's a lot more fun. The adventure is complete with Indian raids; a slow, bumpy ride behind a team of mules; an occasional mud-smeared wagon; rivers to be forded; campfire cooking; and sleeping under the open skies. The silence is broken only by the wind and the melancholy wail of a coyote. They cover 20 miles a day, quite a radical change of pace from driving along America's super-highways or flying coast to coast within a few hours. It's a casual trip, though, lasting 3 days and 3 nights. The trip is offered from early June through August. For additional information on this most unusual journey, contact Wagons Ho, Inc., 600 Main Street, Quinter, Kansas 67752.

## House of Telephones

In the late 1950s, Mr. and Mrs. Oral Watts received a hand-crank telephone as a gift. Almost twenty years later, they had accumulated more than a thousand other phones. About half of that number are collectors' items; the remainder

Watts sold or traded. Besides telephones, Watts has collected parts and has millions of them on hand, down to the smallest screw. "Our collection also includes a score of switchboards, complete with tall, cane-bottom chairs," he added. "The smallest switchboard has six drops or lines, the largest about 300." The Watts home, located on a farm just west of Coffeyville, has become a telephone gallery, including not only the phones but hundreds of photographs of phones. Even postcards showing the use of phones is part of their collection.

Watts and his wife have also donated phone equipment to a dozen museums from Sioux Falls, South Dakota, to El Paso, Texas. The oldest phone in the collection is a wooden box with a goatskin stretched over a hole. It reportedly was made 10 years prior to Alexander Graham Bell's invention. In the Watts kitchen is a 1900 Erickson wall-type phone made of iron. There's a huge sign out front of the Watts home reading: "The Old Telephone Exchange." Anytime you're in southeastern Kansas (Coffeyville is located at the intersection of U.S. 166 and U.S. 169) give the Watts a ring. It shouldn't be difficult to reach them by phone, and they'd be most happy to show you more phones than you've ever likely seen before.

## A Rose Garden

In the late 1950s, Horace Rich, a Coldwater attorney, decided he needed a hobby. That's when he began the enchanted garden he calls the Rich Rose Ranch. The 10-acre garden is part of 740 acres of farmland in southcentral Kansas which Rich inherited in 1949. In 1951, he built a cabin and a spring-fed lake and 6 years later planted the first roses. Now it produces more than 4,000 roses and 3,000 dahlias yearly. The blooms attract several thousand visitors annually. Special events include a spring rose show, usually held in late May, and a Fall Festival, normally held in late September. Rich still practices law; but unless scheduled for a day in court, often takes visitors on an enthusiastic tour of his own garden. "I like people to enjoy themselves," he said. "Some of my most interesting friends are people whom I first met when they visited the roses." Coldwater is located at the intersection of U.S. 160 and U.S. 183; the Rich Rose Ranch is nearby, and anyone in town can give you directions.

## Sod House Community

During the pioneer days on the High Plains of the United States, people built and lived in sod houses. The reason was simple: there were no trees for lumber. The houses were made of blocks of turf and dirt and would virtually last forever. Today at Colby, you can visit an authentic sod house community left over from those pioneer days. Located on U.S. 24, just 60 miles from the Colorado border, the attraction provides great insight into the crude way of life which confronted many of the early settlers.

## Hanging Tree

Not many of the old trees used for hangings in the pioneer days are still standing; but there's one which is still to be seen at Medicine Lodge. Look at it as you pass through, but don't get a noose put round your neck! Near Medicine Lodge are the Gypsum Hills, odd geological formations of weathered rock. A shunpiking drive through the area will lead you past many eerie formations. Medicine Lodge also was the home of Carrie Nation, the antialcohol campaigner. A museum there features displays from her era.

## Liberal's Pancake Race

In Liberal, the International Pancake Race with Olney, England, creates as big a stir as America's Cup competition. The annual running, on Shrove Tuesday, was begun in Olney centuries ago and went international—with Liberal—in

1951. Contestants, all women, must run 415 yards through the main streets of their respective towns three times, flipping pancakes in skillets along the way. Those who drop their pancakes are out of the running. The world champion is determined by transatlantic telephone on the basis of stopwatch times. It's undoubtedly Kansas' most unusual event. To get to Liberal, take U.S. 83 or U.S. 54. It's located in the southwestern corner of the state.

For additional information, contact the Travel Division, Department of Economic Development, State Office Building, Topeka, Kansas 66612.

# Kentucky

## Fancy Horses, Bourbon and Old Mulkey Meeting House

**Keeneland Sales**

Kentucky thoroughbred racing can be seen at several tracks in the Bluegrass State and elsewhere; but there's hardly anything anywhere to match the annual Keeneland sales near Lexington. This is the ultimate event in horse dealing, and any visitor to the auction will realize the vast amount of wealth associated with thoroughbred horse racing.

Traditionally held in mid-July at the Keeneland Race Track west of town, the Bluegrass' most handsome animals are led, one by one, into the flower-decked salesroom to stand in the spotlight while the bidding soars. Prices run phenomenally high; some colts sell for well over $100,000 each. But, of course, it's here that many of the young colts that later become Kentucky Derby hopefuls and even winners are sold. Keeneland is located near the Bluegrass Airport on U.S. 60.

**Court Day**

Bidding is the order of the day at the Keeneland sales, but each autumn at Mount Sterling, east of Lexington, there is another kind of barter: the annual Court Day. It's Kentucky's greatest swapping festival—although a second one is held at Maysville on the Ohio River—and you could end up swapping an Indianhead penny for a mule or a hound dog.

Traditionally held the first Monday of October, Mount Sterling Court Day is attended by thousands, many of whom unload their attics and bring their treasures with them. If they're fortunate, they may be able to trade most of it for something useful; if not, they may cart away two or three times the amount of junk they brought. Some popular items are goats, mules, horses, saddles, hound dogs, guns, old furniture, musical instruments, sorghum molasses and just plain junk. The entire town becomes a swapping festival, and each person bargains for his own trade. There are medicine men, hawkers, magicians and gaily dressed "Indian chiefs" selling their wares. But most of the people come down from the mountains and hill country of Kentucky, not really caring whether they make a swap or not, just wanting to participate in all the excitement. Mount Sterling is located on U.S. 460 and U.S. 60, east of Lexington.

**Bourbon Museum**

In the hills and hollows just south of Frankfort you can visit the Old Taylor Bourbon Distillery and the Bourbon Museum. The making of bourbon has long been a way of life in Kentucky and the museum dramatically displays just how it's done. You'll also see cut-aways of the type of charred white oak barrels in which the bourbon is aged after it's made. Tours are offered through the distillery, as at most distilleries in Kentucky; and you can see the principles displayed in the museum applied to the real thing, although they don't give away samples. When you reach Frankfort, located on U.S. 60, ask directions to the Bourbon Museum and the Old Taylor Distillery.

**Maker's Mark**

Near the little town of Loretto is an old-fashioned bourbon distillery which produces a brand known as Maker's Mark. It's practically made by hand, same as it was a century ago. Located on Star Hill Farm, the Star Hill Distilling Company is the smallest plant in Kentucky. When you enter the grounds, you'll feel as though you've stepped back in time. The old trees provide welcome shade, and fieldstone fences and meandering streams beckon the traveler to pause and enjoy the song of a mockingbird. There's no rushing here, and the men and women who work in the distillery take painstaking care to do an exacting job. You'll see many of the chores you've seen done by machines at larger distilleries done by hand here.

You'll also be able to visit the Toll Gate House, used to collect tolls on a private road before there were public roads. Nearby is the Quart House, the only one of its kind. Before today's modern package stores, the local farmers would drive or ride to the Quart House where their canning jars and jugs were filled from barrels. Star Hill Distilling Company is located on KY 52, between Loretto and Lebanon.

**Boone's Grave**

The grave of Kentucky's greatest hero, Daniel Boone, is located at Frankfort, on a high bluff overlooking the beautiful Kentucky River. Lying beside him is his wife. As history relates, Boone was one of the first white men to explore Kentucky and open up the new frontier. Upstream on the Kentucky River is Boonesboro, named after Daniel Boone. It's here that many admirers and scholars of Kentucky history come to visit and to marvel at the view.

**Renfro Valley**

Kentucky has long been noted for its music, and it was here a particular brand of folk music known as bluegrass became popular. At Renfro Valley, music has long been a way of life. At the center of the preservation of this particular brand of music was John Lair, who became a radio star in the large cities of the North before returning here in 1939 to devote his life to the land he loved best. The famous barn in the valley was built by Lair to house the weekly barn dance. Here folk and country music is presented every Saturday night by local talent.

Also located at Renfro Valley is the great Pioneer Museum building—the largest log structure in Kentucky where many articles and hand-fashioned equipment used in pioneer days have been collected and placed on exhibit. On Sunday morning, the valley residents and visitors get together, much as the early settlers did, to sing inspiring old-fashioned hymns. The Sunday morning gathering and the Saturday night barn dance have, for many years, been recorded and broadcasted over radio stations throughout America.

Lair no longer operates the Renfro Valley facility, but has passed it on to a friend and comrade—Hal Smith—who seeks to preserve it as it has been for nearly half a century. Renfro Valley is located just off I-75.

At Ashland in the northeastern part of the state, a museum of Kentucky folk music is maintained by the region's famous "Traipsin' Woman," Jean Thomas. She also heads up a unique event at the American Folksong Festival. Held during the second week of June, the 3-day program seeks to perpetuate the classic Appalachian folksongs which derive from Elizabethan sources. Costumed singers perform to the lilting music of zithers, dulcimers, lutes and the guitar. Ashland is located on U.S. 60, near the Ohio and West Virginia border.

Costumed singers perform at the annual American Folksong Festival, Ashland, Kentucky.

Berea is one of the most unusual towns in all the United States. The town's activities center around the home of Berea College. The college students are all required to work part time during their tenure in school. In large measure, they provide the labor force of the college and they staff the town's only hotel—luxurious Boone Tavern. They also operate many of the principal industries: broom-making, weaving, candy-making, novelty factories and printing shops. Every student who attends Berea—and most of them are from the Appalachian region of the United States—is required to work a minimum of 10 hours per week. He cannot come from a wealthy family or be financially able to attend college elsewhere.

The visitor to this small town in the Appalachian foothills is impressed with the industrious atmosphere of this small community. The shops and factories are open to visitors who can watch student craftsmen create fine furniture, woven products from the hand loom, candy and other products. And if you should stop at Boone Tavern, you'll find some of the best gourmet food in the entire South (no tipping is allowed). Berea is located on KY 21 and U.S. 25, just off I-75.

## Old Mulkey Meeting House

In the early 1800s, a religious revival swept through Kentucky, bringing with it meetings that often lasted for weeks, with all-day singing and dinner on the grounds. Leftover from that era is the Old Mulkey Meeting House, the oldest log meeting house in Kentucky, and an adjoining pioneer cemetery.

Built by John Mulkey and his fellow Baptists in 1804, the hewn log building is constructed in the shape of a modified cross with twelve corners (believed to represent the twelve apostles) and three doors (for the Trinity). Split log benches with pegged legs sit on the floor beams which are connected with wooden nails.

For history buffs, some of the tombstones in the cemetery are carved with noteworthy names; one represents Hannah and Squire Boone, sister and brother of Daniel. Another marker states that Joseph Gist of Kentucky served as an Indian spy with Seveir's North Carolina Regiment during the Revolutionary War. The shrine, located 3 miles south of Tompkinsville on KY 1446, is open year-round, admission-free.

## Virgin Forest

The giant rows of hemlocks and oaks stood like tall sentinels the day Daniel Boone came through the Cumberland Gap. They still stand in the Lilley Cornett Woods near Whitesburg in eastern Kentucky. Named for the man who spent years accumulating and zealously guarding the 554-acre tract against all intruders, many of the trees of this virgin woodland date back more than 400 years. Their survival is due to Cornett's devotion to the woods.

After a week's work, he would often take his family into the woods for a Sunday picnic lunch. During the fire season, he would pay crews out of his own pocket to go into the woods and protect them from fire. Sometimes the crews would stay as long as 2 weeks. Cornett relentlessly refused to allow any logging operations in the woods. The tract was acquired by the Commonwealth of Kentucky in 1969, and since then trails for hiking and nature study have been laid out. Only a limited number of persons are allowed in the virgin area at any one time and they must be on guided tours. The Division of Forestry conducts tours twice daily and there's no charge for admission. Lilley Cornett Woods, located on KY 1103, can be reached via KY 15 from the Mountain Parkway at Campton.

## Sermon on the Lake

For several summers, a young minister has been conducting Sunday services for boaters on Lake Cumberland. The pastor of the First Christian Church in Monticello opens his weekly service at 5 P.M. at Christian Point, 2 miles from Conley Bottom Dock. While he remains on dry land, boats anchor all over the lake to hear his 20-girl chorus begin the services. His words are inspirational, usually pertaining to the lovely surroundings, the wonders of nature or the beauty of water. The 30-minute service has drawn boaters of every denomination. Christian Point can be reached by automobile. It's located just west of Mill Springs in Wayne County on KY 1275. Incidentally, at Mill Springs is the largest working water wheel in the world, and you can buy water-ground cornmeal there.

## Little Town of Bethlehem

Bethlehem, Kentucky, has a population of about 200 people; it also has a unique acting troupe: a cow, 2 burros, 2 sheep and 36 men and women. Every Christmas season they gather to present a tableau, the "Living Nativity," in keeping with the name of the town. December 22 to December 25 from 6:30 P.M. to 9:30 P.M., the group offers a representation of scripture verses in a motionless scene of the first Christmas. The animals are remarkably well behaved, but usually have to be roped, tied and dragged to rehearsal. The burros ran away one year, and it took eight men several hours to retrieve them. One Christmas Eve, the ewe had a baby lamb. Bethlehem is off the beaten path, but during the Christmas season the roads are clogged with traffic. It's located on KY 22, about 40 miles east of Louisville.

The Belle of Louisville is an old paddle-wheel steamboat which takes passengers on short excursions up the Ohio River from Louisville during warm-weather months.

**Other Points of Interest**

*Belle of Louisville* offers short excursions on the Ohio River, Louisville, Kentucky.

The Pioneer Weapons Hunting Area is located in Daniel Boone National Forest with headquarters at Winchester and provides a special area for hunters with bow and arrow, crossbow and muzzleloading rifles.

The Headley Jewel Museum near Lexington displays some of the most exquisite jewels anywhere, including many of Headley's own art creations using various types of gems. It's located on the Old Frankfort Pike near Lexington's New Circle Road.

Bernheim Forest, 30 miles south of Louisville, is a 10,000-acre privately owned tract and arboretum open to the public. Deer, wild turkey and other animals and birds roam freely through the forest. Admission is free and it's open year-round.

Washington, the first town in the United States named for the first president, has not changed since 1786. Periodically, visiting craftsmen stage demonstrations for the public at one of the town's public buildings. It is located on U.S. 68, south of Maysville.

The Patton Museum, located at Fort Knox, exhibits many types of armored vehicles used by the U.S. Army since World War I. It also includes enemy pieces captured by General George S. Patton, as well as memorabilia related to the General and to armored warfare.

A replica of the Washington Monument, but in honor of Confederate President Jefferson Davis, is located at Fairview. It is the fourth highest monument in the United States, rising 351 feet above the 22-acre state park. It's located on U.S. 68, east of Hopkinsville.

Poke Sallet Festival, a week-long event held at Harlan each June, offers home-cooked vittles with poke sallett greens and all kinds of entertainment including horse shows, sidewalk art shows and crafts shows. Poke sallett is a wild green eaten by pioneers; it was also thought to have special healing powers. Harlan is located on U.S. 421, in southeast Kentucky.

For additional information, contact the Travel Division, Department of Public Information, Capitol Annex, Frankfort, Kentucky, 40601.

# Louisiana

Suckling Pigs, Crawfish and Haunted Houses

**Cajun Land**
When the Acadians, immortalized by Longfellow's poem, "Evangeline," came to Louisiana, they settled mostly in the areas around Lafayette, northwest of New Orleans, and at Saint Martinville. That's where you'll find the strongest Cajun influence today. Drive through the area, get off the beaten path and explore the backroads and the countryside. You'll find French-speaking Cajuns delightful to visit and anxious to show you their way of life.

At Saint Martinville is Saint Martin de Tours Church, a great Cajun landmark behind which is the statue and grave of Evangeline. Down the street on the banks of the Bayou Teche still stands Evangeline Oak.

Crawfish farms are big business in Cajun country, and you might take time to visit one. Consult the chamber of commerce in these areas for directions. Many farms are commercial and allow you to try your hand at crawfishing... you pay a small fee for what you catch. Lafayette is located on I-10; Saint Martinville on LA 31 and LA 96.

**Prison Rodeo**
Rodeos anywhere are crowd-pleasers, but one of the most unique rodeos in America is staged at Angola. It's one of two prison rodeos in the nation. Held by the inmates of the Louisiana State Penitentiary, the rodeo is staged annually each Sunday in September.

Inmates of Louisiana State Penitentiary hold an annual rodeo in Angola, Louisiana.

Inmates participate in such events as bareback riding, bulldogging, bull riding, calf roping and a cutting horse contest. Sideline clown acts are held for the children. The prison rodeo originally took form in 1965 when interested inmates originated the idea and secured the approval of the administrative staff. The first rodeo was such a huge success that it's become an annual event, with each one drawing greater crowds than the one before. Crowds of up to 10,000 can be accommodated. Angola is located near the Mississippi River, at the end of LA 66.

## Suckling Pig Festival

The Cajuns call it *Cochon de Lait,* or festival of the suckling pig. It's held each year in April or May at Mansura—a delight to whet the taste of the most discerning gourmet. Besides eating, the festival also features fais-do-dos (Cajun dancing), parades, Cajun folk music, boudin eating, beer drinking and greasy pig contests. The phrase *cochon de lait* means suckling or milk-fed pig. More than 15 tons of dressed suckling pig are charcoal-roasted; and each pig roasted must dress out around 18 pounds. They are cooked for hours over outdoor charcoal fires, and the aroma of roasting pork is tantalizing enough to make anyone want to attend. Mansura is located on LA 1 and LA 107, northwest of Baton Rouge.

## Pilottown

At the end of the Mississippi River is a small village providing visitors an unusual experience. Located 100 miles below New Orleans, Pilottown is located on the dumping ground of the Mississippi in quivering quagmire. Here the land often becomes a mushy mixture of mud, water and silt; it is so spongy, so shifty, so flimsy that cattle are occasionally lost altogether. The character of the land does shift because of storms and the river. Consequently, the marsh region has been dubbed *prairie tremblant* by the French-speaking Cajuns. ("Prairie tremblant" translates as "trembling prairie.")

Only 100 men and women live in Pilottown, and their homes are built on stilts. The river is on one side and on the other is the trembling marsh. Pilottown has a school, but fewer than a dozen children attend. The town was named for the

Mississippi River pilots who make this their headquarters. For years they have piloted the big ocean-going vessels across the bar and through the passes up to New Orleans and Baton Rouge. Among those who live in Pilottown are fishermen, trappers, boaters, and river people who know but one way of life—the river and the Gulf of Mexico. Charter boats are available at Venice for an historic trip to this unique pioneer town at the mouth of the Mississippi.

## Avery Island

Among the most unique showplaces of Louisiana is Avery Island, a baronial holding of the Avery and McIlhenny families. The island is said by some to be a total kingdom of its own, and one must pay an admission to gain entry. The island is a salt dome pushed up from sea level marshland. Avery Island produces rock salt from its mine, oil from its wells and, in the nearby fields, Tabasco® pepper is grown. The biggest attraction for the tourist, however, is Jungle Gardens, with more than 200 acres of horticultural beauty. Virtually every known variety of camellia and azalea blooms each spring. On Willow Pond in the gardens, the late Edward McIlhenny established a bird refuge; and year-round great numbers of egrets and herons flock to nest there. Observation decks for visitors are provided nearby.

While on Avery Island, you can take a free guided tour of one of the few Tabasco® sauce factories in the nation. Avery Island is located 9 miles south of New Iberia, on LA 329.

## Longest Main Street in the World

Bayou Lafourche, winding 110 miles from Donaldsonville to the Gulf of Mexico, is acclaimed as the longest street in the world. The houses, stores, shrimp boats and seafaring towns have mushroomed so close together that one could throw a baseball from one roof to another all along this stretch to the Gulf. Roads parallel both sides of the bayou, which is a major traffic route for shrimp boats, oyster boats and shell boats, as well as all kinds of barges laden with cargo. Donaldsonville is located on LA 1, west of New Orleans.

## Grand Isle

Among the most primitive and beautiful settings in all Louisiana is Grand Isle, smack on the Gulf of Mexico at the end of Bayou Lafourche. A great haven for wildlife, Grand Isle is headquarters for expeditions into the Gulf in quest of giant fish; and several records have been established here. The Grand Isle State Park offers camping, sunbathing and swimming as well as surf fishing. It is open year-round. Speckled trout and redfish provide plenty of fishing excitement for wading anglers.

But Grand Isle has become more important as a place for pelican watching. A few years ago all the pelicans of the "Pelican State" mysteriously disappeared. Restocking efforts immediately got underway, and Grand Terre, which is within viewing range of Grand Isle, has become headquarters for nesting pelicans. They often feed along the shores of Grand Isle, and many birdwatchers come to watch the small flock which hopefully will replenish the Pelican State with pelicans.

## Ghost Houses

Many of the great old mansions of Louisiana are more than dwelling places for people. No respectable ante-bellum mansion is without one or more ghost forms within its walls or upon its grounds. One of the most substantiated ghosts actually appeared in a photograph published in a national magazine during the 1940s, much to the surprise and mystification of the photographers who had merely meant to take a picture of an old plantation house. This was the best known of several ghosts of The Cottage, which stood a few miles south of Baton Rouge. The mansion was later destroyed by fire, but the ruins may still be visited.

Across the river near New Roads is Parlange, and the sixth generation of Parlanges still live there today. For years, Parlange has been the home of the ghost of a young girl who walks about the yard under the mighty oak trees, her hair blowing in the wind as she entwines herself in strands of Spanish moss. At Saint Francisville in a house called "The Myrtles" is the ghost of an old French lady who roams about the house sobbing. In the French Quarter of New Orleans, at the corner of Royal and Governor Nichols Streets, is another haunted house; however, this one is not open to the public.

## Christmas on the Bayou

Christmas on the banks of Louisiana's bayous and rivers offers the opportunity to see a most unusual custom. Each holiday season, thousands of merrymakers crowd the shores of waterways and levees to light great bonfires, hold floating parades, fireworks displays and candlelit hours of Yuletide caroling. On Thanksgiving, children begin building more than a hundred 30-feet tall, pyramid-shaped bonfires which won't be lit until Christmas Eve. Concentrated in the Lutcher-Gramercy area, the bonfires are constructed on the Mississippi River levee from long poles set in a pyramid frame with logs stacked horizontally, like cabin walls, to the top. Bamboo canes and reeds which pop like firecrackers when heated are woven among the logs just before the fires are lighted. Lutcher and Gramercy are located on LA 20 and LA 44 (Old River Road), about half-way between New Orleans and Baton Rouge.

## Crawfish Races

Each even-numbered year, during the Crawfish Festival at Breaux Bridge, the ever-popular crawfish races are held. There are also crawfish peeling contests for the less-fortunate critters who end up in a boiling pot rather than at a finish line. The races are held on a huge board on which are drawn concentric circles.

The ever-popular crawfish races are held biannually at the Crawfish Festival, Breaux Bridge, Louisiana. *(Courtesy of Louisiana Tourist Development Commission)*

The crawfish contestants are placed in the center of the board under a basket. When the basket is raised, the first crawfish to reach the outer circle is declared the winner. Of course, it's tough to judge the winning crawfish until one has actually crossed the finish line. One may be well ahead of the pack and then decide he wants to go back the way he came, particularly when he sees all those people staring at him from the sidelines. But that's what makes crawfish racing so exciting...and unpredictable. Breaux Bridge is located on LA 31 and LA 347, just east of Lafayette.

**Other Points of Interest**

The Jim Bowie Museum, Opelousas, located at 153 West Laundry Street, is still shaded by the Jim Bowie Oak and boasts a fine collection of Bowie lore and memorabilia.

At the Miniature Church on Old River Road near Bayou Goula, church services are held once a year—August 15, the Feast of the Immaculate Conception. However, the tiny building is open year-round for worship; a key to the church is kept in a box on the church wall.

Duet Moss Gin, Labadieville, located in the backyard of Lawrence Duet, is the last operating moss gin in the world. Duet sells his cured and cleaned Spanish moss throughout the nation; he obtains it from moss pickers who work at nearby Pierre Part in the lower Atchafalaya Swamp.

Cajun Horse Racing with child jockeys is held at many tracks throughout Cajun country. Check with the Louisiana Tourist Commission for individual listings.

For additional information contact the Louisiana Tourist Commission, Box 44291, Baton Rouge, Louisiana 70804.

# Maine

## Fat Man's Ski Races, Windjammers and a Mysterious Tombstone

**World Heavyweight Championship Ski Race**

Near the end of the ski season at Maine's Sugarloaf Ski Resort, one of the world's most unique ski races is held—the participants are all fat. Weighing in from 225 to 465 pounds, the challengers in the World Heavyweight Ski title come from across the nation to compete...and spectators come just to watch. In fact, 225 pounds is the minimum weight required to enter the race. Each is handicapped one second for every 10 pounds over the 225-pound minimum. The entry fee is 3 cents per pound with the proceeds going to the Pine Tree Society for Crippled Children.

Prior to the races is a great feast which is enough to attract anyone who likes to eat (and the public is invited to attend the banquet, too, at $10 per person). The menu, as an example, includes appetizers of spirits and special

Participants weigh in from 225 to 465 pounds for the Fat Man's Ski Competition, Sugarloaf Ski Resort, Maine. *(Courtesy of Dave Luce, Sugarloaf)*

delicacies, an extraordinarily thick cut of roast prime rib of beef, roast suckling pig, roast turkey, steaming baked potatoes, choice of red or white wines, vegetables, mammoth chef's salad, loaves of steaming fresh bread, pink or white champagnes and a special dessert prepared in secrecy by the chef, topped off with cordials and cigars. Some years, a total of more than 18,000 pounds enter the race; and when these behemoths come flying down the slopes, everyone stands back…way back. Sugarloaf is located at Kingfield, on ME 16 and ME 27.

## Baxter State Park

In northern Maine near the town of Millinocket is a most unusual state park; they call it Baxter. This 200,000-acre spread, which includes several mountains, the greatest of which is Mount Katahdin, is the northern terminus of the Appalachian Trail. It was bought piecemeal by a former governor of Maine—Percival Baxter—and presented in good faith to the people of Maine. Today it remains one of the most diversified and unspoiled wilderness parks in North America. Only a single gravel road leads through the park area; campsites are primitive and trails rugged, making this an ideal backpacker's park.

The northernmost part of the Appalachian Trail is at Baxter State Park, Millinocket, Maine.

Moose, bear, deer, grouse and eagles occupy the park, and in its many streams, there are some of the toughest fighting rainbow and brown trout in the East. Mountain climbing is another popular activity here, with Katahdin being the most scaled. Several trails lead up the mountain from various campgrounds in the park. No recreational vehicles are allowed entry into the park, primarily because of the narrow roadways; but tent campers and backpackers are welcome. Millinocket, headquarters for Baxter, is located on ME 157, just 8 miles west of I-95.

**National Dump Week**

Each year in July, at the town of Kennebunkport, National Dump Week is celebrated in a most unique manner. Festivities include a Dump Art Show in which all entries are made of genuine junk. A Miss Dumpy beauty contest is held at the Nonantum Hotel poolside; and in the evenings, a Giant Trash Parade forms at the school grounds and terminates at America's Number One Dump, Kennebunkport's own beloved trash pile. Following the parade, awards of Trash Pile trophies are made for the most outstanding float and then there's a happy hour for trash pickers at the Nonantum. Kennebunkport issues to visitors a Dump Credit Card, permitting one to visit any dump in the United States at any time. The town also issues a Trash Stamp on which are inscribed the words "Absolutely Worthless." The idea behind the festival, of course, is to point out the fact that trash belongs in a dump and not along the roadside. Kennebunkport is located on ME 9, just east of I-95.

**Corea's Seafaring Scenery**

Maine has a most impressive seacoast. There are dozens of picturesque little towns and villages, but none offer the genuine flavor of Corea. On the eastern tip of the Gouldsboro Peninsula, Corea offers unparalleled seafaring scenery. Along the shore, you see lobster boats gliding out of the harbor at dawn, dark silhouettes against the carmine and violet horizon. Once the sun is up, there are miles of surf breaking over red granite rocks with wheeling gulls soaring overhead. The permanent population of the village is under 200, and most of the people are lobstermen. A visit to the dock will tell you lobstering is a primary occupation here, for the homemade traps are piled high and the boats are plentiful. Corea is off the beaten tourist path, although it's across the bay from Acadia National Park and within sight of Mount Cadillac, atop of which the rising sun first strikes in the United States. Corea may be reached by taking ME 195, east to the sea.

**Allagash Canoe Trails**

One of America's greatest wilderness canoe adventures is along Maine's Allagash River. The only way to get out along the route is by float plane and a good bush pilot. Once you enter the Allagash, you're in for some exciting white waters and a close-up look at some inhabitants of the wild kingdom. The trip should be planned for a week or 10 days; but be sure to choose the right time of year. The black fly season usually comes in May and June and may continue until the middle of July and can ruin your trip. The best time is late summer or early autumn until October 1. Outfitters are available, or you can take your own canoe and supplies. Fishing is superb during the seasonal months, and plenty of campsites are available along the route.

**Schooner Museum**

Much of Maine life is devoted to the sea. You'll understand that devotion better after visiting the Grand Banks Schooner Museum. Among the items on display is the seagoing tugboat *Sequin* which you're invited to inspect topside;

there's also a captain's inspection including a below-deck visit and complete tour of the Dory Schooner *Sherman Zwicker*. The tug is the nation's oldest wooden steam-powered tugboat. For an interesting and enjoyable row around the harbor, dories may be rented from the Boothbay Harbor Marine Supply Store next door to the museum. The museum is located along the waterfront, of course, off Commercial Street in Boothbay Harbor.

## Lobsterboat Races

Each August, the Lobster Boat Races are held as part of the Lobster Festival. Off Frazier's Point in Acadia National Park, the one-day event attracts hundreds of people from around the state. The festival also features eating of lobsters which are cooked nearby. Frazier's Point is located on Mount Desert Isle and can be reached by taking ME 3.

## Silversmith Shop

Want to watch a silversmith at work? Then visit the farmhouse shop of Ernest Thompson along Back Meadow Road in Damariscotta, Maine. Heir to the tradition of Paul Revere, Thompson even keeps a horse, for which he forges shoes by hand in his own blacksmith shop. Most unusual is his work in silver chalices, monstrances, tankards, trophies, trays and tea services. His masterpieces are shipped out of Damariscotta to find their way to owners in Chile, England and all Europe and in churches and museums throughout the United States. You won't see an arts and crafts showroom here; but you will see an aproned silversmith at work in a cluttered shop. From mid-June until mid-September and on weekends the remainder of the year, Thompson welcomes visitors, even if they just want to stand around and watch. Damariscotta is located on U.S. 1, northeast of Bath.

## Desert of Maine

It all began with a speck of sand on the farm of William Tuttle back in 1797. Then it began to spread, like a malignancy, until it had devoured the crops and the fields. It grew into a dune, marched on the nearby woodland and inundated the trees. Even today, the colorful sands march on, claiming the countryside for their own. The farm buildings were buried and the Tuttles were forced to retreat.

Today they call it the Desert of Maine; and the multicolored sands—there are more than a hundred shades and hues—have become a tourist attraction. Geologists from across the country have come to study what has been happening to the Tuttle farm. The most logical conclusion seems to be that a pocket of sand was buried under pressure during the Ice Age. As the Tuttles plowed their fields, it ultimately broke through the topsoil. Where the marching desert of Maine will stop, no one knows; but it's baffling to see huge trees with merely their tops protruding as the sand swallows them up. The Desert of Maine is located just west of Freeport, off U.S. 1.

## Bucksport's Mysterious Tomb

Along the main street in Bucksport, the tomb of its founder, Colonel Jonathan Buck, is plainly visible. On one side of the tomb is the image of a woman's stocking foot. According to the legend, it seems that Buck felt that during the days of the Salem witch trials, his town ought to have a witch also. And he found one, an old feeble lady; he had her tried, convicted and executed. With her last breath, she cursed the Colonel and declared when he died his tomb would bear the print of her foot as evidence that he had murdered an innocent woman.

Colonel Buck never forgot that threat; and at the time of his death, his heirs took particular caution to choose a tombstone unblemished in any way. But slowly over a period of months the footprint began to appear. The sexton at the cemetery was the first to notice it. The heirs made many efforts to have it cleaned off the stone, but it always remained. Finally they had the stone taken away and replaced it with a new one. But within a few months, the footprint appeared on that stone, too. A third effort was made and yet the footprint appeared. The heirs gave up cleaning the stone and the footprint remains there today, plainly visible for all the world to see. Bucksport is located on ME 15 and U.S. 1, directly south of Bangor.

**Sign that Diminishes Distances**

Finally there's a sign, at Lynchville, which diminishes distances and shrinks the world...or so it would seem. The sign shows mileages and lists: Norway, 14 miles; Paris, 15 miles; Denmark, 23 miles; Naples, 23 miles; Sweden, 25 miles; Poland, 27 miles; Mexico, 37 miles; Peru, 46 miles; China, 94 miles. Of course, it refers to towns in the vicinity—not the far-off places it might indicate to the traveler. Lynchville is located on ME 35 near Waterford.

**Hus-Skiing Contest**

At Rangeley, one of the state's most unusual sporting events, the Hus-Skiing Contest, is held annually. A humorous affair at best, the drivers on skis are pulled—sometimes yanked—around a circular ¼-mile track by a team of sled dogs. Because many of the drivers and dogs are young and inexperienced and discipline really isn't part of the picture, anything is likely to happen. Many of the dogs swerve from the track, preferring to follow their own routes. Sometimes they even split, going in opposite directions, dragging the skiers with them. Rangeley is located near the New Hampshire border on ME 16 and ME 4.

**Messages from Space**

The reception center for all messages to and from the communications satellite *Telstar* is at Andover. Here you can learn the mysteries of space. The operators call it routine, but you'll think it's fiction. Andover may be reached by ME 120 and ME 5 in western Maine.

**Downhill Canoe Racing**

At Greenville on the shore of Moosehead Lake, some of the most unusual, downhill canoe races are held twice annually. Using the canoe as a toboggan, teams compete for the title of being the fastest canoe on packed snow. With contestants zooming down the slopes at speeds in excess of 40 miles per hour, the downhill canoe races provide the zaniest rides known to the sporting world. The event has become the star attraction at Moosehead's Winter Carnival. It's so popular that one is held in mid-January and another is held in mid-February. Greenville is located on ME 6 and ME 15.

For additional information, contact the Tourism Division, Maine Department of Commerce and Industry, State House, Augusta, Maine 04330.

# Maryland

### Sailing Ships, Clam Festivals and a Gold Mine Near the Nation's Capitol

**Skipjack Races** Just before winter sets in across the icy waters of the Chesapeake, a day of glory is celebrated for North America's only working sailboat fleet, the Skipjacks. The fleet gathers at Annapolis to compete in one of the nation's most unusual sailboat races; and by the end of the day, a captain and crew are decorated the winners.

For 5 months of the year, the Skipjacks are working sailboats pulling heavy dredges across the oyster beds. But on this Saturday in late October, like Cinderella, they are decked out in their finest, scrubbed and washed clean.

On a marked course around the lighthouse off Sandy Point State Park, under the shadows of the giant Chesapeake Bay Bridge, they race throughout most of the day, while spectators watch from nearby boats or from the shores of the state park. The boats rendezvous for a captain's breakfast and briefing at

One of the nation's most unusual sailboat races is the annual Skipjack Race at Annapolis, Maryland.

the Old City Docks in Annapolis, and it's here you'll have the greatest opportunity to talk with the watermen of the Chesapeake and learn something about their way of life. Annapolis, the capital city of Maryland, is located on U.S. 50, east of Washington, D.C.

## Smith Island

Farther down the Chesapeake, on Maryland's eastern shore, is Smith Island. This is the only one of several islands in Maryland waters which has an urban-like population, all of which is devoted to life on the sea. They call themselves the "watermen of the Chesapeake," and daily they go to sea to reap their livelihood in clams, oysters, crabs and fish.

Life on Smith Island is quaint, serene and God-fearing. The island has a mayor, a school, but no hospital or doctor. It has a few small stores, but most islanders travel by boat to the mainland to do their shopping. An ambulance boat, the Angel, is operated out of Tangier Island in Virginia, just south of Smith. It operates in all kinds of weather on missions of mercy, delivering the critically ill or injured to an ambulance on the docks at nearby Crisfield which, in turn, speeds the victims to a local hospital. The people on Smith speak with an Anglo-Saxon brogue which sometimes is difficult for visitors to understand.

Tours are operated by boat out of Crisfield to the island during warm-weather months, and one can catch the overnight mail boat as it makes the rounds of the islands at all times of year. Crisfield is located at the end of MD 413, and Smith Island is nearly an hour's boat ride due west.

## Crab Derby

You've heard of racehorses and greyhounds; but at Crisfield, usually over Labor Day weekend, the Crisfield Crab Derby is held each year. In this race, crabs from various parts of the world, including Washington, Oregon, Louisiana and Hawaii, compete while throngs of spectators cheer them on.

Delaware once entered the crab derby, too, but finally had to refrain, whereupon the governor of that state explained Delaware crabs had become so independent they refused to run without a saddle and jockey.

Nonetheless, the crab derby goes on, year after year, without saddles and without jockeys. There are a lot of other activities connected with the derby, too, such as crab feasts, beauty queens and parades.

## Clam Festival

For 3 days each year at the historic dock in Colonial Annapolis, one of America's most heralded events is held—the Maryland Clam Festival. The U.S. Travel Service in Washington, D.C., once labeled this as an official celebration, while the Discover America Travel Organization named it one of the top twenty festivals in the nation. Usually held in August, the event includes a clam shell pitching contest, string bands, a musical production, dancing, a clam queen contest and all the clams you can eat prepared in a variety of ways. There is also an antique boat show, ecology exhibits and a live marine exhibit.

## National Muskrat Trapping and Skinning Contest

Late in winter, as the fur trapping season is drawing to a close, trappers from up and down Maryland's eastern shore, as well as all parts of the United States, gather at Cambridge to compete for honors. As many as 50 men may enter the event, but it soon narrows down to a few hardy contestants. Each man works with a timekeeper behind him and his friends encouraging him from the audience. When the final result is announced, the cheers are deafening. All this is pure enthusiasm for skill because the awards are indeed modest. Among the nation's muskrat men, however, the honor is great.

The show was started in Cambridge because it is in the heart of great fur country. As a result, the Dorchester County trappers have become virtually a guild. They pass their delicate profession from generation to generation, and children begin to learn the trade when they are only six or seven years old.

In addition to the trapping and skinning contest, there's also a crab pot assembling contest. Entrants in this category are given separate parts of a crab pot and are required to put them together in a race against time. Other events include a beauty contest in which models display the newest fur styles, a hootenanny, duck-and-goose-calling contest, log-sawing contest and vaudeville acts. The event lasts for 3 days. To get there, take U.S. 50, east of the Bay Bridge.

## Assateague Island

Along the east coast of Maryland's shore is Assateague Island, a long narrow strip of land that provides a bunker against ocean storms. Most of the island is either state park or national seashore administered by the National Park Service. It offers camping, swimming and sunbathing opportunities; the island also provides a great habitat for wildlife, including various types of shorebirds, the small Japanese sika deer and the Assateague wild ponies. While the ponies are wild, they graze within close proximity to the campgrounds and children frequently feed them from their hands. Best way to get there is to take U.S. 50 east to U.S. 113, then MD 376 onto the island.

## Bird-Carving Exhibition

Each year in October, the nation's most outstanding exhibition of bird-carving is held at Salisbury. Sponsored by the Ward Brothers Foundation (the brothers are nationally famous carvers), the show often features more than 200 carvings, including replicas of waterfowl, shore birds, upland game birds and some songbirds. A few of the carvings in the exhibit each year are for sale; some carvers accompany their exhibit and accept commissions for future work. The show features the work of more than 25 of the nation's finest bird-carvers, as well as numerous antique decoys, bird sculptures, original paintings and films on wildlife and conservation. Salisbury is located southeast of the Bay Bridge on U.S. 13 and U.S. 50.

## Maryland Gold Mine

Just west of Washington, D.C., no more than a 30-minute drive, is believed to be a rich vein of gold, yet it likely will never be exploited. The site is the old Maryland Gold Mine which closed years ago because of the rising cost of mining and the freeze on gold prices in this country. The mine is being preserved and renovated by the National Park Service which, in 1972, made it part of the adjoining C&O Canal National Park.

The old ruins of the mine tipple, the water tower and the caved-in shaft opening still may be seen today. After a heavy rain, visitors sometimes find gold nuggets upon the ground. However, since it's National Park Service property, you're urged not to take any. Before the property was purchased by the government, some valuable nuggets were taken. At the C&O Canal Museum you'll find many artifacts of gold mining in Maryland, including some of the tools used and some huge nuggets. The mine is located near the small town of Potomac, just off MacArthur Blvd.

## Maryland Line

Each summer at old Fort Frederick, the only extant British stone fort of the Colonial period (1756) in the United States, a group of men who can fire a musket, a cannon or play the drums and fifes reenact the Maryland Line. The roles they play are so realistic it's like stepping into history.

The reactivated First Maryland Regiment was organized for the express purpose of honoring the memory of the vital part that Maryland played in the formation of our Republic. It is a voluntary organization, in no way connected with the military and is composed entirely of young men. Each member makes his own uniform and equipment. Fort Frederick is a state park and is located near Big Pool on MD 56, just off I-70. Camping is available nearby.

## New Market

A few miles from Frederick is New Market, sometimes called the "antique capital of America." This tiny village is entirely supported by the sale of antiques. Nearly 30 shops line its brief street, all of them high quality. Any antiques buff must see New Market, which is located on U.S. 40, just east of Frederick.

## Experimental Aircraft Show

At Frederick, the Eastern Experimental Aircraft Show is held each autumn. Hundreds of antique and experimental aircraft from many states are displayed. During the meet, the airplane builders, many in Wellington boots and jaunty blue and white Experimental Aircraft Association flight caps, flock together to swap stories and look over each other's workmanship. You'll also see gull-wing Stinsons and Stagger-wing Beech 17s...and you'll have the opportunity to see them fly and to inspect them close-up on the field. Frederick is located just off I-70, west of Washington, D.C.

## Topiary Splendors

All kinds of strange *green* animals are to be found on Pleasant Valley Farm outside Jacksonville, Maryland. You will see the fox who has just crossed the road, and close behind is the first of six trailing hounds. A mounted huntsman is about to clear a gate in the groomed hedges, but nothing moves. For the fox, the hounds and the huntsman are groomed hedges.

The farm is privately owned and open only occasionally to the public or by special advance appointment. You can drive by and see one of the most spectacular displays of topiary art in the nation—all the work of the owner, Harvy Ladow. In the several gardens around the rambling farmhouse, there are many topiary surprises: a Chinese junk with genuine red sails, a Buddha and a green giraffe. A long line of swans ride on hedges of waves followed by terrace after terrace of towering obelisks and walls of yew and hemlock. The farm is located on the east side of MD 146, about 19 miles north of Baltimore.

## Nostalgia on Wheels

Just outside of Washington, D.C., at Layhill, is a living museum on wheels that provides not only rides for spectators, but training for fans of the old world of trolleys. It's known as the National Capital Trolley Museum; a visit here offers a nostalgic ride for several miles on one of the old trolleys. Dedicated streetcar buffs pay $10 in annual dues for the privilege of skippering a fleet of antiquated foreign and domestic trolleys, bumping along to the accompaniment of those clang-clang and ding-ding sounds. Visitors pay only pennies for a ride; the trolley runs take about 20 minutes.

Many of the motormen are "moonlighting" lawyers, doctors, government clerks, engineers and park policemen. Some of the conductors are children no older than 12 who like to work with the trolleys. When they are 18, they'll be allowed to learn the operation of the trolley and take along passengers.

Among the trolleys used at the museum is one from Dusseldorf and one from Berlin, Germany; one from Graz, Austria; and a 1926 model from Johnstown, Pennsylvania. All the cars are designed for tracks 4 feet 8 inches wide and operate on 600 volts. In the museum, there is also a comprehensive collection of streetcar photographs.

A nonprofit educational facility operated entirely by volunteers, the museum occupies 65 acres of land in Montgomery County's Northwest Branch Regional Park. Much of the site is in rolling woodlands. The museum is open year-round, but only on weekends from Labor Day to mid-June. To facilitate operations in winter, a snowplow, circa 1899, is used to clear the track for those few hardy passengers who always turn up regardless of bad weather. Layhill is located on MD 182, near Wheaton.

For further information, contact the Division of Tourism, Department of Economic Development, 2525 Riva Road, Annapolis, Maryland 21401.

# Massachusetts

### Heritage of Witches, Turtle Trots, Kiteman of Nantucket and a House Made of Newspapers

## Plymouth Thanksgiving

Each year, on this day of thanks, "America's Home Town" holds an open house celebration in the manner of the Pilgrims of Plimouth Plantation. At no other place in America does Thanksgiving have more meaning or greater atmosphere than at Plymouth. Most of the historic attractions in town throw open their doors to the public free of charge.

Refreshments are served and the mood of the thousands of Americans who come here each year on Thanksgiving is delicately balanced between joy and thoughtfulness. Looking like Priscilla Alden as they stand in the doorways, hostesses in Pilgrim costumes greet you at most of the historic homes. To make your Thanksgiving Day visit memorable, you likely will be served a cup of mulled cider (hot cider with spices) along with oven-fresh donuts and a greeting: "Happy Thanksgiving!"

At the plantation, costumed hostesses go about the daily chores of Pilgrim home life while the men work at the saw-pit or split shingles. The women roast turkeys and haunches of venison on open hearth spits and serve tasty samples along with hot cornbread to visitors.

Perhaps most impressive, though, is the reenactment of the worship procession of the surviving 52 Pilgrims. They assemble by beat of drum, each with his musket and long cloak. They place themselves in marching order, three abreast, and are led by a sergeant. Behind them comes the governor in a long robe; beside him on the right comes the preacher and on the left, the captain with his side-arms. It's like reliving the founding days of this country, and the spectacle makes one more aware of the meaning of Thanksgiving.

A harbor scene of the seafaring village of Gloucester, Massachusetts. *(Courtesy of Massachusetts Department of Commerce)*

Gloucester is one of Massachusetts' most interesting seafaring villages. Its residents are largely of Portuguese and Italian descent, men who have lived from the sea for generation upon generation. For 350 years, men from Gloucester have wrestled with the ocean in small boats. More than 8,000 of them have been lost at sea. About 100 boats with 600 men in their crews ply the waters of the Atlantic for fish, leaving in the wee morning hours and staying perhaps 8 to 10 days on Georges Banks.

Gloucester is a great spot to linger anytime; but it's particularly an attraction during St. Peter's Fiesta, traditionally held in late June. The 4-day fiesta begins with a block dance and includes an evening concert, a boat race, fireworks and more concerts. And to initiate the festivities, a 60-pound statue of Saint Peter is carried through the streets on the shoulders of 11 fishermen, followed by hundreds of families and their friends. It is enshrined on an outdoor altar near the town landing. You can walk along the central waterfront in Gloucester at any time and watch men unload groundfish to be sold at the Fulton Fish Market the next dawn. Come at dawn and you may be invited out for a day of "inshore fishing." Some visitors stop to climb the stairs of the gabled granite home of nineteenth-century marine painter Fitz-Hugh Lane; his works may also be viewed, along with ships big and small, in the Cape Ann Historical Association on Pleasant Street. Gloucester is located on MA 128.

On Hesperus Avenue in Gloucester is the Hammond Museum, a medieval castle complete with drawbridge, battlements, towers, winding staircases and parapets. Built by the late John Jays Hammond to house his pipe organ, the

Great Hall is 100 by 25 by 58 feet. It contains the 10,000-pipe organ which took him 20 years to build. Recordings are played for visitors to give them an idea of the sound of this massive instrument. Summer recitals are regularly held by guest organists. The Great Hall window is a copy of the famous Rose Window in Rheims Cathedral. In the castle towers are original paintings, sculptures and trappings of the Middle Ages brought back from Europe by Hammond. In an adjoining room to the Great Hall is an indoor swimming pool surrounded with tropical vegetation. The castle is just off MA 127.

**Turtle Trots** Among collegiate classics of unusual character are the annual turtle trots at Boston's Northeastern University, held about the time of another and better-known trot, the Boston Marathon in April. Among turtles, zipping over a 29-foot course in under 3 minutes is considered a good track record. Held on the campus, the turtle trots provide a great attraction for students and visitors alike.

**Nantucket** This tiny island 30 miles east of Cape Cod is one of Massachusetts' most unique attractions. At one time, it was a bustling whaling island and riches came to many a family because of it; the wealth is still reflected in life there today.

Nantucket is a restful combination of both the old and the new. A century-old lighthouse at Sankaty rubs shoulders with a modern-style ranchhouse. You won't find stoplights or neon signs on the island, and you won't find a great many automobiles. Most residents transport themselves from one place to another on its 40 square miles (it's approximately 14 miles long and 3 miles wide) via bicycle or motorcycle. The island has a famous artists' colony, and art ex-

An old windmill on Nantucket Island, Massachusetts. *(Courtesy of Massachusetts Department of Commerce)*

hibits are held in the Kenneth Taylor Gallery; and during July and August, they line the streets.

Among the island's unique attractions is the Whaling Museum on Broad Street which houses ship models, logbooks, prints, books and scrimshaw of the era which made Nantucket a leading whaling village. A collection of portraits of whaling masters is also displayed. Nantucket may be reached by ferryboat or plane from Woods Hole on Cape Cod.

## Kiteman of Nantucket

Along the waterfront in Nantucket, there is a small shop distinguished by the kite which almost always flies above it. It's the workshop of New Yorker Al Hartig, once an engineer, but now one of the country's leading kite designers and builders. Hartig invariably has one of his creations tethered to his doorlatch, brightening the Nantucket skies. His kites, which fly virtually on a puff of breath, are among the most popular designs sought across the nation. Visitors are welcome to stop at Al Hartig's shop any time to discuss kite building and kiteflying. He's never too busy to talk...and perhaps demonstrate one of his kites for you.

## Saugus Ironworks

In 1646, the Saugus Ironworks was established with an investment of some $165,000 in English pounds. The Saugus success gave the world its first sustained production of cast and wrought iron and, thus, launched the iron and steel industry.

The American Iron and Steel Institute, over a period of 6 years, invested more than $1.5 million to restore the Saugus works to its original state. Historians, builders, architects and even archaeologists pondered over the site for many months. Excavations produced more than 5 tons of artifacts.

Today, that first ironworks—including the reconstructed blast furnace, forge and the rolling and slitting mill—is open to the public. A museum displays artifacts uncovered in the excavations, including products of the early ironworks plus a 505-pound ironhead used in the original forge building. Nearby is the Old Ironmaster's House, the home of the first proprietor. It stands virtually as it was built in 1648 with 10-foot fireplaces and original hand-hewn beams. The works is open daily year-round. Saugus is located just east of U.S. 1 and just north of greater Boston.

## Salem Architecture

Everyone is well aware of Salem's date with destiny and witchcraft, but few know of Salem's most unusual architecture. You will find some outstanding period architecture, most of it handcrafted by ship's carpenters from the days when Salem was a major wooden shipbuilding center. Besides Hawthorne's House of Seven Gables and the Witch House, there are a number of other historic buildings which form an ideal walking tour. Signs lead the way and a guide is published by the chamber of commerce. Also of interest, not necessarily for its architecture but for its reenactment of witchcraft, is the Witchcraft Museum. Through the use of wax figures, the trials are brought into realistic perspective as you tour the establishment. Salem is located northeast of Boston on MA 114.

## Boston Trout Ponds

In the city of Boston, you'll find excellent fishing in several of the city's trout ponds. One of the best is Jamaica Pond, covering some 63 acres in Jamaica Plain. Its clear, deep, cold waters hold rainbow, brown and brook trout and largemouth and smallmouth bass. It's like a mountain lake, but there are no

An old forge wheel at Saugus Ironworks, Saugus, Massachusetts. *(Courtesy of Massachusetts Department of Commerce)*

mountains and no wilderness. Instead, the background is the hum and throb of a metropolis with a high-rise apartment looming in the north. Other ponds offering good fishing (a most unusual thing for large cities) include Plug Pond and Round Pond in Haverhill, Forest Lake in Methuem, Dug Pond in Natick and Horn Pond in Woburn.

**Mamie**  Along the waterfront of Fall River sits the affectionately named *Mamie*. Officially she's the *U.S.S. Massachusetts;* but to the people of Massachusetts, she's a great deal more than just a battleship.

More than half a million school children chipped in their nickels, dimes and quarters to help rescue *Mamie* from the Navy scrap heap in 1965. She was then brought to Fall River from Norfolk, Virginia, to be established as a memorial to those who fell in World War II. The *Massachusetts* was launched in Quincy more than 2 months before Pearl Harbor and commissioned in Boston on May 12, 1942. Today, visitors may inspect the main deck, gun turrets, bridge and other areas, gaze into the great 16-inch guns or peer through the slits of the 18-inch armor of the Flag Plot. It provides a link with history, and among those most proud of it are the children of Massachusetts who helped to salvage her from the hands of the wreckers. Fall River may be reached on I-195, east of Providence, Rhode Island.

**Jewel Mill**

In the town of Rowley is a jewel mill where you may watch a large iron over-shot wheel operate daily from 9 A.M. to 7 P.M. It grinds and polishes gems from all parts of the country. This site, dating back to 1640, is modernized with a side road bridging the canal and leading to a conventional turnaround spot. The sluice gate is hand-operated, however, with a huge pipe with control valve leading from the bottom of the canal to the top of the water wheel. On the second floor of the mill, mounted jewels are displayed and sold. The mill was first built to finish woolens, but was later converted to grind flour and now to polish jewels. Rowley is located on MA 1A, northeast of Boston.

**Paper House**

At the town of Pigeon Cove is the Paper House. Built entirely of newspapers, the walls are 215 thicknesses of paper, sturdy and tough. All the furniture is made of newspapers, including a desk telling about Lindbergh's historic flight. Pigeon Cove may be reached on MA 127, along the ocean in extreme north-eastern Massachusetts.

For additional information, contact the Travel Division, Department of Commerce and Development, 100 Cambridge Street, Boston, Massachusetts 02202.

# Michigan

Bump-Jumping, Singing Sands and a Town Full of Magicians

**Colon: The Magic Town**

Colon has a magical heritage: it was the home of Blackstone the Magician and Percy Abbott. For one week each August, Colon itself becomes a special side show with magicians performing tricks on every street corner and points in between. For that is the week of Abbott's Magic Get Together which draws magicians and fans from across the country.

The sidewalks are crowded with men and women engaged in showing each other their tricks, whether they are card tricks, a bouquet of flowers that appears from nowhere or a scantily dressed young lady floating in mid-air. The key to all this is the Abbott Magic Company. It was founded years ago by Percy Abbott of Australia. Located just off the main thoroughfare in Colon, Abbott Magic Company employs persons year-round to construct illusions. You can visit the Abbott showrooms any time of year. At the edge of town, you can visit Blackstone's grave in the city cemetery.

During the Magic Get Together, performances are given each evening at the local high school auditorium by amateur and professional magicians. All about town—on the streets, in the park, in the restaurants and in the parking lots—you will see many other tricks performed. Colon is located on MI 86, west of Coldwater.

Magicians perform at the Magic Town, Colon, Michigan.

**Beaver Island**  Off the coast of Charlevoix is Beaver Island, once the only kingdom within the United States. Located 35 miles out in Lake Michigan, today it is largely populated by descendants of Charlevoix Irishmen.

At one time, Beaver Island was under the domain of James Jesse Strang, self-proclaimed king who ruled his isolated Mormon colony with tyranny and oppression. Having founded the colony in 1847, he served in the state legislature with honor and dignity. But to those 2,600 residents who lived under his domain, he was a ruthless and absolute man, determining everything from who was to be whipped in public to the length of the women's dresses. His real undoing was the introduction of polygamy in 1850 and the establishment of his kingdom. Open revolt developed, and eventually Strang was shot, ending a 9-year reign of one of the only monarchies ever established on United States soil. After his death, the Mormons were driven from their homes, taking with them only what they could carry.

Irish fishermen moved into the vacated homesteads, and Beaver Island steadily grew into a resort area populated largely by the Irish. The sign at the ferry dock today extends the greeting in Gaelic, "a hundred thousand welcomes."

The only way to get to the island, of course, is by boat or plane. The island is also the home of thousands of snowshoe rabbits and more than 1,000 deer. It remains today a peaceful emerald gem in the midst of Lake Michigan. The main port of entry is Charlevoix, located on U.S. 31, north of Traverse City.

**Singing Sands**

Southward along the Lake Michigan coastline from Traverse City is Grand Haven, one of two places in the world where you can hear the sands sing. Geologists have made thorough studies and have determined that the sound comes from the winds off the lake as they pass through the various sized and shaped granules. Of course, the whistling, moaning sound of the sand has, over the years, led to many legends and old wives' tales about the area; but many people come there just to walk upon the beach on a windy day and listen to the song of the sands. It was once believed that walking in this sand would provide relief from rheumatism and arthritis, and some people still believe it.

**Musical Fountain**

Also at Grand Haven is the world's largest musical fountain, located at the base of Dewey Hill. During summer evenings, two performances nightly are given of the fountains dancing to a musical score while colored lights play on the constantly changing formations. The spectacle may be viewed from across the river. Grand Haven is located on U.S. 31.

**Golf on Ice**

Each February at Spring Lake near Grand Haven, one of the nation's most unusual sporting events is held—a golf tournament on ice. An 18-hole course is set up on Spring Lake, and golfers come for miles to participate. Awards are made in three divisions—men, women and children. The balls are sprayed with brightly colored paint, the latter supplied by the chamber of commerce, which sponsors the event. Another such golf tourney is held each winter on Lake George in New York; but there only a 9-hole course is played.

**Snow Snurfing**

North of Grand Haven at Muskegon, the National Snow Snurfing Championships are held annually. The event is sponsored by the students of Muskegon College and is held in the Muskegon State Park. Snow snurfing is a word coined from snow and surf—it resembles using a surfboard on snow. A rope tether allows the rider to hold onto the board, however, for greater control. Speeds close to 30 miles per hour can be attained on the slopes, and many age groups enter the competition, usually held in February.

Snow snurfing was developed in Muskegon at the home workshop of Sherman Poppen. He made the snurfer for his young daughters from a set of old wooden skis; he later developed the idea and patented it. Today snurfers are sold in sporting goods stores across the snow belt. Muskegon is located on the shores of Lake Michigan on U.S. 31.

**Bump-Jumping**

Each winter, the International Bump-Jumping Contest is held at Petoskey. As a featured attraction of the Petoskey Winter Carnival, the bump-jumping competition draws participants and spectators from several states and Canada. The little bump-jumper was first made in the North Woods country of Michigan and has largely remained a sport unique to this area for nearly half a century. Made of wood, the bump-jumper appears as a single runner sled which, when it hits a bump in the snow, has a tendency to broad-jump for several feet, depending upon the speed, before touching down again. The downhill performances are spiced with a slalom course. Petoskey is situated on Lake Michigan's Little Traverse Bay, 36 miles south of the Straits of Mackinac on U.S. 31.

Bump-jumpers compete on Suicide Hill at the International Races, Petoskey, Michigan.

## Canoe Sledding

Grayling, on I-75, is the center for canoeing on the world-famous AuSable River. But in winter, the canoes take to the slopes like toboggans; and each year, usually during the month of February, the Downhill Canoe Races are held. Most of the canoes used are of aluminum structure, highly waxed and polished and ridden by a team of two racers. There's little steering once the canoe is set in motion at the top of the slope. It swooshes downhill at tremendous speeds, often hitting rates of 50 miles per hour. The little control and guidance is provided by the occupants leaning in unison from one side of the canoe to the other.

## Archery Museum

Also at Grayling is the home of Bear Archery and the Bear Archery Museum. The museum is open year-round and is loaded with items relating to the sport, many of them centuries old and from all parts of the world. It is the world's largest private collection of archery artifacts; it also contains the largest collection of trophy animals shot with a bow and arrow by archer Fred Bear. The museum also includes a complete archery tackle shop featuring Bear Archery bows and equipment and a fascinating gift shop with unusual collections from many continents.

## National Mushroom Hunt

Each spring, just after the last snow melts, a certain breed of people begin combing the countryside. They're the mushroom hunters; and in north Michigan woods, the morels grow huge. At Boyne City south of Petoskey, the National Mushroom Hunt is held each May, usually during the second week.

Supervised by the State Department of Natural Resources and sponsored by the Boyne City Chamber of Commerce, the hunt brings spectators and participants from several states. Prizes are given for the largest and greatest number of morels found during a specified time in the restricted hunting area. In town, the menus of several restaurants feature mushroom delicacies that week, and there's a prevailing carnival atmosphere throughout the area. Boyne City is located just west of U.S. 131.

**Frisbee Fling**

If Frisbee is your game, you'd enjoy attending the annual Frisbee-flinging frolic of the International Frisbee Association held annually in Michigan's copper country. The fanciest flinger is awarded the Julius T. Nachazel Memorial Trophy, an empty beer can mounted on a used tomato can. This magnificent prize is reputed to be named for a Frisbee fanatic who followed a floating Frisbee into the forest and just faded away, never to be seen again. For the exact location of the contest in a given year, write to the Michigan Tourist Council (see address at end of Chapter).

**Stone Skipping Open**

If golf opens don't excite you, perhaps you'd like to attend the National Stone Skipping Open Tournament, held annually at Mackinac Island, Michigan. The meet is traditionally held in early July—or whenever enough skippers can be rounded up to make the competition worthwhile. Anyone can enter and, since the chamber of commerce voiced the opinion that interest was lagging, perhaps it's time for the stone-skippers of the world to reunite and get things going again. Mackinac Island is located in the Mackinac Straits and can be reached by ferryboat from Mackinac City or from Saint Ignace, just off I-75.

**Mackinac Bridge Hike**

One of the most unusual Labor Day celebrations is the annual hike across the 4½-mile Mackinac Bridge. Each year, more than 20,000 people gather for the trek across the engineering marvel that links Michigan's two peninsulas.

Labor Day is the only time you can cross the bridge on your own two feet—on all other days pedestrian traffic is banned since the bridge is not so designed. The first walk was held in response to a number of requests for a walking race to be held as part of the bridge dedication ceremonies in June 1958. Further requests led bridge officials to try the idea out on Labor Day, 1959. The crowds of walkers have increased ever since. The walk begins at Saint Ignace and terminates at Mackinac City on the south end of the bridge.

**Ore Mine Tour**

Much of Michigan's Upper Peninsula country is underscored with iron ore, and some of the nation's largest mines are located here. Several of the mines offer tours; one of the most interesting is the Ore Mine at Iron Mountain. Here, well-versed guides take visitors underground for an educational tour of an ore mine in operation.

You'll travel through 2,600 feet of underground drifts and tunnels, see a wide array of working mine equipment, an amazing lighted underground cavern and many examples of nature's freakish handiwork. The tours take you 400 feet below the Earth's surface; and once you've taken the tour, you'll be delighted to see some open sky over your head again. Iron Mountain is located on U.S. 2, near the Wisconsin border.

For additional information, contact the Michigan Tourist Council, 300 S. Capitol Avenue, Lansing, Michigan 48926.

# Minnesota

## The Northwest Angle and the Otter Man

**Geographic Mistake**

Jutting into the western waters of Lake of the Woods in Canada is a most unusual peninsula called the Northwest Angle. It lies within the natural borders of Canada, but is part of Minnesota. Until Alaska was admitted as a state in 1958, this section of 130-square miles of wilderness was the northernmost point in the United States. This patch of Minnesota is actually a geographic mistake; it was included as part of the United States through ignorance of geography at the time the Canadian boundaries were created.

The Treaty of 1783 stated the boundary would extend through Lake of the Woods to its northernmost point and then due west to the Mississippi. When geographers later realized the Mississippi did not come anywhere near Lake of the Woods, the treaty was changed to make the boundary extend from the northern tip of the inlet south in a straight line to the forty-ninth parallel. The freakish result was slightly more than 130-square miles of American territory

Fort Saint Charles is an important landmark on the Northwest Angle, Minnesota.

created in the northern wilderness, accessible only by boat, float plane or—in winter—snowmobiles.

Three small communities exist today on the Northwest Angle: Angle Inlet, Oak Island and Penasse. One of the most important landmarks on the Angle is Fort Saint Charles, restored by the Knights of Columbus. The fort was the first white settlement and trading post on the shores of Lake of the Woods. Though acquired by mistake, the Northwest Angle today is probably the most unusual and unspoiled portion of Minnesota.

## Wasioja— Minnesota's Ghost Town

Wasioja is not a ghost town in the usual sense, but its population has virtually dwindled to zero. Once, like many boom towns throughout the nation, Wasioja was prosperous and saw no worries for the future. Its population numbered more than 1,000, and it was located on an important Territorial Road stage-coach stop. It had a new seminary, a fairgrounds and racetrack and many fine stores and buildings circled by limestone slab sidewalks cut from local quarries. It even had a weekly newspaper—*The Wasioja Gazette.*

However, when a new railroad bypassed the town, its hopes for the future were crushed and the esprit de corps of the people diminished. Soon the people themselves vanished, moving to other communities with more promise and leaving only a few scattered homes and landmarks.

The landmarks make Wasioja worth seeing. The stone schoolhouse, built in 1856, is preserved, complete with a huge rock which wore out many pairs of trousers and shoes as children used it for a slide. When parents threatened to remove the rock, the local cobbler said he'd have to close his shop and leave town. Not wanting this to happen, the townspeople let the rock remain.

At the southeast edge of town in a grove of Norway spruce are the ghostly remains of Wasioja Seminary, opened in 1860 by the Free Will Baptists. The school had hardly opened when the Civil War began and 90 students marched to the town recruiting station to enlist. None of them returned. The school was forced to close and not until 1873 was it reopened again—this time by the Wesleyan Methodists. In 1905 it burned, leaving only the ruins which can be seen today.

The small square stone building constructed as a bank in 1855 is the only Civil War Recruiting Station still standing in Minnesota. It was dedicated in 1961 as a Civil War Centennial project. At the historical museum in neighboring Mantorville is an elegant, old horsedrawn hearse with carved wooden tassels and fringed curtains at the windows. This was used in Wasioja until 1901. At no other place in the state will one find so many remnants of the past and reminders of the demise of a community. Mantorville is located on MN 57, just west of Rochester.

## Mayo Tour

In the middle of the nineteenth century, a brilliant surgeon, Dr. William Mayo, and his two sons, William and Charles, founded the Mayo Clinic at Rochester. Today, it not only is a mecca for ailing persons around the world, but a considerable tourist attraction as well. The huge clinic, affiliated with the University of Minnesota's Graduate School of Medicine and the Mayo Foundation for Medical Education and Research, consists of a number of large buildings connected by underground tunnels. Many additional hospitals and hotels have been added to the city's facilities to accommodate the thousands of patients and visitors from all parts of the world. Tours of the Clinic and Medical Museum are conducted twice daily, Monday through Friday. They last 1½ hours and include a ½-hour film. On Saturdays, there is a single morning tour. Rochester is located on U.S. 52 and U.S. 14, south of Minneapolis–Saint Paul.

## Grange Farm

Overlooking the Mississippi River near Elk River is a spacious farm house known as "the birthplace of organized agriculture in the United States." The Oliver H. Kelley Homestead has 11 rooms with 12-foot ceilings and is filled with authentic furnishings from the Civil War era. Kelley, who moved to Minnesota from Boston in 1849, was convinced that by banding together farmers could improve their life-style. He became an almost fanatical crusader.

In 1867, after traveling for two years through farm states as an emissary for the Department of Agriculture, Kelley and six other men formed the National Grange of the Patrons of Husbandry. Its purpose was to help educate farmers, enrich their social life, obtain the latest information on marketing and crops, set up markets in large cities where farm produce could be sold and reduce high shipping rates. The Grange movement ultimately spread into every state. The National Grange, which purchased the 200-acre farm in 1935, has spent thousands of dollars on its restoration. In 1961, they turned the farmstead over to the Minnesota Historical Society which keeps it open to visitors daily from Memorial Day to Labor Day. The farm is located on U.S. 10 near Elk River.

## Artificial Canyon

If you'd like to drive through an artificial canyon as colorful as the Grand Canyon, take a trip from Chisholm along MN 73 to Hibbing. The highway actually goes through a mined-out ore pit of the Pillsbury Mine.

At Hibbing is the Hull-Rust Mahoning mine, the largest open-pit mine in the world–3 miles long and at one point a mile across. The pit walls are in terraces, created by various stages of ore removal. So brilliant and varied is the coloring on the walls—reds, browns, yellows, oranges and blacks—that some people compare it favorably with the Grand Canyon.

## Mystery of the Petroglyphs

In Minnesota's Cottonwood County, there are many mysterious petroglyphs. Some of them depict turtles, deer, buffalo and other creatures, and some are human figures or parts of figures—hands, faces, feet. Others—the more mysterious ones—are symbols, lines and abstract forms which archaeologists have never really been able to figure out. Scientists do believe the petroglyphs, carved in rock walls, were done long before white men came to America; and they say, indeed, the pictures may be thousands and thousands of years old. The Minnesota Historical Society has built a modern, interpretative shelter containing many of the exhibits; but what the symbols mean is anybody's guess. The picture rocks are located 3 miles north of MN 30, on County Road 2 near the community of Jeffers. Admission is free and the site is open daily from May to October.

## Jasper Quarry

Near the little town of Jasper in southwest Minnesota is one of the few jasper quarries in all North America. In the past, jasper blocks were used to pave streets. But now, because it is such a hard stone, it is in great demand for industrial grinding purposes. Most of the cutting work, because of its hardness, has to be done by hand. Watching a mining operation can be a fascinating way to spend a sunny afternoon. Jasper is located on MN 23, near the South Dakota border.

On the banks of the Mississippi stands the living museum of the otter kingdom. **Otter Man**
Emil Liers, known as the otter man, has spent most of his life training otters
and other small animals and usually keeps a number of them as pets. He's written several books, including one on the otter and another on the beaver. Of all
wild animals, he most respects and loves the otter. Otters trained by Liers have
starred in Walt Disney movies. Liers' otter sanctuary is located on U.S. 61,
south of Winona near the town of Homer.

Emil Lier's otter sanctuary near Homer, Minnesota.

Each year at the town of Viola, there is an event which wildlife enthusiasts may **Gopher Count**
find distasteful. It's called the Gopher Count. Thousands of people turn out for
this event which features the counting of feet of gophers, killed by persons
participating in the contest. Cash awards are made for the persons turning in
the most gopher feet.

    The event was begun in the early part of this century when gophers
created so much havoc with farmers' crops that they became a nuisance. Since
that year, the gopher count has been tradition. A gopher count king and queen
are selected and a parade is held; other attractions include a doll buggy race,
talent show, a ladies' nail-driving contest and a foot race. The event normally is
held in June. Viola is located on MN 2, a few miles from Rochester.

    For additional information, contact the Division of Tourism, Department
of Economic Development, 51 E. 8th Street, Saint Paul, Minnesota 55101.

# Mississippi

Tobacco Spitting Champions, Stick Ball Tournaments and a
Singing River

You can hear the spurt of amber a thousand yards as America's greatest tobacco chewers and spitters step up to the platform and fire away. In 1972, the
distance title was held by a Mississippian from Europa, Don Snyder, who fired
a distance of 24 feet, 1 inch, while Dwight Hunt of Ackerman, Mississippi,
held the accuracy title. Snyder already had set a record, in 1970, of 25 feet, 10
inches; one he's not been able to break. But during practice sessions prior to the
big event, he did even better than that—31 feet even.

In 1952, the National Tobacco Spit evolved from an event in the annual
Forestry Field Day sponsored by the U.S. Forest Service. It was discontinued

Participants in the Tobacco Spitting Championships at Raleigh, Mississippi. *(Courtesy of Ger-
trude Gibson)*

in 1963 and revived again in 1965. The Raleigh Jaycees began sponsoring the
event in 1966, and proceeds from the event now are used on various civic proj-
ects. Although tobacco spitters from Missouri and Wisconsin have also entered
the contest, no women have made an appearance.

The Tobacco Spit is held each year at Billy John Crumpton's pond, 5
miles from Raleigh. Look for signs directing you to the spot. Normally held in
August, the event also includes an auction and flea market, coon dog field trials,
a mule race and a chicken barbecue. Raleigh is located 55 miles southeast of
Jackson on MS 18.

Some say it resembles the musical classic, *Flight of the Bumble Bee;* others say it has no resemblance to anything but a pleasing sound. It's for this sound that the Pascagoula River has become known as the "Singing River." The singing sound is best heard in late summer and autumn months in the stillness of late evening. Barely audible at first, the music seems to grow nearer and louder until it sounds as though it comes from directly underfoot. No concrete theories have been arrived at by scientists studying the source of the sounds, but an old Indian legend gives it a touch of romance that suits the purpose.

The legend connects the sound with the mysterious extinction of the Pascagoula tribe of Indians. The Pascagoula were a gentle tribe of contented, innocent and inoffensive people; on the other hand, the Biloxi were a tribe who called themselves the "first people" and were extremely jealous of their position. Anola, a princess of the Biloxi tribe, though betrothed to a chieftain of her people, fell in love with Altama, a young Pascagoula chieftain; and she fled with him to his tribe. The Biloxi chief led his braves to war against Altama. Chief Altama begged his people to let him give himself up to the Biloxi, but the tribesmen refrained, saying they would die with him. Outnumbered in battle, they were faced with the decision of subjection to the Biloxi or death. They chose the latter. With their women and children leading the way into the river, the braves followed with joined hands, each chanting the death song until the last voice was hushed by the dark engulfing waters. The river continues to sing the song after these many years. The Pascagoula is located on U.S. 90, between Biloxi and Mobile, Alabama.

One of Mississippi's most unique calendar events is the Choctaw Indian Fair, held every summer on the Choctaw High School campus near Philadelphia. This strange mingling of past and present is considered one of the most outstanding and authentic festivals of the South.

Traditional ceremonies and activities at the Choctaw Indian Fair, Philadelphia, Mississippi.

Traditional ceremonies and activities performed during this 4-day event date back countless centuries and include demonstrations with blowguns, still used by the Choctaws in hunting, stickball games, Indian style shows and dancing. There are displays of various types of handicrafts and a beauty contest to select an Indian princess. A nightly drama entitled "A Chosen Land for a Chosen People" is staged. Philadelphia is located on MS 16, northeast of Jackson.

**Leake County Sportsmen's Day**

Traditionally on the Fourth of July, the Leake County Sportsmen's Day celebration is held. This event includes a pallet race for babies, pistol shoot for ladies, greasy pole climbing, turkey calling, a rabbit roundup for children, horseshoes, duck calling, horn blowing and the crowning of "Miss Freckles." The event is held at Carthage on MS 16, just 22 miles east of I-55, near the Choctaw Indian Reservation.

**Big Mama**

On the banks of the Mississippi at Vicksburg sits the *Big Mama,* favorite nickname for the riverboat *Sprague.* Built in Dubuque, Iowa, shortly after the turn of the century, the *Big Mama* is one of the most famous boats ever to operate on the Mississippi. In 1907, she set a new riverboat record by towing a fleet of barges carrying 67,307 tons of coal. In 1948, she was sold to the city of Vicksburg for $1, and today the old sternwheeler houses the River Hall of Fame. She is also the home of the Dixie Showboat Players; and from March until November, visitors can watch melodrama performed by the players aboard the boat. Vicksburg is located due west of Jackson on I-20.

**Floundering**

One great nighttime activity along the Mississippi Gulf Coast is flounder fishing. All you have to do is dress in some old clothes, roll up your pants' legs, carry a lantern in one hand and a spear in the other and go wading in the surf. You'll soon see these delectable fish; and once you've speared a meal, you're in for a most delicious treat. Most fishermen prefer to fillet them and cook them over an open fire built from driftwood on the beach. The best place to fish for flounder is in the area east of Biloxi.

The *Sprague,* a Mississippi River sternwheeler, is docked at Vicksburg, Mississippi. *(Courtesy of Mississippi Travel Department)*

There are several islands off the Mississippi Gulf, among them is Ship Island. Located about 12 miles offshore, it can only be reached by boats which are available along the waterfront in Biloxi. It was settled in 1721 by the French who sent over young French girls to become wives of the colonists. Ship Island is a fascinating place; on the island is old Fort Massachusetts, built by Union forces during the Civil War as a prison. Also lying offshore are Deer Island, Cat Island and Horn Island. All of these provide excellent beachcombing opportunities.

For additional information, contact the Travel Department, Agricultural and Industrial Board, 1504 State Office Building, Jackson, Mississippi 30205.

# Missouri

## Tom Sawyer Land, Castle in the Ozarks and a Train to the Top of a Rainbow

**Painting Tom Sawyer's Fence**

Each July, the National Tom Sawyer Fence Painting Contest is held in the Mississippi River town of Hannibal where Mark Twain spent his boyhood years. The contest is held on the weathered wooden fence outside the home of Samuel Langhorne Clemens; it is the very fence he wrote about in the *Adventures of Tom Sawyer.*

Kids in coveralls and straw hats show up to compete for the best painter for prizes in U.S. Savings Bonds. Contestants are selected by the governor of each of the 10 states bordering the Mississippi and are flown to Hannibal the day prior to the contest. The expense of their trips as well as their stay in the city is absorbed by the Hannibal Jaycees, who sponsor the event.

Early in the morning, the boys are armed with the tools of battle—a bucket of whitewash and a brush—and line up before their assigned stations along the fence. Judging is based 50 percent on costume, 25 percent on quality of work and 25 percent on speed. The boy who wins receives, in addition to the savings bond, a large trophy which he in turn presents to the governor of his state. It is then displayed in that state's capitol building for one year before it is returned to the contest the succeeding year. The previous year's national champion returns to the contest to help judge the new champ.

On the day prior to the contest, all youngsters in the Hannibal area are invited to participate in a Junior Olympics Carnival under the supervision of local youth physical fitness activities personnel. Candidates for the Tom and Becky contest are selected from the seventh grade classes of the city's schools; the winners represent the city at various civic functions throughout the year.

Next door to the Mark Twain home is the place where Twain's father

Young boys and girls compete in the annual Tom Sawyer Fence Painting Contest at Hannibal, Missouri. *(Courtesy of Missouri Tourism Commission)*

practiced law. And next door to the law office is the home of Becky Thatcher. The buildings are open to the public. A visit to each gives an insight to the world that inspired Twain to write the stories about Tom Sawyer and Huckleberry Finn that have been read and enjoyed world-wide. Hannibal is located on U.S. 36, upriver from Saint Louis.

**Hermann's German Festival**

Hermann is Missouri's most renowned Bavarian town. More than 3,000 fun-loving sons and daughters of German immigrants live here. Long before prohibition, the town's export of fine wines was widespread. As early as 1870, there was an annual output of over 350,000 gallons of wine from Hermann. Hermann's wine industry has declined somewhat over the years. However, during the third weekend in May, it manages to put itself back on the map with a gay, old-world festival called Maifest.

The hub of activity during this magnificent German festival centers in the city park. You can smell the sauerbraten all over town, and draft beer flows in endless supply. Maifest gives the visitor an opportunity to participate in the traditions that make up the German heritage. Featured attractions include an Oldtimers Parade, complete with bouncing polka band and native-costumed street dancers. Hermann is located on the Missouri River on MO 19 and MO 100.

In 1903, a wealthy Kansas City industrialist, R. M. Snyder, decided he would build a castle in the Missouri wilderness by a huge spring, which earlier had been the site of an Osage Indian campground. In fact, the grounds had been named Ha Ha Tonka and were widely known.

## Crumbling Castle of the Ozarks

Stonemasons and gardeners were imported from Scotland and England to build the finest castle this side of Europe. An 80-foot watertower, a large stable and greenhouses were constructed. An extensive European-type garden was planted. Exotic orchids and other rare plants flourished in the greenhouses, which covered two acres. A miniature railroad was built to haul quarried stone to the worksite as well as transport oak and walnut timbers used in the edifice.

For nearly 3 years, construction progressed. Then one evening tragedy struck. Only a few months before Snyder planned to move into the four-story stone castle, he was fatally injured in an automobile accident.

The following day, construction on Snyder's dream halted. The workers and other artisans were stranded, but soon drifted to other jobs. For more than 10 years, the great, nearly completed home stood idle. Then it was used by the Snyder family as a summer home. In 1942, the wooden shingles on the roof caught fire, and the interior of the castle was gutted. Today the great walls still stand.

The ruins and several large beautiful caves in the area and the huge spring just below the castle which pours out 158-million gallons of water daily are just a few of the sights open to the public. Sinkholes and natural amphitheaters dot the area, and there's a huge natural bridge under which the Osage Indians camped. Three Missouri governors have recommended the area be purchased and preserved as a state park, but the state legislature has never seen fit to act. And so Ha Ha Tonka remains a rejected, crumbling castle in Missouri's Ozarks. It's located on the edge of a large chasm, 3 miles southwest of Camdenton on U.S. 54, not far from Lake of the Ozarks.

## Grant's Farm

At Grant's Farm, a 281-acre tract once worked by President Ulysses S. Grant, one may get a look at some of the most magnificent draft horses in the world. Although the farm offers a number of attractions such as roaming deer and

The largest number of Clydesdale horses in the United States can be seen at the Clydesdale Stallion Stable and Paddock Area at Grant's Farm, Missouri. *(Courtesy of Todd Studios, Inc.)*

buffalo herds, performing elephants and long-horn steers, by far the greatest attraction is the Champion Clydesdale Stallion Stable and Paddock Area. Grant's Farm is the home of the largest number of Clydesdale horses in the United States; among them are those used to pull the Busch Beer wagons seen on television and in parades throughout America. Free tours are given at Grant's Farm, April through October, Tuesday through Saturday, 9 A.M. to 3 P.M. Reservations are required, however, and can be made by contacting Grant's Farm Tours, Saint Louis, Missouri 63123. Out-of-town visitors are advised to make reservations a month in advance.

## House of Little Boy Blue

In Saint Louis, you can visit the modest home of Eugene Field, poet and newspaper columnist whose creations, "Little Boy Blue" and "Wynken, Blynken and Nod," have become known and quoted around the world. Built in 1845, the house, three-stories high with only six rooms, was one of twelve connected brick dwellings called Walsh's Row. It was located on land once owned by Pierre Laclede, founder of Saint Louis.

The house was about to be torn down in 1935, but was saved at the last minute by a newspaper editorial that ignited a flame of enthusiasm for it. School children contributed $1,800 in pennies and nickels for the renovation. The poet's widow, sons and daughters donated personal treasures and furniture. The second-floor bedroom and den were fashioned to closely resemble Field's Sabine Farm home in Chicago, so that visitors to the house today can see how Field lived and worked. Many of his original manuscripts are displayed. In one room, Field's poetry is recited via tape recorder. The house is located at 634 S. Broadway, Saint Louis.

## Melody Museum

The Melody Museum is an adventure in sight and sound. Open since 1967, the museum includes displays of nickelodeons and band organs dating back to the 1800s. Most of them were collected, assembled and restored by Mr. and Mrs. Paul Eakins of Sikeston, Missouri, over a 20-year period. Also included in the display is the Emteror, an ancient Belgian Band Organ with gilded trappings and fascinating carved figures. This machine contains 418 pipes, 22 xylophone bars, snare and bass drums, cymbals and double castanets. Its original cost was $14,000.

Some of the magic music machines in the Melody Museum play from paper rolls, others from metal discs; while the large band organs play from cardboard books and perforated books of music. In addition to the music machines, authentic antiques and rare Arcade pieces are displayed. Open daily year-round, the Melody Museum is located at 320 S. Broadway across from Busch Stadium in Saint Louis.

## Train to the Top of a Rainbow

Ever wish you could ride up a rainbow? Well, in Saint Louis, you can do just that; only this rainbow is made of steel. It's more appropriately known as the Gateway Arch. Carrying 40 passengers at a clip, the little trains climb to the top of the arch to offer a magnificent panoramic view of Saint Louis, the meandering Mississippi and a hunk of Illinois. The great arch commemorates the westward movement of America. A ride to the top takes about 4 minutes, the return trip about 3 minutes.

## National Transport Museum

Displays at the National Transport Museum provide an educational background on the implements of transportation and communication. Here one can see locomotives, railway cars, automobiles, street cars, buses, trucks, horse-drawn vehicles and even motorcycles. Visitors may sit in a locomotive cab, board a double-deck bus or walk into a railway tunnel. The museum, which is still expanding, is a chronicle of mankind's accomplishments in the movement of people, things and ideas. It's open daily throughout the year. The museum is located at 3015 Barretts Station Road, Saint Louis.

B&O *Camelback* on display at the National Museum of Transport, Saint Louis, Missouri. *(Courtesy of Convention Board of Greater Saint Louis)*

## Skidding School for Safety's Sake

At Central Missouri State University is a most unusual driver training school. It deals mostly with emergencies, and students are put through nerve-shaking episodes of the road: skids, blowouts, breakdowns, the works. The skidding is done on a large slab of asphalt slicked down with water. Each skid car comes equipped with a roll bar, treadless tires and two extra brake pedals on the instructor's side, giving him the option of freezing the front, rear or all four brakes to throw the car into a skid. Cars have tires with blowout simulators.

Spectators are invited to watch from the sidelines; and sometimes, if scheduling allows, demonstrations are staged. Occasionally, they are allowed to get into the act. The driver's training course is acclaimed as one of the toughest in the nation; but once students have graduated from the course, they're capable of handling practically any emergency that arises on the highway. Central Missouri State University is located at Warrensburg, on U.S. 50, east of Independence.

For additional information, contact the Missouri Tourism Commission, 308 E. High Street, Box 1055, Jefferson City, Missouri 65101.

# Montana

Big Sky Country, an Unusual Wildlife Museum and an
Earthquake Phenomenon

## Madison River Earthquake Area

In the Gallatin National Forest not far from West Yellowstone, you can witness the world's most unusual and dramatic display of earthquake phenomena. As you enter the area, you first notice two bodies of water. One, called Hebgen Lake, was created in 1915 when Hebgen Dam was built across the westward flowing Madison River. The second—appropriately named Earthquake Lake— was formed overnight.

The two bodies of water are part of the Madison River Canyon Earthquake Area, 37,800 acres of land virtually untouched since the night of August 17, 1959—the night the mountain fell. The force was equivalent to that of 2,500 atomic bombs. The evidence is still visible; abandoned homes and resorts cling tenaciously to the shores of Lake Hebgen, half submerged in water.

Parts of old MT 287 remain, cracked and twisted. On a knoll is a sign labeling Refuge Point as the spot where survivors of the quake who escaped from a campground in the canyon gathered to wait for daybreak. At the end of the drive is a visitor's center with a working seismograph and a museum display of the pictorial results of some of the world's most devastating earthquakes. Lectures are given daily during the summer months. Across the way from the quake-proof visitor's center is the slide on the mountain which buried many campers in the canyon below. Nearby is a memorial to those who perished here. This area is one of America's most impressive attractions on the site of a tragedy. To get there, take U.S. 191 and MT 287, northwest of West Yellowstone.

## Model T Race

One of the nation's most unusual auto races is the 500-mile competition featuring Model T Fords. In late June or early July each year, the race is held on a loop drive in Montana's Big Sky Country. For 3 days, the race continues, drawing a cross section of Model T fanciers. Ranchers, telephone linemen, salesmen, engineers, physicians and shopkeepers, ranging in age from 20 to 70, come from both ends of the continent to compete or to watch.

Most antique car buffs treat their cars as though they were rare pieces of Chinaware; not so with the Model T racers. They stoutly maintain Henry Ford built his jalopies to trundle over uncertain roads and still be absolutely reliable. To prove their point, they do just that in the big Montana race.

To qualify, one needs only a Model T and a small entry fee. Autos are inspected before and after the race by experts armed with a checklist of permitted and forbidden technical extras. Sometimes the spunky Model Ts ride three and four abreast, fighting for the lead. When the Model Ts were new, their top speed was 42 miles per hour; but on some of Montana's steep downgrades, speeds of 57 miles per hour have been recorded. Every contestant earns a plaque and there are trophies for the first three finishers. There's even a prize for the first mechanical collapse. Headquarters for the crosscountry Model T race is Ledger, located on Route 366, just east of I-15 in the northern part of the state.

North of Helena is an adventure cruise through a 14-mile canyon on the Missouri called Gates of the Mountains. It's an optical illusion of nature—the opening and closing of the Gates of the Mountain; it's an experience you won't want to miss. The boat ride includes a trip through a 2,000-foot gorge in the Missouri named by Captain Meriwether Lewis. Uneasy about what he would find in the Rockies, he felt the gorge the most spectacular he had seen—but "dark and gloomy." The boat trip takes 2 hours and only operates during the summer months. Headquarters for the cruise is 16 miles north of Helena on I-15.

**Gates of the Mountains**

Located at Browning is the Bighorn Foundry, built by Bob Scriver in an attempt to rediscover the techniques of bronze casting during the last century and to use them in casting his own work. Every step from wax to patina is

**Museum of Montana Wildlife**

One of the world's most unusual earthquake phenomena, the Madison River Earthquake Area in the Gallatin National Forest, Montana.

supervised by the artist. Visitors are welcome to the Bighorn Foundry to watch the casting of bronze statuary and to see the elaborate display of Montana wildlife statuary. Browning is located on U.S. 89, on the Blackfeet Indian Reservation in northern Montana.

## Custer's Last Stand

One of the most realistic dramas ever staged is the reenactment of the Battle of the Little Big Horn. Staged only 3 days during the middle of summer, the outdoor drama brings this historic event to life. To see this performance is to experience the event on the Little Big Horn, in the Indian camp with the wagon trains west. A cast of hundreds includes members of the Crow Indian tribe in authentic costume. It's staged only one mile from the actual site of the battle. Five performances are held during the 3 days. For further information, contact Custer's Last Stand at P.O. Box R, Hardin, Montana 59034. To get there, exit off I-90 at Crow Agency or Custer Battlefield Interchange and follow the signs.

## Territory Junction

When you visit Territory Junction at the Montana Historical Society Museum, you'll take a trip back in time. The mini-village recreates the typical Montana town of the 1880s. You can sense its history in the mirrored and ornately carved bar of the old Mint Saloon from Great Falls, the place where cowboy artist Charlie Russell played cards and drank sarsaparilla. Filling the twelve units of Territory Junction are a dressmaker's shop, blacksmith, jail, dentist's office, newspaper, Wells Fargo station, saloon, gun and saddlery, pharmacy, doctor's office, barber shop and a general store. The museum is located at 225 N. Roberts Street in Helena, which is on I-15.

## Aerial Fire Depot

Seven miles west of Missoula, a large barracks-like facility is headquarters for the U.S. Forest Service smokejumpers' operations and training. Aerial fire fighters from this base serve as shock troops in fire fighting in the sixteen national forests of the Northern Region, extending over 29-million acres in five states. Among the items to be seen are the visitor center, the Northern Forest Fire Laboratory, fire warehouse where their equipment is stored, the parachute loft used by smokejumpers and a smokejumper training area.

## Pryor Mountain Mustangs

In the Pryor Mountain Range, most of which is in Montana, there are roving herds of wild mustangs. Backpackers and horseback riders are sometimes afforded the opportunity of seeing them through binoculars. Founded in 1968, under the auspices of the Interior Department, the Pryor Mountain wild horse lands are managed by the Bureau of Land Management in cooperation with the state livestock commission and an advisory committee of interested citizens. Much of the Pryor Mountain area is accessible only on foot, horseback or jeep. Motorists sometimes report seeing the wild stallions and their harems from a road along the west edge of Bighorn Canyon. Additional attractions in this area are Indian "vision quest" sites and wall paintings; ice caves; archaeological features; wildlife including the Rocky Mountain bighorn sheep; and unique scenic beauty. The Pryor Mountain Range is southeast of Billings, most of it lying south of U.S. 87 and 212.

For additional information, contact the Advertising and Travel Unit, Department of Highways, Helena, Montana 59601.

# Nebraska

Tracks of the Westward Movement, Roaming Longhorns and the
Ghost of Buffalo Bill

Anywhere you enter Nebraska, you'll sense its strong historical significance; perhaps you can imagine the creak and rumble of the Conestoga wagon. That wagon has great significance, for many of the great pioneer trails ran through Nebraska—Oregon Trail, Mormon Trail, Lewis and Clark Trail, the Pony Express and many others. Between 1840 and 1866, more than 2.5-million people crossed this prairie region in Conestogas; and along much of the way today—particularly if you fly over the Platte River Valley—you can easily spot the rutted tracks of the prairie schooners that brought on the western movement. All across Nebraska, you'll see reminders of the pioneer days when this land was rugged, raw and untamed.

**Oregon Trail**

Among the traces of yesteryear, there is what is commonly referred to as "the Gibraltar of the West" or Scotts Bluff. Today it's a national monument administered by the National Park Service. This pilot rock remains a unique attraction. You need not use your imagination here to envision what the Oregon Trail was actually like, for you can walk, as most pioneers did, ½-mile of the trail. Dun-colored sand and clay cliffs rise around you. The fact that the journey was tough is evident from the graves along the trail—some say there's one every 200 feet. You can still see the ruts made by the wagons; daily, park rangers give lectures at the ruts, 250 yards from the modern visitor's center, and lead hikes to the pioneer campsite. And you shouldn't miss the drive to the summit of Scotts Bluff, some 800 feet above the valley floor. There is a small charge, but it's worth every penny. Three tunnels carved out of the cliff add to the suspense of the steep 1½-mile climb. The views are spectacular. Scotts Bluff is located just off U.S. 26, near the town of the same name in western Nebraska.

**Gibraltar of the West**

Just outside the town of North Platte is another reminder of Nebraska's rich heritage—Scout's Rest Ranch, the home of Buffalo Bill Cody. The rambling, two-story ranch house was built during the affluent period of Cody's famous Wild West Show. He once owned some 4,000 acres here and engaged in the raising of cattle and horses. He introduced blooded stock to this portion of the country through the purchase of thoroughbred horses and high-grade Hereford, Shorthorn and Polled Angus cattle.

**Scout's Rest Ranch**

The house, barn and original outbuildings are Cody's handiwork and are preserved and maintained as a State Historical Park. To walk under the giant shade trees and to visit the stables is to feel a closeness to one of the West's

Historic Scotts Bluff National Monument along the Oregon Trail in western Nebraska. *(Courtesy of Nebraska Game Commission)*

greatest historical figures. Every schoolboy in America would be quick to assert that claim. Each summer, to bring Cody's lifestyle into proper perspective, a reenactment of Buffalo Bill's Wild West Show and Congress of Rough Riders of the World is staged only 200 yards from the ranch. It includes many of the attractions of Cody's original show and more. North Platte is located just off I-80.

**Pony Express Station**

Near Gothenburg, in the Platte River Valley, you'll find Midway Station on 96 Ranch, a bonafide Pony Express station in its original location. Other things you'll find include an old dispensary of frontier Fort McPherson; an old stage stop with bullets still imbedded in the walls and a new no-charge campground at LaFayette Park in Gothenburg.

There's another original Pony Express station in the city park. Just south of U.S. 30, on the back trails between Gothenburg and Maxwell, you can explore the hills denuded of their once-rich cedar forests. The trees were used as poles for the old Overland Telegraph and as ties for the building of the Union Pacific Railroad. Gothenburg is located just off I-80.

**A Wildlife Refuge with Texas Longhorns**

Three miles out of Valentine is Sears Falls and Fort Niobrara, an army post built in 1879 to protect settlers from the Indians. The fort has a weapons museum and preserved specimens of wildlife. Surrounding the fort is one of the nation's most interesting national wildlife refuges. Besides herds of antelope, elk, deer and buffalo, there are Texas longhorn cattle. This is one of two herds in the entire nation, or in North America, for that matter. Therefore, it presents a unique opportunity to see and photograph these unusual animals which played such an important role in the Old West. Valentine is located on U.S. 20 in north central Nebraska.

**Smith Falls**

The highest falls in Nebraska cannot be reached by automobile. You can take an inflatable raft or canoe down the cliff-draped Niobrara River from Cornell Dam and, after some 15 miles of white water, you'll reach the falls. Regardless of how many times you get dunked on the way, the trip is worth the effort. Because of its inaccessibility, however, few tourists actually visit this spot. For 80 feet, the falls plunge to the valley floor, spreading a veil of fine mist before reaching its destination. It's located near Valentine.

**Popcorn Festival**

At the turn of the century, citizens of North Loup gathered to celebrate one of the most unusual festivals in the nation: North Loup's Popcorn Days. Free popcorn was distributed to the hungry crowds who gathered to enjoy 2 days of

Scouts Rest Ranch, home of the famous William F. (Buffalo Bill) Cody, near North Platte, Nebraska. *(Courtesy of Nebraska Game Commission)*

contests, games and fun. So well do the people respond to the event that it has become an annual affair. North Loup's Popcorn Days sees more than 30,000 bags of hot popcorn devoured.

Formerly known as the popcorn capital of the United States, North Loup is still a major area of production with an estimated 7-million pounds of corn grown on about 2,500 acres. The festival features not only buttered popcorn but also free entertainment, including horse shows, parades, games, music, dances, exhibits, carnivals and a horseshoe pitching contest. Since 1925, a queen contest has been an integral part of the celebration. North Loup is located on NB 11, northwest of Grand Island.

**Interstate Lakes**

Along I-80, one of the nation's most distinguished lakeland playgrounds has been created for superhighway travelers. Between Grand Island and North Platte are 116 excavated lakes, 46 of which are open to the public. All of them offer fishing, swimming and limited boating. The lakes feature bass, bream and crappie fishing; it is a restful interlude to motorists who are weary of concrete and asphalt and want to take a break.

**Cedar Canyon**

Among the most interesting and unusual canyons of the West is one that's hardly known outside the state of Nebraska—Cedar Canyon. The canyon slashes through Pine Ridge, a tribute to beauty and tranquility. Its towering walls create a cathedral-like atmosphere as they fall away to merge with the tabletop flatness of Oglala National grasslands, northwest of Crawford. Cedar Canyon is the kind of place that must be experienced by walking the floors, climbing the walls, examining the unique shades and formations that line its many coves and inlets. Crawford, the nearest town, is located on NB 2 in northwest Nebraska.

**Boys Town**

If you've ever had any doubt about the youth of America, visit Boys Town and you are likely to come away feeling everything is going to be fine for years to come. This 1,500-acre ranch has facilities for 1,000 boys who operate the establishment with much enthusiasm. The government of this well-kept community consists of a boy major and six commissioners. The farm and dairy are also operated by the boys. You'll find the huge fieldhouse, chapel and trade schools of particular interest, too. Stamp and coin collections and other items of considerable historic interest are displayed in the Philomatic Center. The grounds are open daily year-round, and there's no admission charge. Boys Town is located 10 miles west of Omaha on U.S. 6.

**Homestead Monument**

More than 100,000 settlers came to Nebraska as a result of the Homestead Act of 1862 that provided for distribution of public lands, free of charge, to those who settled on them, cultivated and improved them for a period of 5 years. Today, the Homestead National Monument on NB 4, near Beatrice, marks the land where the first home was built under that act.

For additional information, contact the Tourism Coordinator, Department of Economic Development, P.O. Box 94666, State Capitol, Lincoln, Nebraska 68509.

# Nevada

A School for Gamblers, a Basque Festival and a
Valley of Fire

In Las Vegas, several casinos sponsor schools for gamblers. They first began at the Mint Hotel in downtown Las Vegas with courses conducted 7 days a week on the basic rules of playing 21, roulette, craps and keno. Baccarat instruction is offered on a personal basis at the gaming table. The course is free and is offered in several languages. The Mint combines the gaming school with a behind-the-scenes tour of the casino. Tours limited to about 15 persons are led to the upper levels. Amid the rafters, there are rows of one-way glass used to spy on the gambling tables of the casino. To the gamblers, the ceiling appears to be paneled with mirrors.

At graduation exercises, the instructor hands out diplomas, adds a free keno card, then leads his class into the Mint casino where class is dismissed and the pupils are left to the house's own devices. At other casinos such as the Dunes, the Frontier and the Stardust, classes are offered on keno, dice, 21, blackjack and slot machines. For those wanting to enroll in post-graduate training with aspirations of becoming a professional gambler or dealer for one of the casinos, courses are available. Gambling schools are advertised locally.

The National Basque Festival at Elko is held annually during the first weekend in July. The Basques, one of the most unique ethnic groups in America, are a fun-loving people. Mostly sheepherders and farmers, the Basques still consider Europe their real home and make frequent trips there. About half of the 4.5-million Basques in the world today live in the Pyrenees Mountains between Spain and France. Their language, called Euzkera, is so unique even the best scholars are totally defied by it.

Among the festivities of this event are colorful dances and a game of pelota or jai alai which requires skill, strength, endurance and courage. There are also weight lifting and carrying, sheep hooking, foot races and wood chopping. The wood chopping is done standing barefoot on top of the log and hacking away with a short-handled single-bit axe. Chips fly and spectators encourage contestants with shouts and threats and many bets among themselves. Basque food is delicious and a feast is served. Hearty soups and meat dishes prepared in a Dutch oven are the main fare. Roast lamb is very popular, as are fresh fruits and vegetables. Also during the festival, there is an outdoor mass with Basque music and a huge parade. Basque people come from many western states to attend the festival. Even a brief visit to the festival is a most unusual, educational experience. Elko is located in northeast Nevada on U.S. 40.

**Wild Jackass Race**

In the little town of Beatty is held one of the most ornery races in the world—the World Championship Wild Jackass Race. Sponsored by the Lions Club of Beatty, the event attracts wranglers from all over the West to drag their wild jackasses over 40 miles of Nevada terrain for prizes ranging from $5 to $750.

The race takes 3 days, and sometimes it takes a couple of days prior to that to round up the wild burros from the desert. On the day prior to kickoff, festivities get underway with a wild burro haltering, followed by a riotous polo match in which donkeys are ridden instead of ponies. The rules state: "Players may not kick, bite or beat the burros at any time. Burros may kick, bite, stomp,

The 40-mile World Championship Wild Burro Races at Beatty, Nevada.

gouge, buck or otherwise conduct themselves in burro-like manner without fear of penalty." Other events include a burro-roping competition, burro branding, the crowning of a Burro Queen and a Wild West Parade. Beatty is located on U.S. 95, northwest of Las Vegas.

**Mysterious Petroglyphs**

Possibly no place in the world offers more questions and frustrations for archaeologists than a small range of mountains in southeastern Nevada, bordering Lake Mohave. More specifically known as Grapevine Canyon, here is one of the finest collections of Indian Petroglyphs remaining today; but no one has been able to fully interpret them. After more than 50 years of intensive study, an aura of mystery still prevails. One authority says they are not a form of communicative writing and there is no reason to assume they are texts or messages. Other authorities aren't so sure. Some believe the writing has religious significance; others feel they represent clan or family symbols. Still others claim the Indians were merely doodling and that perhaps psychiatrists could make something of them. At any rate, for those who wish to study petroglyphs, there's no better place than in the Lake Mead National Recreation Area, 7 miles west of Davis Dam.

## Valley of Fire

Just below the dairy city of Overton, there is a wonderland of rock elephants, dragons and beehives. It's a menagerie packed into 30,000 acres known as the Valley of Fire. The name comes from the brilliant red sandstone, which changes in form and hue with each hour of sunlight. This sight had a semi-religious meaning in the minds of the early Pueblo dwellers. They produced petroglyphs you can still see—stories told in pictures from the weird formations they saw. It's mighty easy to get lost in the strange winding passages through the Valley of Fire, however; and you're advised to either take a compass or stay on the marked trails. In the town of Overton, you'll find the Lost City Museum, a pueblo building which displays and interprets the ancient cultures of the Valley of Fire. Overton is located on NV 12, on the northernmost arm of Lake Mead.

## Ruby Valley

Originally, Ruby Valley was intended to be an Indian reservation, but the United States government decided it was too barren to support even the Indians. A Kentucky gentleman named Colonel J. B. Moore, who had initially scouted the valley, decided it would make fine grazing land; to back up this

The Valley of Fire contains 30,000 acres of brilliant red sandstone, just south of Overton, Nevada.

theory, Ruby Valley today is one of the finest ranching areas of the entire West. Moore, with the help of soldiers from nearby Camp Ruby, taught the Indians to plow and planted an acreage of grain that not only took root and flowered, but yielded so bountifully that the soldiers, as soon as their enlistments ended, hustled in to stake homestead claims.

Today, a fifth generation of some of those families lives in Ruby Valley. To see the valley at its best, take a shunpiking drive south of Elko and over Harrison Pass. The view, which embraces a whole skyful of lakes, ranges and peaks, is one you'll never forget. Some of the ranchers in the valley accept guests for a day or two. The valley's best known citizen is former movie star, Joel McCrea, who keeps a working ranch in the upper end; you just might see him herding Herefords. The valley was named for tiny garnets panned from a tumbling mountain stream that glowed like a ruby in the sunlight.

For further information, contact the Tourism-Travel Division, Department of Economic Development, Carson City, Nevada 89701.

# New Hampshire

### Mystery Hill, a Cog Railway and the Old Man of the Mountains

**Mystery Hill**    Mystery Hill has been called America's Stonehenge; some say it dates back to 2000 B.C. No one has yet disputed that, nor fully confirmed it; for that is part of its mystery. In fact, there's some thought that Europeans may have landed at the southeast corner of New Hampshire at least 3,000 years ago, maybe more, thus striking down the belief that Columbus discovered America, or even that the Vikings were the first to arrive here.

The village on Mystery Hill is comprised of a number of dwellings built around the hill. At the peak, in the center of the dwellings, is what appears to be an amphitheater in which a huge stone slab rests on pillars. Around the top of the slab has been carved a groove. Some scientists feel this slab was used for sacrifices and that the groove was chiseled out to allow for the run-off of blood. Because of the size of the stone buildings, it's believed the people who used them were less than 5-feet tall.

While the buildings here actually resemble no other construction known to man, they do bear some resemblance to buildings found in England, France and Spain, dating back to the Stone Age. While the truth may never be revealed, Mystery Hill has indeed provided New Hampshire with one of the most puzzling pieces of archaeological masonry in the world today. America's Stonehenge is located at North Salem, located off I-93.

A sacrificial table at Mystery Hill, North Salem, New Hampshire. *(Courtesy of Robert E. Stone)*

**Mount Washington**

It's said that the world's worst weather is recorded atop Mount Washington in New Hampshire's White Mountains. Blizzard conditions are common throughout much of the year, and wind velocities greater than 200 miles per hour have been recorded. Once the wind hit an unbelievable velocity of 231 miles per hour. Atop the boulder-strewn mountain are two television antennae, a weather observatory, a cluster of buildings (one of them fortified with chains across its roof) and a hostelry called Summit House. The summit is actually a rocky heap, a moon-surface crag from which, on a clear day, one can see five states and Canada. The average snowfall here is 16 feet and snow has fallen there every month of the year. Seldom does the temperature, if ever, exceed 71 degrees, even in summer, and the lowest temperature recorded is 46 below zero.

**Cog Railway**

The most unusual way to see Mount Washington is aboard the oldest cog railway in the world. When you climb aboard the base station, you'd swear this little engine could not possibly push those cars loaded with people up the steep incline, but it does. Open since 1869, this crazy little train with the bright red and green locomotive grabs into the cogs of the track and pushes its train upward. It takes an hour and a quarter each way and you can browse around the summit as long as you like, or sleep over if you've made arrangements. To get to Mount Washington, take NH 16, south of Berlin.

**Clock Museum**

Ever see a horological wonderland? In Newport, Esley Hallett has accumulated more than 400 timepieces, covering five centuries. Acclaimed as the second largest collection of clocks in the country and the largest in the East, the museum contains water clocks, hour glasses, sundials, digital clocks, self-winding clocks and even one clock run by an old wagon spring. The oldest clock in the museum is dated at 1590; it is made of iron and has a painted face. One of his novelty clocks, when wound, sets in motion a gigantic tableau of a rocking sailboat on a pond, a turning water wheel and two trains passing over a bridge. It strikes every half hour and plays a music box on the hour. The museum is located on the Common in Newport, which is on NH 11.

The largest collection of clocks in the East can be seen at the Clock Museum in Newport, New Hampshire. *(Courtesy of Newport Clock Museum)*

## Old Man of the Mountains

As you visit one of New Hampshire's finest state parks—Franconia Notch—you will see the Old Man of the Mountains. Perched on a steep precipice that plunges down toward the gorge, the old man was once the subject of a story written by Nathaniel Hawthorne called *The Great Stone Face.* Geologists say it was formed over 200-million years ago. Farther along the notch is a remarkable basin, a granite pothole 20 feet in diameter at the foot of a waterfall. Experts theorize it was formed some 25,000 years ago as the Ice Age glacier receded. The Flume, a natural chasm 800 feet long with walls 12 to 20 feet apart rising above you, terminates at Avalanche Falls, with a drop of 25 feet. Franconia Notch is located off U.S. 3, north of Woodstock.

Along New Hampshire's short seacoast is a renovated pioneer town which allows one to step back to early seafaring days. It's known as Strawbery Banke, located within the confines of bustling Portsmouth on the banks of Puddle Dock. Shops, stores, a blacksmith shop and a boat-building works, along with historic houses such as the Daniel Webster home, make up Strawbery Banke. You may watch craftsmen work and see women spinning and weaving in the costume of the original colonies.

**Strawbery Banke**

Students of Colonial architecture and travelers interested in America's heritage will find the restoration of the village an exciting program; a dramatic arrangement of Colonial architecture and an unrivaled opportunity to view original workmanship and materials. The restoration project is well underway, but it will continue for many years to come. Signs in the city of Portsmouth direct you to Strawbery Banke, which is near the downtown area.

Another New Hampshire restoration project underway is a Shaker village between Concord and Laconia. Starting as a one-building museum in 1959, more buildings and displays are opened to the public each year. Eventually, the village will allow the visitor to walk through the pages of history and time and see re-created the home, furnishings and farms of one of America's Shaker settlements. This Shaker village was one of nineteen in the United States based on the principles of the early Christian Church, living in a commune-type environment and devoting their labor to the general good. The village is located on NH 106 and is open late May to Labor Day.

**Shaker Village**

A Shaker sect settlement at Canterbury, New Hampshire. *(Courtesy of Eric Sanford, State of New Hampshire)*

**Peterborough**  Few towns in America can lay claim to harboring as many well-known men and women of literature as can Peterborough. It all began with the MacDowell Colony just north of town. After the famous composer Edward MacDowell died, his wife and friends established a hideaway workshop for writers, artists and musicians. Among those to visit the workshop over a period of time were Stephen Vincent Benét, Edwin Arlington Robinson, Hervey Allen, poet and playwright Padraic Colum, William Rose Benét and Thornton Wilder. The list goes on and on. Many of the works they produced had their beginnings at Peterborough, which is located on U.S. 202, north of Jaffrey.

**Cathedral of the Pines**  In a deep pine forest atop a hill, there is a most remarkable memorial. Begun in 1945, the altar is made of stones from practically all parts of the world given by people of every known religious faith. These stones form the Altar of the Nations. The Congress voted unanimous recognition of the cathedral as a memorial for all American war dead—but no government, state, local or federal, has jurisdiction here; neither has any religious faith, except at the time of conducting services. The only cathedral housing the altar is the pine forest. It's located on Cathedral Road, off NH 119 near Rindge.

For additional information, contact the Vacation Travel Promotion, New Hampshire Division of Economic Development, P.O. Box 856, Concord, New Hampshire 03301.

# New Jersey

## A Genuine Ghost Town, a China Exhibit and the Boy Scout's Museum

**Ghost Town**  Visitors to the Garden State may see a quiet, unrestored ghost town by taking a county road due east from Mount Holly, along Rancocas Creek to the old village of Smithville. Hezekiah Smith of Vermont moved here as a manufacturer in 1865; and in no time, the tiny village had an opera house, ballroom, gaming casino, an actress in residence, conservatories and the Smithville Brass Band. The peak of prosperity came when Smith began making the Star high-wheeled bicycles.

Smith and one of his inventors later developed the first commuter monorail—for bicycles—that ran all the way to Mount Holly. As early as 1879, Smith had a working steam automobile whose boiler was fired by kerosene. Today the town is all but deserted and in a state of ruins; it is one of the most authentic ghost towns of the entire East. Mount Holly is located on NJ 38, only a short distance east of the New Jersey Turnpike.

Today the most illustrious name in American china is Lenox, the dinner service used in the White House. On Prince and Meade streets in Trenton are the Lenox showrooms, which feature a museum of china, including American Beleek perfected by Walter Lenox and plates made for noted persons. The showrooms are open to the public on any weekday and on Saturday from 9 A.M. to 3 P.M. **China Exhibit**

Scouts enjoy the many museum exhibits that they can operate. Here scouts learn basic meteorological principles at the model weather station in the Boy Scouts Museum, New Brunswick, New Jersey. *(Courtesy of the Boy Scouts of America)*

The national headquarters for the Boy Scouts of America and the Boy Scout Museum is in New Brunswick. Here is a variety of exhibits on outdoor life and camping that make it a must for families with boys. In the spring, a marked **Boy Scouts** nature trail is open for public hiking. New Brunswick is located just west of the New Jersey Turnpike on NJ 18.

## Rockhound's Heaven

The mines of the New Jersey Zinc Company are located at Franklin, atop the largest zinc deposits in the world. Tours are offered of the plant; but rockhounds will be interested in at least 190 other minerals found in the area, too. At least 30 of them are found nowhere else in the world. One of these, franklinite, was named by the physician, Dr. Samuel Fowler, who in the 1830s founded Franklin in order to mine the ore. At least 25 different fluorescent rocks which emit a multicolor glow under ultraviolet light have been discovered here. Nearby is headquarters for the world's largest mineralogy club. The mineral dump of Buckwheat Mine, now owned by the town of Franklin, is open to the public for a small fee. You may keep what you find and use the ultraviolet light in nearby "sentry boxes" so as to see your fluorescents in vivid color. You can also see the small replica of the original mines, the "black light" display of fluorescent rocks and the exhibit of 257 different minerals. Franklin is located on NJ 23, 2 miles south of Hamburg.

## Cherry Blossoms in Newark

In the heart of Newark is Branch Brook Park with the most elaborate display of Japanese flowering cherry trees in the nation, even surpassing the display in Washington, D.C. In the 500-acre park each evening, the flowering trees (which are usually in full bloom by the last of April) are lighted until 11 P.M., creating a unique site that draws hordes of photographers.

## Edison's Laboratory

Located at West Orange are numerous brick buildings which once served as laboratories for Thomas Edison. Now a National Historic Site, the buildings are crammed to the rafters with original working models, cylinder phonographs

Now a National Historic Site, Thomas A. Edison's chemistry laboratory and home may be visited in West Orange, New Jersey.

and early kinetoscopes. Visitors can see one of the most famous pioneer silent films, *The Great Train Robbery,* made for Edison's company. If you obtain a ticket at the laboratories, you can see the multigabled mansion where Edison and his family lived from 1886 until his death in 1931. West Orange is located on NJ 10, just west of Newark.

The New Jersey Fire Museum is located at South Orange. With a real fire-house setting of the 1840s, the display includes an original engine, old-time paraphernalia of fire fighters and expertly executed scale models of street scenes. You may reach South Orange on NJ 510, west of Newark.

**Fire Museum**

The Great Swamp in northern New Jersey is proof that wilderness can some-times be found, and preserved, in the midst of a megalopolis. Only 25 miles from Times Square and surrounded by numerous urban centers, The Great Swamp has somehow survived. It remains distinctively a part of America's pre-civilized past. Migrant hawks and waterfowl rest here on their way up and down the Atlantic flyway. Wood ducks, deer, foxes, muskrats, mink, weasels and other animals thrive in the swamp. Northern trees mingle with those of the South.

**The Great Swamp**

Today the Great Swamp is a National Wildlife Refuge and may be visited in some detail on any day of the week, year-round. The swamp is located just west of New York City and south of Morristown, New Jersey.

For additional information, contact the Environmental Protection Office, P.O. Box 400, Trenton, New Jersey 08625.

# New Mexico

Billy the Kid, a Christmas Tour and Music from the Hills

Each August, at the Palace of Governors in Santa Fe, there is a unique Indian market—perhaps the most noteworthy one in all North America. Sponsored by the Southwestern Association on Indian Affairs, a nonprofit organization, the funds from the market are used to provide financial aid to Indian students and to foster better understanding of Indian culture and greater appreciation of Indian arts.

**Santa Fe's Indian Market**

In the Indian Market, held on the sidewalks of Santa Fe, shoppers are assured of finding genuine products, often sold by the craftsmen who created them. Invitations to sell their products go only to recognized artists and crafts-men from the Indian nation. Among the crafts are pottery from the Santa Clara and San Juan; jewelry from the Navajos, Hopi and Zuni; Navajo rugs; wood-carvings; and Kachina dolls. As many as 300 Indians occupy the booths and spaces along three sides of the Plaza; even if you purchase nothing, it's a sight to behold.

**Mercado**    On another summer weekend (the dates vary) is the Mercado—a market and showcase for the work of artists of Hispanic origin. Totally limited to Chicano people, this market offers fine silverwork, furniture and traditional and contemporary art. It, too, is held in front of the Palace of Governors in Santa Fe.

**Madrid**    In the hills and sandwashes south of Santa Fe is the state's most unusual and largest ghost town—Madrid, once famous for its Christmas ceremony. When this writer was last there, the town was for sale—lock, stock and ghosts. For $1 million, one could purchase 240 bungalows, one church, two schools, a movie theater, two coal-burning locomotives, a restaurant, coffee shop, barber shop, boarding house, art gallery, half a dozen vintage cars, one Model T truck, a service station and an assortment of other ghost town accessories.

Once very much alive with a population of more than 2,000, Madrid today is a haunt for only the wind that rattles its shutters and sweeps its streets. Not so long ago, Madrid was the third largest coal-producing community in New Mexico. The Spanish began mining there in 1803 and the town thrived for many years. It later became a company town from one end to the other; and one gentleman, Oscar Huber, owned it all. But when the railroads—the principal user of coal from Madrid—began using diesels, Madrid's economy began to crumble.

Today Joe Huber, an Albuquerque furniture dealer and son of Oscar Huber, owns the town. He occasionally leads visitors on tours of the old mill and the scarred hillsides. Huber will tell you how, during Madrid's heyday, Christmas was a most unique experience. Every family opened its house. Scenes of the Nativity were recreated on the hillsides; and more than 40,000 lightbulbs spotlighted Mary and Joseph leaving Nazareth, shepherds tending their flocks, the birth of the Christ child and various other scenes. By the beginning of World War II, more than 100,000 visitors flocked to Madrid during the Yule season. Now, all is dark and silent on Christmas night, and every other night throughout the year. Madrid is located on NM 10, south of Santa Fe.

**Opera in the Hills**    From the hills, there is the echo of music floating up into the starlit New Mexico night. The trill of a soprano's voice carries across the mesas. A Steinway echoes against an old, weathered barn. Two violinists rush up a pinon-studded hill in the shadows of the Sangre de Cristo Mountain Range.

Each summer, on a bluff 5 miles north of Santa Fe, the hills come alive with music from the Santa Fe Opera; it's a stunning outdoor theater. Sante Fe Opera has become one of the most outstanding and unusual opera companies in the world. Every year during a 6 to 8-week engagement, more than 50 young singers from all parts of the nation begin their apprenticeship in such performances as *Madame Butterfly, Don Giovanni* and *Salome*. At least one American or world premiere is scheduled each summer.

**Toltec Railroad**    Railroad buffs and others who are looking for a unique and different experience will love the Toltec Railroad and its ride through the mountains of northern New Mexico. Goggle-eyed passengers can still ride this old smoke-belching train over trestles, through tunnels, around towering cliffs, over high mountain passes and through near-deserted river valleys on the Cumbres & Toltec Scenic Railroad. It's an all-day excursion into yesterday, aboard one of the last re-

Through the northern part of the state, visitors can ride the Cumbres & Toltec Scenic Railroad, New Mexico. *(Courtesy of Tom Brown)*

maining coal-fired, steam-powered narrow gauge railroads on the continent.

It began in 1880 as a mining railroad on a roadbed 64 miles long connecting two towns—Chama, New Mexico and Antonito, Colorado. Although these towns are only 35 miles apart, the railroad takes the long way around, giving the rider an exciting experience amid some of the West's most impressive scenery. The train passes through two national forests, and a Forest Service ranger rides on every trip to keep watch for fires in remote areas. Be sure to take your sunglasses along; a cinder in your eye can ruin the entire journey. Chama, headquarters for the Toltec, is located on U.S. 84, northwest of Santa Fe.

## Albuquerque's Luminaria Tour

Luminarias are a carry-over from the old Spanish religious folk custom of placing little bonfires along the path to the church on Christmas Eve to light the way for the Christ child. Today's luminarias are a bit different, consisting of an ordinary brown paper bag about 10-inches high with a cuff turned down at the top to hold it upright. An inch or two of sand is placed in the bag and a votive candle set in the sand. The gentle, flickering light, when multiplied by thousands, casts a golden glow.

On Christmas Eve, individual homes, institutional buildings and the historic, old town all put out luminarias outlining roofs, garden walls, sidewalks and streets. The Greater Albuquerque Chamber of Commerce provides free tours to out-of-town visitors, picking them up by bus at various hotels and motels in the city and taking them through some of the most outstanding luminaria display areas. It's a special gift to out-of-town visitors, Albuquerque's way of saying, "Merry Christmas Everyone."

**Centuries-Old Apartment House**

At Chaco Canyon stands one of the nation's oldest apartment houses. Centuries ago, the 800-room dwelling was home for Indians and today is intricately preserved for all posterity. Chaco Canyon is located 70 miles southeast of Farmington on NM 57.

**Billy the Kid Still Lives**

The Lincoln County Range Wars were waged approximately a century ago; but the legends surrounding one of the dispute's most active participants—William Bonney, alias Billy the Kid—continue to live and grow. Each year at Lincoln State monument in the town of Lincoln, Billy the Kid's last escape from the hoosegow is reenacted. Any schoolchild in Lincoln knows Billy the Kid as if he were his neighbor; for the Kid's deadly exploits are a part of the area's heritage. The event normally is staged in August. To get to Lincoln, take U.S. 380, southeast of Albuquerque.

**Town of Outlaws**

If you'd like to drive through some of New Mexico's back country, don't miss the town of Las Vegas, east of Santa Fe. Just off U.S. 84, the town once was green pastures for the scum of the Southwest. In the latter part of the nine-

The Four Corners Monument in northwest New Mexico connects Arizona, Colorado, Utah and New Mexico.

Hoop dancers performing at an Intertribal Ceremonial, New Mexico.

teenth century, Las Vegas' *Who's Who* included such notorious characters as Soapy Smith, Pegleg Dick, Rattlesnake Sam, Kickapoo George, Scarface Charlie and Split-Nose Mike. Some of them never left town; they were hanged from the windmill that used to be on the plaza. Today, you can visit the exact spot of the executions.

**Gateway to the Land of Enchantment**

Clayton, a small town in eastern New Mexico, is known as the "Gateway to the Land of Enchantment." But the most noteworthy event that ever occurred there was as unique as they come. Clayton always was a cowtown; and when cowpokes drove herds up the Goodnight-Loving Trail, it was home for Black Jack Ketchum and his train robbers. The law finally caught up with him; and in 1901, he was hanged to the tune of a violin at his request. Dressed like a dude, he helped the nervous hangman adjust his noose, then yelled: "Let 'er go! I'm due in Hell for dinner!" Staff reporters from a number of newspapers, including *The New York Times,* covered the story. Clayton is located on U.S. 56.

**Four Corners Monument**

At a remote spot in northwest New Mexico along U.S. 164 is a most unique monument—a cement slab across which are two intersecting lines, forming an X. Where the lines cross in the center of the slab is the only place in the United States where four state boundaries meet—Arizona, Colorado, New Mexico and Utah.

**Pony Express Races**

That glorious hero of American history—the Pony Express rider—is reincarnated each year with the reenactment of the Pony Express race from White Oaks to Lincoln. Begun in 1969 as a one-time event, the race attracted so much attention that it's been held every year since. Broken into four laps involving three exchanges of horses, the race is held over a 41-mile course. The first lap is 9.7 miles, the second 10 miles, the third 8.3 miles and the fourth 13 miles. Riders take virtually the same course Sheriff Pat Garrett rode from White Oaks when he heard Billy the Kid had killed his guards and escaped from jail. To add to the spice of the race, only the rider's first and third horses can be previously saddled; the rider must change the saddle at the start of the second and fourth laps. That's where many of the races are won or lost. Spectators watch the event from the roadway all along the 41-mile route, but most of them gather at the relay points. White Oaks is located on NM 349; Lincoln on U.S. 380.

For additional information, contact the Tourist Division, Department of Development, 113 Washington Avenue, Santa Fe, New Mexico 87501.

# New York

## An Antique Flying Museum, an Easter Eggs Exhibit and Uncle Sam's Grave

**Rhinebeck Aerodrome**

Above the Hudson River Valley, amid the roar of straining engines, comes the staccato burst of machine fire as old triplanes and biplanes stage aerial dogfights that set the heart throbbing with excitement. It's the weekly show at the old Rhinebeck Aerodrome, where some of the nation's best pilots—flying vin-

Weekly shows are staged at the Rhinebeck Aerodrome, up the Hudson River, New York.

tage World War I Fokkers, Sopwith Pups, Spad XIIIs and Flying Jennys—soar through the air with the greatest of ease.

More than 20 of these old planes have been collected by flying ace Cole Palen at a cow pasture outside Rhinebeck to represent what he calls a living museum of the air. A number of the planes are not used in the aerial demonstrations, but are available for visitors to take a closeup view on the ground. Near the flying strip is a building housing many items of memorabilia connected with flying, including some planes.

For 3 hours, the show holds thousands of visitors spellbound as the pilots put the old planes through their paces at low altitude above Rhinebeck. There also are demonstrations with a hot-air balloon and comical skits involving Sir Percy Goodfellow and the Black Baron. At no other place in the nation can one find so many flying models of vintage aircraft. To get to Rhinebeck, take U.S. 9, north of New York City up the Hudson. Once there, anyone can direct you to the Rhinebeck Aerodrome.

## Village of Violets

Rhinebeck is noted for other offbeat attractions, including its millions of violets. In fact, it's become known as the village of violets. The self-styled Violet Capital of America has specialized in violet production since the 1890s and is now the largest producer in the United States.

Its principal grower, Trombini Brothers, has been in the business for several generations. Visitors with a hankering for this special harbinger of spring are welcome any time during the season from November to April. The purple tide of violet production hit its peak between 1900 and 1908 when violet houses mushroomed in the backyards of 200 individual growers. Since then, the citizens of Rhinebeck have dedicated a Violet Hill Road, a Violet Place and a Violet Avenue to the little flower that brought their village fame. Trombini's greenhouses contain more than 150,000 plants and yield an annual crop of some 5-million violets. An average day's harvest is 65,000 blossoms.

Another Rhinebeck attraction is the Beekman Arms Hotel, claimed to be the oldest hotel in America. During its 228 years of continuous service, it has hosted such distinguished guests as George Washington and Alexander Hamilton; it still serves the public today.

## Deep Hollow Cattle Ranch

Because of its location and history, the Deep Hollow Cattle Ranch is unquestionably the most unique ranch in North America. Located on Long Island, just a short distance from bustling Manhattan, Deep Hollow Ranch was once training grounds for Teddy Roosevelt's Rough Riders. Today it remains a cattle and guest ranch with a western flavor. It occupies the unique distinction of being the oldest cattle ranch in the United States.

Located at the very tip of Long Island on Montauk Point, where the Long Island Sound meets the Atlantic Ocean, you can ride the dunes and sweeping moors on horseback or go down to the sea and fish for cod and porgies. The ranch is also on the Atlantic flyway, and birdwatching is so great that devotees of the sport congregate here each autumn.

There are some 2,000 acres for riding, including the Deep Hollow Ranch and adjacent state and county-owned land. Although the horses prefer the solid ground above the beach, you can ride down to the breakers as Teddy Roosevelt often liked to do. Today a small herd of Black Angus cattle roams the pasturelands of the ranch; but in 1661, there were approximately 6,000 head of cattle here. Lodging, as well as meals, is provided at the ranch. The ranch is open from May until October or November, depending on the weather.

## Museum of Immigration

In the base of the Statue of Liberty is a most unusual and interesting attraction little known to visitors outside of New York...the Museum of Immigration. It tells the history of America through the story of its immigrants. Operated by the National Park Service, the museum is designed so the visitor can proceed chronologically through the story of United States immigration, although those early Indians who are believed to have crossed the Bering sea from Asia are represented only by a map. More than 200 exhibits and dioramas, many with special voice and sound effects, tell the story. The focus of the exhibit is on the century of immigration that began in the 1820s when some 34 million persons came to these shores. The theme of the museum points out that the fabric of the United States today has been woven from various immigrant groups.

## Magic Store

High above New York's Times Square is one of America's most colorful retail establishments—the Louis Tannen Magic Store. Colorful silks and flags of all nations hang from the ceiling and are draped on the walls. Photos of every notable professional magician festoon the counters. Ventriloquists' dummies gape from showcases. In a corner, a brightly painted guillotine stands menacingly—but is guaranteed not to harm the "victim." On a single day, one may see world-famous personalities come and go from this store. In one corner, the familiar magic enthusiast and television personality Johnny Carson may be seen demonstrating a series of bewildering card tricks. In another corner, Dunninger, the famous mentalist, may be reading a fellow customer's mind. Elsewhere, a clergyman from Quebec may have dropped in to buy a magic book and is showing an impromptu audience how to make golf balls appear and disappear.

The Tannen Magic Store is one of the world's largest, serving more than 10,000 customers. Over the years, the clientele have included such famous professionals as Harry Blackstone, Carl Ballantine, Frank Garcia and Shari Lewis. The store is located on the seventeenth floor of the Wurlitzer Building, facing Forty-second Street.

## Author's Room

Tucked away on the first floor of the huge New York Public Library is a room in which authors have worked on many of the best-known books in circulation today—the Frederick Lewis Allen Memorial Room. It is to this room that authors come to do research, write and, if they wish, smoke.

Named for the editor of *Harper's* who wrote "Only Yesterday," an account of the 1920s, the Allen Room has eleven carpeted, open cubicles.

With space for so few writers at a time, it isn't easy to gain admission. A writer must have proof of a signed contract with a known publisher. More than 200 books have been written over the past few years in this room. Betty Friedan worked on *The Feminine Mystique* here. Nancy Milford wrote *Zelda* and Robert Massie turned out *Nicholas and Alexandra* here. Theodore White worked in this room on his *Making of the President* books.

You'll probably never get to see the interior of the Allen Room unless you become a writer meeting the established qualifications; but you can see the entranceway and, if you're there at the right time, you may see many of the writers coming and going. Nonetheless, it's a most unusual place and worth knowing of its existence in the "Concrete Jungles" of Manhattan.

**Polo on Wheels**

In New York's Central Park each Tuesday, weather permitting, there are practice sessions and occasional games of one of the nation's most offbeat sports—polo on wheels. The bicycle-riding players are members of the U.S. Bicycle Polo Association which has started a new fad in American sports. The activity is not new, however. Bicycle polo was first played 80 years ago in Ireland. It soon spread to the United States where a charter club was formed at Milton, Massachusetts, in 1897. In the past few years, the sport on horseback has become particularly expensive because of inflation and the high cost of keeping horses. So many polo players have turned to bicycles. Clubs have been organized in several states, but the most active seems to be in New York.

In addition to the practice sessions in Central Park, tournaments are held on weekends on Long Island. The Central Park sessions are quite democratic; volunteers are allowed to join the fun when one of the riders becomes winded. Some of the replacements are pony-polo players anxious to give the game a try. Most of them go away disappointed, however, and as one remarked: "At least you don't have to pedal a pony." For further details on the polo games, check with the New York Convention and Visitors Bureau, 90 E. Forty-second Street, New York 10017.

**Unicyclists' Rendezvous**

Each summer in Central Park, the annual Unicycle Invitational is held. Unicyclists gather from around the nation to participate in competition, fun and games. They range from six years of age to eighty and offer the visitor an opportunity to view this unusual activity. There are usually more than 250 participants in the affair, which includes unicycle racing, stunts and tricks, jumping and hurdling. During one meet, an eleven-year-old girl rode the unicycle while twirling a hula hoop around her waist and a young man did a juggling act while riding a unicycle.

**Bears and Bulls**

If you don't know the difference between the Bears and the Bulls, you'll enjoy a trip to the American Stock Exchange's new Visitors' Gallery. There are exhibits, movies, literature and a bird's-eye view of the Amex trading floor with telephones at hand which provide interpretations of the buying and selling below. A most captivating aspect of the exhibit is a replica of Wall Street at the turn of the century. The Gallery is open on business days from 10 A.M. to 3 P.M. at 78 Trinity Place. The New York Stock Exchange at 20 Broad Street also has a visitors' gallery with similar facilities.

**Uncle Sam**

At the town of Troy on the Hudson River is the grave of Uncle Sam, symbol of our nation. While the majority of American people believe Uncle Sam to be alive and well, hundreds of others through the years have visited his grave in the public cemetery at Troy.

A local meat packer, Uncle Sam's real name was Samuel Wilson. During the War of 1812, Samuel Wilson was contracted to deliver some of his products to the U.S. Army. Because of his avuncular appearance, Wilson became known as "Uncle" to the soldiers he served; and since he already stenciled his army meat barrels "U.S.," someone got the idea the initials stood for Uncle Sam. A slogan was added: "Uncle Sam—he feeds the army." The slogan stuck and so did the name. Other army property marked U.S. soon became known as Uncle Sam's. Long before Samuel Wilson died in 1854 at the age of 88, he had become a legendary figure. The cemetery in Troy is open daily 8 A.M. to 5 P.M., and markers plainly point the way to Uncle Sam's grave. Troy is located on NY 2, along the east bank of the Hudson.

## Museum of Fire Fighting

The American Museum of Fire Fighting, at Hudson, is dedicated to those intrepid firemen everywhere who give so freely of themselves to protect the lives and property of the American public. Located on the grounds of the Firemen's

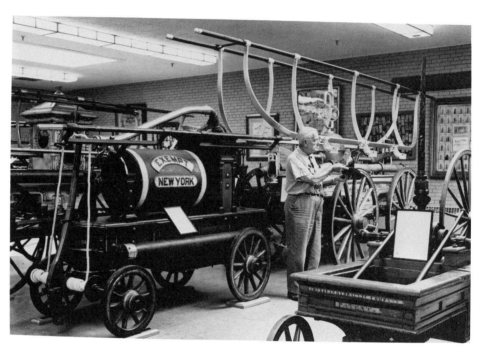

The American Museum of Fire Fighting is open to the public at Hudson, New York. *(Courtesy of New York State Department of Commerce)*

Home, the museum is maintained by the Fireman's Association of New York and is open free to the public 9 A.M. to 5 P.M. daily.

Displayed are thirty-five pieces of fire apparatus dating from 1731 to 1926, as well as several thousand items relating to the fire service, including fire models, fire hats, speaking trumpets, badges and banners. A fine collection of oil paintings, prints and lithographs can be seen in the art gallery. Among the pieces is a Newshame Engine built in London in 1725 and imported in 1731 to Manhattan, where it was used by volunteers for 154 years. Hudson is located on NY 66, just a short distance east of the New York State Thruway.

## Preheater Inner Tube Regatta

Each year in May, the Air Preheater Inner Tube Regatta is held at Wellsville. The competitors race down a swift stretch of the Genessee River in one of the most outlandish convoys of floating vessels ever gathered at one spot. The vessels range from a wide conglomeration of boards, broomsticks, chicken wire and old kitchen doors to some looking like homemade flags, potted plants or floating caskets. Each has to carry two people, and the one thing they must have in common is inner tubes. Their main means of flotation have to be no more than four automobile-size inner tubes.

The river is fast and full of snags and the crafts are difficult to maneuver, all of which make the race more interesting. Prizes are given for the most flamboyant craft and for the best dressed team. Of course, there are prizes for the winners. Check with the Wellsville Chamber of Commerce for a schedule of the event. To get there, take either NY 17 or NY 19 (Wellsville is in western New York).

**Easter Egg Exhibit**

At the Mary Beatrice Cushing Memorial Library in Schoharie each year just before Easter, there is the Easter Egg Exhibit. The exhibit started in 1953 when two of the townswomen—librarian Mildred Vrooman and library trustee Elizabeth Warner—decorated two trees in the yard of the library with eggs. The project was inspired by a book called "The Egg Tree" which described the Easter customs of the Pennsylvania Dutch. The exhibit has now become so popular, it's spread virtually throughout the community.

The exhibit, which goes on display 2 weeks prior to Easter, includes more than 3,500 hand-painted and decorated eggs—goose, turkey, duck, hen, bantam, game, guineahen, peahen and pigeon eggs. More storybook themes are created each year. Some of the most popular are the Egg Brothers Circus, the Holland scene, Snow White and the Seven Dwarfs, Toy Parade, Cinderella, Wedding of the Painted Dolls, Treasure Eggs and Eggshell Pictures. Several individuals supply eggshells, and one local farmer annually donates a thousand eggs. The contents of each egg is blown out after a small opening is made at each end, and they are used to make custards and omelets. Schoharie is located on NY 30, directly west of Albany.

**Soaring at Harris Hill**

Harris Hill, near Elmira, is the center of soaring in America. Factories producing sailplanes are located nearby. On top of Harris Hill is the Soaring Museum of America, as well as the landing strip from which sailplanes, providing weather conditions are right, are towed into the skies over New York to ride the thermals like giant birds. Pilot instruction is offered here as well as rides for the public. In the museum, one can sit in the cockpit of a sailplane and imagine zooming along with the wind currents at 4,000 feet, free as a bird, with only the sound of the wind for companionship. Movies on sailplaning are shown at the museum periodically.

Visitors are welcome at the gliderport on Harris Hill from 9 A.M. until

Harris Hill, near Elmira, New York, is internationally famous as a gliding center. *(Courtesy of New York State Department of Commerce)*

dusk, between the last week in June and the first week of September and on weekends and holidays year-round. At various times during the summer months, national and regional sailplaning meets are held here (for details and schedules contact the Harris Hill Soaring Corporation, Route 1, Elmira, New York 14903). Elmira is located on NY 17 and NY 14.

## Brotherhood Winery

An opportunity to see America's oldest winery, reminiscent of the Old World and of pioneer days, awaits you at the Brotherhood Winery, located in the Hudson River Valley. Open throughout the year, free guided tours take you to historic underground cellars, the largest in the United States, to view huge white-oak casks which line the native stone walls. A free wine-tasting session is a feature of every tour. The tour takes about 2 hours. The winery is nestled in the foothills of the Catskills, near Washingtonville on NY 94, just off the New York State Thruway.

## The Scythe Tree

On an October day in 1861, an apple-cheeked farm boy named James Johnson answered the call from President Abe Lincoln for volunteers, placed his scythe in a nearby sapling and said: "Leave it here—I'll get it when I return." For 3 years, he fought in the Civil War before dying in a prison camp. The scythe remained in place and the tree grew around it. Over the years, the tree towered 100 feet and 5 feet in diameter. In 1918, two more farm boys left this place to fight in World War I and left their scythes in the great tree, too. Both returned, but the blades of their scythes remain in the tree today.

Located some 2½ miles west of Waterloo, the farm is now owned by another family, but visitors are allowed to look at the scythes and the tree. For the tree is an oddity itself, one that rarely grows in this area—they call it a balm of Gilead. Waterloo is located on NY 96, south of the New York State Thruway.

## The Cardiff Giant

On October 16, 1869, workmen discovered a 10½-foot stone giant on a farm outside Cardiff and created a furor that spread across the nation. It came to be known as the Cardiff Giant and will probably pass into history not as a great scientific discovery but as the "Great American Hoax."

Creator of the Cardiff Giant was George Hull who set out to purposely hoax the American public. He hired two sculptors in Chicago to carve the giant out of a piece of Iowa gypsum. After experimentation, he was able to give the giant an aged look by applying sulfuric acid to the surface. Originally he considered burying the giant in Mexico, but decided against it because of the distance and expense. He then chose a farm owned by a relative near Cardiff, New York.

It was 6 months later that men were hired to start digging a well behind the barn where the giant had been buried. The owner of the farm, not aware that it was a hoax, began charging an admission as crowds gathered to see the giant. On some days, as many as 3,000 people came, traveling by buggy, horseback and wagon for many miles. Scientists soon discovered it was a fake, and today the giant lies in the Farmers' Museum at Cooperstown surrounded by farm implements, a church and a country store. As in 1869, people still come to look and utter their disbelief that such a thing could happen. It is probably the oldest tangible example of a great American hoax. Cooperstown is located on NY 80, south of I-90.

For additional information, contact the Travel Bureau, Department of Commerce, 112 State Street, Albany, New York 12207.

# North Carolina

Rubies, a Mule Festival and a Hollerin' Contest

**Ruby Fields**

Millions of rockhounds search the woods and meadows of America every year, and a good percentage of these enthusiasts have been to the Cowee Valley ruby fields. The center for the activity is the town of Franklin. The town calls itself the "Gem Capital of the World," and it may not be far from wrong.

In the area, there are approximately fifteen mines, and the territory is blessed with rubies. The chamber of commerce will supply a list of mines. At many of them, you can pay a small fee and dig for your own rubies. One of them—the Jacobs Ruby Mine—employs men who dig bucketfuls of dirt, hoping to find gems which are later sold to panners. Mine operators rarely try to appraise stones, but they will give an estimate if the find is a really good specimen. One time a woman invested $1 for soil and came up with a $5,000 ruby; and more recently, a man at the Gibson Ruby Mine discovered a 295-carat blue sapphire.

At Spruce Pine is the Museum of North Carolina Minerals, where samples of gems and minerals are displayed. Exhibits feature minerals in their commercial application to include kaolin, which is used to make fiberglass, and Halloysite®, which gives shine to china and industrial porcelain. On display, too, are gem stones in the rough and cut forms, some huge chunks of crystal and garnet and casts of large gold nuggets found in the state.

Until 1849, North Carolina was the main gold-producing state in the United States. Franklin is located on U.S. 23 and U.S. 441 in western North Carolina. Spruce Pine is just off the Blue Ridge Parkway on U.S. 19E and NC 226.

You will also find other worthwhile minerals in North Carolina. For instance, the largest emerald found in North America—a 1,438-carat specimen—was found at Hiddenite, near Statesville. The "Carolina Emerald" now owned by Tiffany and Company in New York was also found at Hiddenite in 1970. When cut to 13.14 carats, the stone was valued at $100,000 and became the largest and finest cut emerald on this continent. Emeralds may be found at several mine sites, including the Emerald Valley Mines at Hiddenite and Big Crabtree Mine at Spruce Pine. Hiddenite is on NC 90, just north of I-40 in the western part of the state.

**Gaddy's Geese**

In central North Carolina is one of the nation's most unique wayside inns for wild Canada geese. Since 1934, the rambling Gaddy farm near Ansonville has provided a winter home for thousands of wild Canada and snow geese. That was when Lockhart Gaddy hung up his gun, quit shooting geese and, with his wife Hazel, began converting his farm into a wildlife refuge.

**149**

The late Mrs. Hazel Gaddy feeding one of the more than 20,000 wild Canada geese that winter at Gaddy's Wild Goose Refuge, Ansonville, North Carolina. *(Courtesy of Department of Conservation and Development)*

Today thousands of tourists come to watch the geese closeup and to feed them grains of golden corn from their hands. Visitors were once welcome free of charge, but with several thousands of geese dropping in to spend the winter, the Gaddys were often hard put to provide enough feed for them, so a small gate fee was instituted to help defray food costs.

The farm pond has been enlarged twice to provide enough water surface for the geese; it now covers 15 acres and still is too small. The first year the honkers began stopping here was 1934, and that year only nine stayed the winter. Each year, however, as the Gaddys and the geese became closer friends, more and more came until there were thousands. They stay from October until April; then they head for their northern nesting grounds, with only a few stragglers remaining behind. Come October, everyone in the Ansonville area is on the lookout for the geese returning to Gaddy's Boarding House. Since the deaths of Mr. and Mrs. Gaddy, a great-nephew, Thomas Pond, has taken over as the refuge manager. Ansonville is located on U.S. 52.

**Wagon Train** The first wagon train to cross the mountains in this century was initiated by North Carolina and Tennessee in 1957 to call attention to the need for a road from Tellico Plains, Tennessee to Murphy, North Carolina. With the road assured, the wagon train has continued as an annual event, and it has become one of its most popular tourist attractions. Sponsors of the wagon train plan to continue it as a feature of the Fourth of July holiday season.

Another adventure called Daniel Boone Wagon Train was begun in 1963 by the citizens of Watauga and Wilkes counties in the Blue Ridge Mountain country north of Asheville to commemorate the 200th anniversary of Boone's crossing the Blue Ridge. This wagon train has also become an annual event between North Wilkesboro and Boone, with overnight encampments enroute. Participants in both the wagon train events dress in pioneer costumes, but visitors who join the trip wear anything suitable for the rugged trail. Wilkesboro is located on U.S. 421 in northwestern North Carolina.

**Highland Games**

In the shadow of Grandfather Mountain in the Blue Ridge Mountains, the most outstanding Scottish Highland games in the nation are held annually. MacRae Meadows on the slope of the mountain resound with the strains of marching bagpipes. Scottish bands and pipers from across the country gather at this spot near Linville in early July to spend a few days renewing the Scottish spirit. Events include dancing (the Highland Fling, Sword Dance and Sean Truibhas); drumming, tossing the caber, tug of war, highland wrestling, standing broad jump, running high jump, pole vault, crosscountry run, tossing the sheaf and archery. Kilts and bonnets are favored attire. Linville is on U.S. 221 in the northwestern part of the state.

**Hollerin' Contest**

At Spivey's Corner, the rural folks were accustomed to raising their voices as a way of communication long before Alexander Graham Bell invented the telephone. They hollered then and they still holler today. It's the best way, they felt, to let your neighbor, who lives across the valley, know that everything is all right at the end of day. Every man had his own pitch, tone and vocal variations, and each had a special meaning.

The annual National Hollerin' Contest is held at Spivey's Corner, North Carolina.

This means of communication is being fostered and preserved in that section of North Carolina to this day with the National Hollerin' Contest. Scheduled in June, the art of hollerin', you'll see, has nothing to do with hog calling, yelling, shouting, screaming or screeching. It's just plain hollerin'. Of course, the contest draws entries from outside the Spivey's Corner vicinity... some of them even come from foreign countries. Various activities are held in conjunction with the Hollerin' Contest, such as the Prettiest "Possum Pickin" Contest, a square dance, a "Miss Spivey's Corner" beauty contest and an old-time wagon train and country barbecue—and there's a rabbit race. For the ladies, there's a "callin'" event; and for the children, a hollerin' event. Spivey's Corner is located on U.S. 421 east from I-95 near Dunn.

## Flying Saucers or Brown Mountain Lights

Were you aware there's a place in North Carolina where you can see UFOs on almost any clear night? Their behavior pattern varies from sudden, instantaneous flights to slowly ascending, wandering flights. What they really are, no one knows, but they are there and they can be seen. The location is the lower end of the Blue Ridge Mountain chain at a place called Brown Mountain, a few miles off NC 181 between Morganton and Lenoir. The National Forest Service has even put up a sign, giving some background information on the Brown Mountain lights. In 1919, the U.S. Weather Bureau physicists, after studying the matter, wrote an article based on a report by Dr. Herbert Lyman, a noted scientist. The article, subsequently published in *National Geographic Magazine,* suggests the Brown Mountain Lights are akin to the Andes Lights, which are caused by flashes of electrical discharges, similar to lightning, passing from clouds to the Brown Mountain Peak. But the article doesn't seem to be correct, for the Brown Mountain lights are multicolored and in no way resemble lightning. The U.S. Geological Survey and other agencies have done studies from time to time, but no one has come up with a good explanation for these mysterious lights. Thus, many people are calling them UFOs. However, it remains to be seen whether or not they're really from outer space.

## Mule Festival

The lowly mule is king at Benson... at least for 3 days in September during the community's annual Mule Day celebration. A community park called Singing Grove is the site of the Mule Day program, and there is keen competition for the title of grand champion mule. The animals compete in weight-pulling contests and a scoop race in which cowboys in heavily reinforced trousers are towed along on large shovels by their mules. As they hang on desperately, the shovels sometimes slip away and they scoop up the dust with the seats of their pants. The mules usually don't think much of being crowned king. In recent times, one mule rubbed off its gold paper crown against a wall and showed obvious irritation with the fancy blanket that went with the award. After the judging and declaration of a grand champion, there's a Mule Procession for the public. Benson lies just off I-95, northeast of Fayetteville.

## Folkcrafts School

Deep in the valley of the Great Smoky Mountains is a colony of mountain craftsmen who invite you to come and camp with them and learn the ancient folk arts of the Southern Highlands. At the John C. Campbell Folk School, Brasstown, North Carolina, you can camp in the school's own campground while taking one or two weeks of classes. The school, which encourages the pursuit of old-time arts and crafts and perpetuates the traditions of this rugged mountain country, offers courses in weaving, woodcarving, woodworking, enameling, lapidary, creative crafts and sketching, along with folk dancing and music. Brasstown is located near the North Carolina–Georgia border on U.S. 64.

**The Clock Place**

In an old schoolhouse at the edge of Leasburg is a most remarkable collection of clocks. The schoolhouse contains hundreds of old clocks of all ages and descriptions collected by Carl Fisher and Crother Doolin. Along with a thousand or two other antiques they're all for sale. Known as The Place, you can get there by taking U.S. 158.

**Wilmington's Christmas Tree**

If you're in the Wilmington area at Christmastime, you won't want to miss the coastal city's Christmas tree. It's acclaimed as the world's largest living Christmas tree—a 90-foot water oak decorated with thousands of colored lights which are turned on nightly between mid-December and New Year's Day. Wilmington is located on U.S. 17.

For additional information, contact the Division of Travel and Promotion, Department of Natural and Economic Resources, Box 27687, Raleigh, North Carolina 27611.

# North Dakota

## A Mysterious Lake, a Giant Buffalo and a Burning Coal Mine

**Mysterious Devils Lake**

Devils Lake was named "Bad Spirit Lake" by the Indians because of its restless attitude, its turbulence during storms and its undrinkable water. For years, visitors to the town of Devils Lake complained of the city's drinking water, which was obtained from the lake. Since then, new facilities have improved the situation, but the lake retains its aura of mystery. Among the more than 1,000 Sioux Indians living on Fort Totten Reservation, bordering the lake on the south, there are still tales and legends of the lake.

One tells of an Indian brave who stuck his knife into a log while sitting on the shore. The log slid into the lake and turned into a sea monster which, it's said, still lives at the bottom of the lake and occasionally may be seen, usually during severe storms crashing across the waters. During certain weather conditions, the lake is shrouded in a vapor which tends to magnify the waterfowl swimming in the water, making them appear several times their size. There are also stories told about phantom ships seen upon the waters during stormy nights. And some of the natives actually claim the monster of Devils Lake is no different from the Loch Ness monster of Scotland. Thus far, no research studies have been made. Devils Lake is located on ND 57 and U.S. 2 in the northeastern section of the state.

**World's Largest Buffalo**

You wouldn't want to pass through North Dakota without seeing the world's largest buffalo. The giant concrete statue, three stories tall, is located on I-94 and U.S. 281, near Jamestown. Also on the grounds are a pioneer schoolhouse, drugstore, print shop, church, railway depot and caboose, log headquarters building and blockhouse gate.

The world's largest (concrete) buffalo near Jamestown, North Dakota. *(Courtesy of North Dakota Travel Division)*

**Burning Coal Mine**

Near Amidon is a coal vein approximately 30 feet below the earth's surface that's been burning since before white men came to this country. Efforts once were made to extinguish the slow burn, but they produced no results. A campground and beautiful columnar-shaped junipers are close-by, but the earth is hot and sometimes emits wisps of smoke from cracks in the soil. The coal vein is located 15 miles northwest of Amidon, which is located near the Little Missouri National Grasslands.

**Sauerkraut and Wieners**

Each October in Wishek, the town folks treat the country folks to a Sauerkraut and Wiener Day. Since 1925, the event has been staged annually, an old German custom designed to repay the country folks for their business interest during the year. The sauerkraut and wiener lunch is held in the Wishek auditorium, and the high school band plays during the meal. Free entertainment is provided in the afternoon and evening. Wishek is located on ND 13 and ND 3 in the southern part of the state.

Across Lake Sakakawea is the Four Bears Bridge, named after a Mandan Indian chief. However, the Mandans had other chiefs they thought should be honored, as did the Hidatsa and Arikara tribes. A squabble ensued over many months, and finally other names were added to appease all the different parties in the squabble. As a result, the bridge has nineteen names, all of which are listed on the span. The bridge is located on ND 23, near New Town.

**Bridge of Nineteen Names**

This 1,100-acre ranch is a study in social behavior, a nonsectarian home for neglected boys. The boys live on the ranch and help to operate it; you can see them riding herd on cattle, building fences and tending crops. They attend public school and hold a Champions Ride Rodeo, open to the public each August. The ranch is located just ½ mile north of I-94, west of Sentinel Butte.

**Father Cassady's Home on the Range for Boys**

One of America's most unusual ethnic groups are the Hutterites of North Dakota. In some ways, they have been compared to the Amish people, and yet they are quite different. Their lands are manicured, but they often retain their old ways of farming and ranching and maintain their own schools. The Hutterite country makes excellent territory for shunpiking; even though these people don't cater to tourists, you may find some interesting conversationalists. School children and other groups are welcome by prior arrangement. Hutterite colonies are located near Berlin (just off ND 13) and Fullerton (east of U.S. 281) in the southeastern section of the state; and at Fordville (just east of ND 32) in the northeastern part of North Dakota.

**Hutterite Country**

For additional information, contact the Travel Division, State Highway Department, Capitol Grounds, Bismarck, North Dakota 58501.

# Ohio

An Antique Airline, a Buzzards Festival and a
Bottomless Waterhole

Serving the islands of Lake Erie out of Port Clinton is what is claimed to be the airline with the world's shortest flights. Named Island Airlines, the firm flies its passengers and cargo to and from a half dozen islands via antique Ford trimotor planes, a corrugated metal lumbering craft that appears unable to become airborne. Yet thousands of people come to Port Clinton annually just to see them or to fly to the islands aboard one.

The Fords, which have been flying here since 1935, provide a year-round

**Ford Trimotors**

A Ford trimotor airplane used by Island Airlines in Port Clinton, Ohio.

life line to the island residents. School children commute on the planes daily. All necessities—mail, freight, supplies of every description—as well as passengers, are transported to the islands by the trimotors. Conducted tours originating from many foreign countries have included a flight on the "tin goose." On some of the islands, accommodations, as well as rental cars, bicycles and golf carts, have been provided by the airline for tourists. Aluminum fishing boats are also available. Port Clinton is a small town along Lake Erie's southern shore and can be reached by taking OH 2, east of Toledo.

## The Buzzards of Hinckley Ridge

Each year, it's said that precisely on March 15 the buzzards return to Whip's Ledges on Hinckley Ridge. They've been doing it for a hundred or more years. Now when the buzzards come, so do the people. Gathering from a dozen states, thousands drive past Hinckley Ridge to see the buzzards and to celebrate the coming of spring. The Cleveland Metropolitan Park District sets up a tent and nature center for the occasion and keeps several naturalists on hand to answer questions. Special observation points are provided where visitors may watch the buzzards spiraling over the ledges.

In the small hamlet of Hinckley, a pancake breakfast is served all day on Sunday at the elementery school cafeteria. After breakfast, visitors may tour the halls to see an art exhibit staged by the school children; the theme of the exhibit is Hinckley's buzzards. It's safe to say that never before or since has the buzzard been given so much acclaim, but Hinckley is proud of them. To get to Hinckley, take OH 94 or OH 303 to the intersection where they cross. You'll see a traffic light and, on Buzzard Week, a large sign prepared by cartoonist Al Capp welcoming you to one of America's rarest events.

Buzzards gather on Whip's Ledges on Hinckley Ridge, Ohio.

**Blue Hole**

In Castalia is a natural phenomenon known as the Blue Hole. One can look down into the blue waters to a depth of 50 to 60 feet and from there it's all darkness. Attempts by scientists to measure the depth of the hole have failed, for it goes on and on, deeper and deeper. The temperature of this remarkable spring is 48 degrees year-round. The brilliant blue water is dead, devoid of air, and fish cannot live in it until it is aerated by passing over small waterfalls and waterwheels specifically built for that purpose. After the water is aerated, it flows through streams in which rainbow, brook and brown trout can be seen and fed by spectators. Open from late May to early November, there is a small admission charge. The Blue Hole is located at 502 N. Washington Street in Castalia on OH 269.

**Cranberry Island**

Another natural phenomenon in Ohio is Cranberry Island in the northern portion of Buckeye Lake. This bog is a relic of the Ice Age, left behind more than 17,000 years ago when Ohio's last glacier receded. Cranberry Island is the only sphagnum bog known which is floating in a lake, surrounded by water. Almost all others grow out into the water from the shore. Along with the little creeping vines of cranberry, there are also rare and unusual northern plants such as poison sumac, elder bush, pitcher plants and sundew. Exploration should be undertaken with extreme care, however, and never alone. One can easily sink into the marsh above the ankles and be unable to free himself. Buckeye Lake is located east of Columbus, just off I-70.

**Blue Heron Welcoming Committee**    In the town of Wapakoneta each spring, the Blue Heron Welcoming Committee gathers (usually the last weekend in March) to visit a nearby private marsh where a large colony of blue herons have nested for more than half a century. The herons traditionally return to the marsh from their wintering grounds by mid-March; and the welcoming committee, made up of some of the town's business and civic leaders, treks to the woods to spend the day watching the herons. Since the woods is alongside Freyburg County Road, other visitors have also come to park along the road and watch the herons as they build their nests. Wapakoneta, the home town of Neil Armstrong, is located some 20 miles south of Lima on I-75 and Freyburg is located some 3 miles south of Wapakoneta on old U.S. 25.

**TOSRV**    Sponsored by the greater Columbus area YMCAs, the Tour of the Scioto River Valley (TOSRV) is one of the nation's most popular bicycle rides. Held traditionally on Mother's Day weekend, the 210-mile ride from Columbus, the Ohio state capital, to Portsmouth on the Ohio River and return attracts bicycle riders from nearly 50 states and some foreign countries. Hundreds of riders of all ages participate in the event. They travel over all types of terrain, flatland and steep hills, along the scenic Scioto River. Overnight lodging is provided in Portsmouth, and the return trip is made on the second day.

**Delta Queen**    An Ohio floating landmark is an old paddlewheel steamboat, the *Delta Queen*. Its home port is Cincinnati. Sailing on river cruises to New Orleans, Saint Louis, Saint Paul and points in between, the *Delta Queen* is the only overnight steamboat operating on the inland waterways of America today. It carries passengers from all parts of the nation and the world, giving them a taste of river life not unlike that described a century ago by Mark Twain. Entertainment is provided nightly, along with some of the finest gourmet cooking to be found in the United States. Cincinnati is located on the Ohio River and I-71, I-74 and I-75.

**National Trap Shoots**    At the Dayton suburb of Vandalia, the National Amateur Trap Shooting Competition is held annually. Incorporated in 1923 to promote and govern the sport of trapshooting in the United States and Canada, the Amateur Trapshooting Association, with headquarters at Vandalia, is the largest organization of clay-target, shotgun shooters in the world. Using a modern data processing system, the ATA records all scores shot by its more than 30,000 members at more than 600 gun clubs holding registered shoots. Since 1924, the national shoot has been held at Vandalia, where more than 3,000 shooters compete on the mile long, 50-trap firing line. Many of the shooters camp on the grounds. Vandalia is located 7 miles north of Dayton on I-75.

**Bed Races**    Each spring at Ohio State University in Columbus is held a most unique competition—bed racing. Students at the university modify old beds by fastening them to high wheels. They race them around the football field, two beds competing at a time. Men students push the beds while the girls ride in them. All participants wear outlandish costumes. Most bed entries are jointly sponsored by various fraternities and sororities while some dormitories enter representatives in the competition. Admission is free to the event, which is part of the traditional May Week celebration.

## Warther's Woodcarving Museum

Mooney Warther worked most of his life carving the history of steam-powered vehicles. His collected works can be seen at his personal museum at Dover, and they include the miniature replicas of the Lincoln funeral train and the DeWitt Clinton, the first locomotive of the New York Central Railroad. Also on display in the museum are more than 4,000 Indian arrowheads Warther personally collected while roaming over the northeastern Ohio hills. A total of 50 hand-carved and operating miniature steam locomotives may be seen at the museum, along with many other steam machines and conveyances. The museum is on the outskirts of Dover which is located on OH 800 near I-77.

## Ohio's Japanese Teahouse

Once you enter the gate leading to the Japanese Teahouse, a restaurant in the college town of Westerville, you enter an Oriental world. Large, brightly colored lanterns sway amid ancient ornaments, complementing the mood of the plum-colored wooden building. They call it the Kyoto Teahouse, an authentic Japanese structure patterned by its owners after similar buildings in Japan. Inside, one walks barefoot across the tatami, a floor covering of reed matting, sits cross-legged at a lacquered table and quietly contemplates the surroundings. The building is filled with objects of Oriental art. There are no clocks to measure the passing of time.

There are other Japanese restaurants in America, but there are none like this one. The Japanese consider a house like a picture, with the garden as the mat around the picture and the fence as the frame. That's the way it is at the Kyoto Teahouse. Guests are greeted by a barefooted hostess wearing a kimono. The visitor then passes through the sliding shoji panels of kiri wood and paper. There's a cloisonne vase 5-feet high, a 32-inch Imari plate weighing 50 pounds and a teakwood tea cabinet which holds the china. Westerville is located 13 miles from Columbus on OH 3.

## Sassafras Tea

Hermie Kerner has one of the most unusual businesses in the world—he whips up a strange concoction known, but little sampled, throughout the nation... sassafras tea. In an immaculately refurbished chicken house, just north of Columbus Grove, Hermie has a sassafras factory. He uses some 12 tons of sassafras root bark annually in making instant tea concentrate and in packaging prepared bark. From earliest times in America, sassafras was held in high esteem. Early explorers cherished it as a spring tonic. Ponce de Leon savored it; and when samples were brought to Europe, a sassafras craze was spawned. The demand for Hermie's product (Pappy's Tonic Sassafras Tea) has doubled each year since 1969. If you'd care to drop by his plant and watch him and his small staff work, you'd be more than welcome. For Hermie figures you'll want to take home some sassafras tea or maybe some bark to make your own. Known locally as H&K Products, anyone in Columbus Grove can direct you to his plant. Columbus Grove is located on OH 65, a few miles north of Lima.

## Pumpkin Show

Ohio is known as the festival state, for it has more annually than any other state in the nation. The Circleville Pumpkin Show, the last festival of the year, could easily be labeled the most genuine. For its theme runs true—practically everything is pumpkin. There are servings of pumpkin pie, pumpkin cake, pumpkin ice cream, pumpkin fudge and pumpkin fritters. The world's largest pumpkin pie, which measures several feet across, is annually baked and on display at a local bakery. Pyramids of great pumpkins fill the streets of Circleville; and on the sidelines are related activities such as pumpkin carving, pumpkin weight lifting (some pumpkins weigh more than a hundred pounds) and pumpkin pie eating contests. The pumpkins are also sold; you'll see visitors carting them away in baby carriages, on wheelbarrows and atop their heads. The festival goes on for 4 days, making one wonder if the world has not indeed turned into a pumpkin. The only thing missing is Cinderella and her pumpkin carriage. Circleville is located on U.S. 23, south of Columbus.

Pumpkin pyramids are built in the streets at Circleville Pumpkin Show, Circleville, Ohio.

**Chicken Flying Meet**   On Bob Evans' Farm in southeastern Ohio, the International Chicken Flying Meet is held each year, usually in July. Chickens are weighed in and accordingly placed in four classes—lightweight, medium weight, heavyweight and extra heavy. The chicken entries are placed on a platform about 10 feet tall and their owners then coax them to fly to them. The chicken flying the longest distance is proclaimed the winner. The Chicken Flying Meet is held as a part of Bob Evans' Farm Days, a free farm festival with square-dancing, old-time farm demonstrations in molasses making, candlestick making, lard rendering, cider squeezing, sheepherding and shearing. The farm also features a small band of wild mustangs. Bob Evans' Farm is located on U.S. 35, near Rio Grande.

The International Chicken Flying Meet is launched by the call of the trumpets on Bob Evans' Farm, near Rio Grande, Ohio.

## Moonshine Festival

During Prohibition, the community of New Straitsville was known for its moonshining activities. Now New Straitsville is noted for its annual Moonshine Festival during which the activities of the Prohibition era are reenacted, except there's no corn squeezin's. Activities at the festival include mock raids by the police force and the Perry County sheriff's officers, parades and a Moonshine Queen beauty contest. And there's a Little Miss Moonshine contest, too, for the little girls. Volunteer firemen hold a greased pig and greased pole contest; there is also a horseshoe tournament, a costume contest, a pie eating contest, a sack race, a wheelbarrow race and a tug of war. Other features of the festival include a display of a confiscated moonshine still and the opening of Robinson's Cave where secret meetings took place leading to the formation of the United Mine Workers' union. New Straitsville is located on OH 93, east of Logan.

## Other Points of Interest

Rena's Handcraft Miniature Rooms on display, at New Philadelphia, includes twenty-four breathtaking one-inch to one-foot scale rooms, made entirely by Rena Poteet. The rooms are completely furnished with furniture made to scale. It's open daily 10 A.M. to 7 P.M. June to September, for a small admission charge. New Philadelphia is located on I-77.

Back in 1838, Nathaniel Wilson III deeded a plot of ground to President James Monroe and "all United States presidents to follow" as a private burial place. Around it, he erected a strong stone fence; and although it was located in

A still on display at the Moonshine Festival, New Straitsville, Ohio.

the midst of a cornfield in rural Ohio, the place became known as the Presidential Cemetery. However, to this day, no president has been interred here. The cemetery is located 2 miles west of Lancaster on Stonewall Cemetery Road, 2/5 of a mile from U.S. 22.

For additional information, contact the Travel and Tourist Division, Ohio Department of Development, P.O. Box 1001, Columbus, Ohio 43216.

# Oklahoma

America's Smallest National Park, the World
Cow Chip Throwing Contest and a Cowboy Hall of Fame

**Nation's Mini Park**   In south central Oklahoma is the nation's smallest national park—Platt. In only 912 acres, the mini-park encompasses a wide variety of attractions such as mineral springs, waterfalls, meandering streams, well-planned campgrounds, a nature museum, trails for hiking and biking, scenic vistas and a buffalo herd. Platt is a mixing ground; for here are deer indicative of the west and whitetails indigenous to the east.

Some claim Platt is the most intensively used park, per square inch, of any national park in the country. Thousands come here just because they're intrigued by the novelty of visiting the nation's smallest national park. A multitude of others come here simply to enjoy themselves.

All roads leading to Platt bisect grasslands and rolling plains, and then suddenly they lead to this little oasis of heavy foliage and woods. Some people come to drink the mineral water from the ever-flowing springs, probably the reason Platt was established as a national park in the first place. Whatever your reason, if you're traveling through Oklahoma, it's worth a visit. The park is located at the town of Sulphur, just east of I-35 and south of Oklahoma City.

## Cowboy Hall of Fame

On Persimmon Hill on the Old Chisolm Trail stands the National Cowboy Hall of Fame. From the high vantage point, one can see what the great American West was like. Today, the great American West comprises seventeen states beyond the Missouri River; and those seventeen states are represented in the National Cowboy Hall of Fame and Western Heritage Center. Included are the paintings, sketches and statues by cowboy artists Charles W. Russell and Frederic Remington, as well as Joe Beeler and Willard Stone, a native of the Sooner State and a Cherokee Indian. You can see a western sod house and displays of old cattle trail camps, including chuckwagons and a wax model of the trail cook. There's a collection of saddles, spurs and other memorabilia and some of the most dramatic western sculpture to be found anywhere.

The exhibits are timeless; they represent the West from the earliest days of the pioneers to the present. Displayed with equal prominence are the rifle of Charley Russell on which he etched intricate drawings of animals and the saddle in which Gary Cooper rode to fame in western movies. Occasionally during summer weekends, Indian dances are performed at various times of the day in the large auditorium.

The Cowboy Hall of Fame project was started in 1952 by a Kansas City executive who stopped at Claremore, Oklahoma, to see the Will Rogers Memorial. Chester A. Reynolds was so impressed by the tribute to Rogers that he decided other great westerners ought to be honored. After visiting the governors of all seventeen western states—Arizona, California, Colorado, Idaho, Kansas, Montana, Nebraska, New Mexico, Nevada, North Dakota, South Dakota, Oklahoma, Texas, Oregon, Utah, Washington and Wyoming—he was able to raise enough money to make his dream come true. To understand the West and to realize what it was really like, visit the Cowboy Museum and Hall of Fame.

## World Cow Chip Throwing Contest

Perhaps you've heard that old expression "slinging the bull"; in Oklahoma, it's more than talk. They really do sling the bull at a little community named Beaver, site of the World Cow Chip Throwing Contest. The contest is held each April and is open to men, women and children. Throwing cow chips climaxes the week-long Cimarron Territory celebration.

Cow and buffalo chips played an important role in the settlement of what once was the rugged panhandle territory of Oklahoma. In a land without trees, fuel was scarce; and when the north winds swept down out of Canada, to have life was to have fuel. Many a youngster's chore was to gather up all the buffalo and cow chips (dried manure) he could find to be burned as fuel. The chips burned slowly, yet with intense heat and left little ash. Had it not been for cow and buffalo chips, the Cimarron Territory may not have been settled for another 50 years.

The original cow chip throwers learned their skills out of necessity. A strong arm and careful aim allowed them to plunk the chip into an accompanying wagon rolling over the prairie, thus saving a lot of footsteps. When the first World Championship Cow Chip Throwing Contest was staged in Beaver, it became immediately popular. Beaver is located on U.S. 270.

The World Champion Cow Chip Throwing Contest at Beaver, Oklahoma. *(Courtesy of Oklahoma Tourism and Recreation Department)*

## World Championship Cornstalk Shoot

Each year during the Cherokee National Holiday, a most unusual athletic competition is held—the World Championship Cornstalk Shoot. A revival of one of the historic competitions of the Cherokee Nation, the cornstalk shoot attracts much attention. Here's the way it's done. Two targets of thoroughly dried cornstalks are placed approximately 100 to 110 yards apart. The number of cornstalks penetrated by the bowmen's arrows determines the score.

The original idea behind the sports activity was to distinguish the more experienced and more powerful bowmen, since an arrow coming directly at the target would penetrate more cornstalks than one sent into a high trajectory which would give only the impact of a fall arrow rather than the impact of an arrow driven by the force and strength of the bowman.

In the old days, this was a frequent activity among the Cherokee; but for many years it was lost and was only recently revived as part of the Cherokee National Holiday. Shooters compete in two divisions—one for modern bows and one strictly for native bows and arrows. Thirty to forty bowmen shoot at the targets at the same time. Since each archer knows his own arrows, it is not difficult to determine the winning scores. The cornstalk shoot and Cherokee

National Holiday celebration are traditionally held in September at the town of Tahlequah, located on U.S. 62, east of Tulsa.

## Rattlesnake Roundup

One of the largest rattlesnake roundups in the nation occurs annually at Eastertime in the rock hills of Salt Creek Canyon near Okeene. The roundup draws hunters from across the United States and Canada. The rattlers den in this part of the canyon and emerge sluggish from hibernation at this time of year.

The snakes are brought live to the snake corral where the venom is milked. The finest specimens are auctioned to zoos. Two large canneries compete for the snake meat, increasingly popular as steaks and tidbits used at cocktail parties. Shoe, belt and bag manufacturers always want more skins than can be supplied. The heads are in demand to be mounted and the rattles are variously used. Prizes are plentiful. A large marked snake is released on the morning of the hunt, and the catcher is awarded $100. There are also prizes for the longest and the heaviest snakes and the runner-up in each class. Rattlesnakes sold on the open market often bring in excess of 50 cents per pound. Okeene is located on OK 51 and OK 8, northwest of Oklahoma City.

The annual Rattlesnake Roundup at Okeene, Oklahoma. *(Courtesy of Oklahoma Tourism and Recreation Department)*

## Watermelon Seed Spitting Contest

In Pauls Valley, the great Watermelon Seed Spitting Contest is held each summer, usually in July. One year, the champion spat a seed some 48 feet.

One story has it the reason spitters can fire so far is because of the special hybrid watermelon produced in Pauls Valley. It seems each watermelon contains 6 ounces of rich red pulp and averages 25 pounds of seed...usually five

The annual Watermelon Seed Spitting Contest in Pauls Valley, Oklahoma.

seeds at 5 pounds each. And, according to the story, they really carry against a strong headwind. Pauls Valley is located just off I-35, south of Oklahoma City.

For additional information, contact the Oklahoma Tourism and Information Division, 500 Will Rogers Building, Oklahoma City, Oklahoma 73105.

# Oregon

## A House of Mystery, Sea Lion Caves and a Rooster Crowing Contest

**Sea Lion Caves**  Along Oregon's rocky coast are caves inhabited by sea lions. The present owners of one cave claim it to be the world's largest sea cave, and apparently it's the only mainland rookery of the Steller sea lion. Since the construction of a gravel highway above the caves in 1932, the general public can view this natural wonder. Originally, the cave could be reached only by descending an arduous set of steps, making the climb impossible for some. But now, access to the cave is by elevator built through the solid rock cliff. It takes riders down into the cave as well as to the outside observation deck.

The giant animals are constantly moving about on the rocks, diving into the ocean and leaping out again. During the spring, gray whales can be spotted offshore, surfacing periodically to breathe and spurt mighty exhalations of air and moisture into the sky. The rocky cliffs are always thickly populated with gulls and cormorants during the nesting season. Inside the cave, you may see the pigeon guillemot which nests there. The entire population of the Steller sea lion is estimated in excess of 275,000, most of which live in Alaskan coastal waters. But the most convenient place to see them is at Oregon's Sea Lion Caves. The elevator entrance can be reached by U.S. 101, just north of the Siuslaw River.

## Portland's People Park

A *New York Times* critic once wrote: "The Portland People Park may be one of the most important urban spaces since the Renaissance." Situated in the heart of downtown Portland in front of South Auditorium, Portland's People Park takes up an entire city block. It's surrounded by concrete waterfalls, 18-feet high by 80-feet wide, over which cascades 13,000 gallons of sparkling clear water per minute. The design is irregular and at the base is a large pond dotted with concrete islands. In areas not covered with water there are pathways, stairs, alcoves and even a place where you can stroll behind the waterfall. Since its opening in 1969, thousands of townspeople and visitors have come to look; invariably a large percentage of them end up wading in the water.

Designed by famed landscape architect Lawrence Halprin of San Francisco, the park has been described as a sculpture, a fountain, a waterfall, a plaza and a park. The sound of waterfalls in a busy downtown section of the city has a charming effect upon passersby; and at night, when the falls are illuminated, the park is particularly beautiful.

## Oregon Vortex

Walk into the area surrounding the House of Mystery and you find, provided you stand relaxed, that you're leaning. It's perfectly natural to do so here, for you are standing on the Oregon Vortex, a spherical field of force half above the ground and half below. In this circle, even the trees are drawn toward magnetic north. The Indians knew this area long before the House of Mystery was built here; and to them, it was forbidden ground, a place to be shunned. It was not until the present century that scientific studies were made to analyze the area and only in 1943 was a solution found. It's a strange feeling to visit here, but great fun.

Nearby is the Old Oregon Historical Museum on Sardine Creek Road with a wide collection of Indian artifacts, antique guns and early mining equipment. The House of Mystery and the Oregon Vortex are located near Gold Hill some 4 miles off I-5.

## Rogue River Mail Boats

At Gold Beach you can experience one of America's most unusual adventures—a ride aboard the mail boat, up the scenic Rogue River. The Rogue, one of the designated wild rivers of America, offers a lot of whitewater rapids. The boat goes 32 miles upstream to the little community of Agness, climbing 257 feet through a series of rapids. The hydro-jet boats, especially designed for the river, seat 45 people per boat. On the banks and cliffs along the way, bear, deer, blue heron and wild creatures are often seen. The 6½-hour trip, which includes a 2-hour stopover, allows time for stops to photograph along the route. Gold Beach is located on U.S. 101, just north of the California border.

**Rooster Crowing Contest**

Traditionally on the last Saturday in June at Rogue River, one of the noisiest championship events is held—the Rogue River Rooster Crowing Contest. Sponsored by the Rogue River Jaycees, the event is one of the most unusual occasions in the entire West. By mid-afternoon, the roosters have been assembled, each in his own private cage and each with his own private judge. The contest gets underway as the flag drops to signal to the judges to start counting the sometimes frequent, sometimes seldom utterances of the contestants. For 30 minutes, the crows of each rooster are recorded by his private judge. Scores are then tallied and awards made. First prize is $150. Cash prizes are also awarded for the most unique cage entry in the adult division, the most unique cage entry in the youngsters' division and the owner who traveled the greatest distance with his rooster. Other events include an old-fashioned pit beef barbecue, antique car judging, an art exhibit and a parade. Rogue River is located on I-5.

**Fleet of Flowers**

This event dates back to October 1936, when two Depoe Bay fishermen tried unsuccessfully to save a fisherman and two fourteen-year-old boys from a high sea and a black fog that took them by surprise. Their bodies were buried at sea

Residents carry floral pieces to vessels during Fleet of Flowers ceremony in Depoe Bay, Oregon.

and they were posthumously awarded the Carnegie Award for bravery; the state of Oregon erected a monument facing the harbor in their memory. Greater than that monument is the living memorial reenacted each Memorial Day at Depoe Bay. It is known the world over as the Fleet of Flowers.

In the spring, brigades of volunteers trek into the Coast Range foothills and neighboring areas to gather loads of evergreens, huckleberry fronds, ferns and flowers. Others spend many tireless hours making wreaths and sprays. Among the special floral pieces made up annually are replicas of the U.S. Navy submarines *Thresher* and *Scorpion,* both of which disappeared at sea in recent years. Friends and relatives of those who have perished in storms, shipwrecks, coastal accidents or as the result of enemy action on the high seas are invited to attend.

Thousands gather on the bridge and along the shores of the harbor to watch as clergymen bless the fleet and, in column formation, more than 50 flower-laden vessels thread their way through the twisting, rocky-gorge channel leading to the Pacific. Seaborne, they churn westward over the swells and circle a Coast Guard cutter hovering a mile offshore. Then, as National Guard jet fighter aircraft from Portland fly in formation overhead, those aboard the vessels—many of them loved ones of those who lie beneath the waves—cast their floral offerings onto the sea in silent tribute. The ceremony will unquestionably make a lasting impression on those who see it. Depoe Bay is located on U.S. 101, just a few miles north of Newport.

### Children's Festival

The events of this 3-day festival held in Peter Britt Gardens in Jacksonville are designed for little children. The festival includes demonstrations of potters, handweavers, spinners, woodcarvers, farriers and dancers; there are also storytellers, animals to pet, chess and medieval games, puppeteers and performers. The first festival was planned around a story-telling theme. On-stage performances include plays and dramas written and presented by children enrolled in local schools. Youngsters learn to dip candles, hammer nails, paint pictures and work with clay. Jacksonville is located on OR 238, just west of I-5.

### Lava Butte

Oregon is not generally known for its volcanic activity, but there has been some over the centuries and the remains are there for all to see. Among them is Lava Butte, a cinder cone which rises some 500 feet above the adjacent forest-covered countryside. Lava Butte came into existence centuries ago on a fissure which can be traced to the south. From the Lava Butte viewpoint, you can see much of the spectacular volcanism of this area. Other attractions of the area include the Lava Caves State Park, 3 miles to the south, and the strange lava cast forests of the Paulina foothills. Lava Butte is located in the Deschutes National Forest on Road 1926, just off U.S. 97 near Bend.

### Wild Horse Rodeo

At Tygh Valley, the Indian wild horse rodeo is held annually. The wild horses are from the Warm Springs Indian Reservation. All contestants must be full-blooded Indians; they come from all parts of the United States and Canada. Among the featured attractions is a wild horse race. The wild horses are turned loose in the arena and the Indians, working in groups of three, must rope, saddle and ride the mustang through a designated barrier. Other features include bareback riding, bull riding, calf roping, wild cow milking, bull dogging, team roping, a girls' barrel race and a western dance. Indian war dances and a buckaroo breakfast also are held. The event held each May is sponsored by the Tywama Saddle Club. Tygh Valley is located on U.S. 197.

**Turkey-Rama**   Each July, hundreds of Oregon citizens engage in a festive event at McMinnville called a Turkey-Rama. It features a giant turkey barbecue, a give-away of 300 turkeys and Oregon's only official turkey races. Then later, a Wacky Vehicle Race is staged in the city parking lot, featuring any type of unconventional vehicle or automobile. McMinnville may be reached on U.S. 99W.

**Green Cobras**   Oregon's unusual Darlingtonia are rare plants which get their food by capturing insects. Their cobra-like hoods are not flowers, but tubular leaves of translucent pale green, mottled with red or orange. An opening under each hood allows insects to enter; once inside, they are unable to climb out, and thus become food for the plant. You can see them in the Darlingtonia Wayside north of Florence, an area set aside by the state to preserve the plant. Florence is a seacoast town on U.S. 101.

For additional information, contact the Travel Information Section, Oregon State Highway Division, 101 State Highway Building, Salem, Oregon 97310.

# Pennsylvania

A Pretzel Factory, Mysterious Ringing Rocks and a
Stargazer's Stone

**Grand Canyon**   Pennsylvania's Grand Canyon is one of the most picturesque canyons in all the East. Fifty miles long and a thousand feet deep, it embraces some 300,000 acres in the north central section of the state. The state-owned canyon is heavily forested and laced with deep valleys and rocky tumbling streams. Geologists estimate the canyon was formed some 25,000 years ago, during the glacial period. In 1968, Pine Creek Gorge, commonly known as Pennsylvania's Grand Canyon, was designated a Federal National Landmark by the National Park Service. A monument and plaque noting that designation are located at Leonard Harrison State Park which encompasses a portion of the canyon. Headquarters for the canyon is Wellsboro, located on U.S. 6.

**Pretzel House**   At a weathered stone building in Lititz, a modest sign proclaims "Pretzel House—Restaurant, Museum". The two sets of words are separated by a traditionally shaped, twisted pretzel. Owner and operator of the shop is Lewis Sturgis, an octogenarian pretzel bender. He claims there's something special about the twist in every pretzel; it all started with the way pretzels were invented.
About 610 A.D., an imaginative monk somewhere in southern France or northern Italy used up his dough scraps to make treats for children who said

Pennsylvania's Grand Canyon has become one of the most popular scenic attractions in Eastern United States near Wellsboro, Pennsylvania.

their prayers properly. He put the distinctive twist in the dough to represent children's arms folded in prayer; he called the result *pretiola*, Latin for *little reward.* So, Sturgis contends, the pretzel is a religious symbol.

The Pretzel House Restaurant serves Pennsylvania Dutch food. In the museum area of the building, Sturgis' old pretzel-making implements still stand in their original places. One item of particular interest, though definitely not an original piece, is the mechanical pretzel-twisting machine that shows how modern bakeries keep up with the ever-increasing demand for pretzels. It's uncanny the way the machine repeatedly crosses its "hands" as tireless steel fingers produce the traditional three-hole pretzel shapes. The Pretzel House is located in Lititz, on PA 501, north of Lancaster.

## Ephrata Cloister

At the town of Ephrata, in the midst of Pennsylvania Dutch country, stands a neat complex of immaculate, weathered wooden buildings surrounded by a split-rail fence. Known as Ephrata Cloister, they represent a monastic order of a by-gone era; an epoch in early American history when many examples of religious freedom flourished in the states. Rich farmlands still surround the 24-acre museum.

The unique order was founded in 1732 by Conrad Beissel, a German mystic who came to these shores intent on becoming a hermit. In a short time, his religious beliefs stimulated the interest of several followers. Soon after that, they established the Cloister as a place to work and express their religious fervor, a place to perform acts of charity.

The fascinating tour through these old buildings, with original furnishings more than 200 years old, is easily done on foot. During its peak in 1750, some 300 persons lived at Ephrata Cloister; but after the Revolutionary War, its population began to decline and by 1800 it had virtually become a thing of the past. The Ephrata Cloister is located on U.S. 322, northeast of Lancaster.

## Bird-in-Hand Village Store

The name of the town is as unusual as its central attraction; for who could pass through Bird-in-Hand without being intrigued enough to pause and visit awhile. There are things of interest to be found at Bird-in-Hand, for example, the Gay Nineties General Store which first opened in 1890 and hasn't changed much since. At one time, Ford and Overland cars were assembled and sold here. They no longer are, of course, but there are penny candies, a pot-bellied stove and a charming atmosphere. There's a distinct lack of neon and glitter, too. Also at Bird-in-Hand, you'll find the world's shortest covered bridge, a Gay Nineties Museum and, in one of the back rooms of the old Village Store, a honky-tonk piano. The Village Store is closed January and February, but open the remainder of the year. It is located on PA 340, 7 miles east of Lancaster in the heart of Amish country.

## Johnny Appleseed Festival

Of all the festivals held in the Keystone State, none can quite compare with the Johnny Appleseed Festival, traditionally held in early autumn. The festival honors the name of John Chapman, fabled in story and song as the beloved "Johnny Appleseed." He established his very first apple tree in Warren County, Pennsylvania, in 1797 through 1799, supplying the pioneers with their first apple orchards. Of course, as history relates, Johnny moved West, spreading apples wherever he went. This big festivity honors a humble man and his quest to seed the new country with apples. Included in the festival are contests in chain sawing, crosscut sawing, log rolling, wood chopping, horse-pulling

The old village store in the heart of the Pennsylvania Dutch-Amish countryside, Bird-in-Hand, Pennsylvania.

contests and a tour through a modern sawmill. The festival is staged at Sheffield, located in the Allegheny National Forest on U.S. 6, south of Warren.

## Ringing Rocks

Of the seven areas of ringing rocks in Pennsylvania, three are located in Bucks County. There are ringing rocks in Bridgeton Township on a plateau 350 feet above the Delaware River, 3 miles east of Kintnersville; in Stony Garden in Haycock Township on the north slope of Haycock Mountain; and in Rocky Valley in Springfield Township, about 3 miles east of Coopersburg on the flank of a knob whose top is 880 feet above sea level.

Best known and most readily accessible to the public, however, are the ringing rocks of Upper Black Eddy on the Delaware River—Bucks County Park. Only 70 acres in extent, it provides 4 acres of boulders lying exposed as if dumped from a giant truck. When struck with a hammer or similar object, many of these rocks will ring. Geologists explain this metallic resonance by the unusual crystal structure. If you want to go rock-hopping or try your hand playing musical notes on the ringing rocks, bring a metal hammer and sneakers or rubber-soled shoes. It's a fascinating and a most unusual phenomenon. The Bucks County Park is located near Revere on PA 32.

## Stargazer's Stone

In the midst of a field, surrounded by bushes and weeds, you will find the Stargazers' Stone, a most fascinating remnant of history. On a plaque are these words: "Erected in 1764 by Mason and Dixon in locating the Pennsylvania-

Maryland boundary line being 15 miles north thereof and 31 miles due west of Philadelphia." Here, they also measured a degree of latitude on the earth's surface southward, and made other astronomical observations; hence the name. At KOA, the campgrounds in Chester County, you can ask for directions; it's located on PA 162, near West Chester.

## Ride a Gondola into Space

One of the most exciting and fascinating rides in the nation is offered by aeronaut Buddy Bombard, whose Chalet Club owns two hot-air balloons. Weather permitting, balloon rides are offered in the basket gondola; you can float around the skies at speeds of 5 to 25 miles per hour, depending on the winds. The pull of gravity is broken by heating the air pumped into the balloon with a double-barreled propane burner. The balloon will run for 3 hours, and there's always a chase vehicle on the ground to pick you up when you land. The direction you take is beyond your control; you must go wherever the winds carry you. However, your pilot can control altitude by adjustment of the burners delivering heat into the balloon. The balloons are operated from the New Hope Balloon Port located on U.S. 202, north of Philadelphia.

## Steam Lokie

Ever ride an old-fashioned steam locomotive? You will have the opportunity when you visit the Pioneer Coal Mine Tunnel at Ashland. Named the *Henry Clay,* the little train takes you around the side of Mahanoy Mountain to give you a look at modern-day strip mining. You can also ride the train back to its stopping place and take a tour in an electric mine train to see coal-mining operations underground. It runs for 1,300 feet straight into the heart of Mahanoy Mountain. The miner-guides tell you the history of anthracite coal mining. For further details, contact Ashland Community Enterprises, 19th and Oak Streets, Ashland, Pennsylvania 17921.

You can ride the *Henry Clay,* an old steam lokie, at the Pioneer Tunnel Coal Mine and Railroad at Ashland, Pennsylvania.

The Mary Merritt Doll Museum is a rare collection of antique dolls; it is located 10 miles east of Reading on PA 422.

In the Coudersport Ice Mine, during the summer months, strange and striking formations of beautiful ice appear. It is located 4 miles east of Coudersport at the entrance to Black Forest on U.S. 6.

The Morris Rattlesnake Hunt is traditionally held in June with prizes for the most and largest rattlesnakes caught during the hunt. It also features a chicken barbecue. It is located on PA 287 and PA 414.

For additional information, contact the Bureau of Travel Development, Department of Commerce, 420 South Office Building, Harrisburg, Pennsylvania 17120.

Other Points of<br>Interest

# Rhode Island

### Two Independence Days, an Island with No Roads and a Carnivorous Tree

While the United States celebrates the Fourth of July as Independence Day, Rhode Islanders actually celebrate two Independence Days; for Rhode Island declared its independence on May 4, 1776, a full 2 months before the remainder of the colonies. Thus, the most important historical date celebrated in this state is May 4; and to highlight the activities, the officers and men of the Newport Artillery Company (the oldest active military organization in the nation) fire a salute with a 1750 cannon (oldest cannon in actual use in the world). The men dress in exact replicas of the uniforms worn by the artillery company in 1741 when the unit was organized. Each year, the celebration is held on the Sunday following May 4. Newport is located on RI 138.

Twin<br>Independence Days

Roger Williams, one of the leading pioneer citizens of Rhode Island, died in 1683 and was buried alongside his wife on their farm. A fitting, but by no means elaborate, headstone was used to mark their resting place.

Many years later, a commission was authorized to dig up the remains for a more elaborate interment and a more fitting memorial. When the group opened the two graves, they found them empty. Roger Williams and his wife were gone, bones and all. Nearby stood a great spreading apple tree, known widely for the fine quality of its fruit. When investigators could figure no other way the graves could have been robbed, they turned to the tree.

Sure enough, the roots of the tree had entered the coffins. A large root curved where Williams' head would have been and entered the chest cavity,

The Apple Tree<br>That Devoured<br>Roger Williams

growing down the spinal cord. It branched into two roots representing the two legs and then, at the end, upturned into feet. The roots, consequently, bore a remarkable resemblance to the bodies they had devoured; and today they are displayed in the museum of Rhode Island Historical Society, located at the John Brown House, 52 Power Street in Providence. It's open Tuesday through Sunday, year-round for a small admission charge.

## Block Island: Resort in the Sea

Block Island, a modest strip of sand, bluff and moor lying 10 miles south and seaward from Rhode Island, is reminiscent of England. The multihued clay cliffs rise more than 200 feet above sea level and stretch along the seacoast for about 5 miles. Called Mohegan Bluffs, they are so named because they appear as profiles of Indians. Skin divers and surf fishermen flock to the island where world records for fish are common. The waters off Block Island are plentiful with giant bluefin tuna, school tuna, swordfish and marlin. The best way to get to the island is by ferryboat, although many come by private boat and by plane. Cars are scarce on the island. Many prefer to bicycle along the 21-square-mile countryside to explore the old graveyards, abandoned lighthouses and Settler's Rock where the island's first colonists stepped ashore in 1661. Ferries run from New London, Connecticut and Galilee and Providence, Rhode Island.

## Oscar Green's Railroad

If you're a railroad buff, you'll want to see Oscar Green's Railroad, probably the shortest railroad in the nation and perhaps the world. The Warwick Railroad, as it's called, is operated over a 1.3-mile track entirely within the city of Cranston;

Mohegan Bluffs rise 200 feet above the Atlantic Ocean and stretch for 5 miles on the coast of Block Island, Rhode Island. *(Courtesy of Rhode Island Development Council, Providence, Rhode Island)*

and annually it moves about 700 cars, grosses more than $50,000 and burns in excess of 2,000 gallons of diesel oil. It racks up 80 train-miles a month.

Oscar Green is the operator of this railroad; he also serves as president, brakeman, conductor, engineer and auditor. Working with Oscar is Paul Wessel, engineer and maintenance man. The Warwick Railroad links the main line of the Penn Central Railroad with the Geigy Chemical Corp., the Atlantic Tubing and Rubber Company, and two lumberyards. If he has time, Mr. Green will be more than happy to talk to anyone interested in his railroad. His headquarters are on Elmwood Avenue, in Cranston, located on RI 12 in the suburbs of Providence.

**Marble Dome**

In the midst of Providence is one of the stateliest buildings in the nation; it has a dome made of white Georgian marble, the second largest unsupported dome in the world. The building is the state capitol. Its dome is particularly eye-catching at night when illuminated by a battery of floodlights. The bronze statue on top is the Independent Man, clothed only in a lion's skin and holding a spear in his extended right hand while his left hand rests on an anchor. The figure is 11-feet tall and weighs some 500 pounds; its lofty perch is 235 feet from ground level.

**The Great Swamp**

Among Rhode Island's most unique attractions is the Great Swamp, rich in history and animal life. This 2,600-acre marsh created by a glacier some 100 centuries ago is swarming with an infinite number of creatures and vegetations of all types. The Great Swamp became a part of colonial history on a frigid day in 1675 when militia troops surprised the Narragansett Indians by making their way across the frozen swamp. They burned the Indian village and a granite shaft marks the site of the encounter. The Great Swamp is located off RI 2, near Kenyon.

**Prudence Island**

In Narragansett Bay is an island of particular significance. Only 150 people live year-round on Prudence Island; but in the summer vacation season, the population swells. Prudence comprises colonies of cottages. One is named Bristol Colony after the people from Bristol, Rhode Island, who went there years ago to build summer cottages. There are no highways on the island; the roads (if you wish to call them that) are legally called driftways. Since there are no town or state highways on Prudence Island, it isn't even necessary to have an automobile registration plate. However, the island's dwellers have developed an honor system whereby they have appended tags to their cars. The principal driftway, which is little more than a trail going across the island east to west, carries a very auspicious name—Broadway.

For additional information, contact the Tourist Promotion Division, Rhode Island Development Council, Roger Williams Building, Providence, Rhode Island 02908.

# South Carolina

Ghost Country with a Chitlin Strut and
Arthur Middleton's Birthday Celebration

**Ghost Country**

Along the low tidewater areas of South Carolina is an area known by natives and visitors as ghost country. It's a kingdom under the reign of the Gray Man, the Country Doctor and a host of other free spirits that appear occasionally along the seashores and in the salt marshes, sometimes to warn people of impending danger. Throughout this area are great rambling, haunted houses with creaky doors and shutters that bang in the middle of a still night. On Pawley's Island is a house with a ghost banquet room and at Georgetown and on Hilton Head Island the stories of the Gray Man and the Country Doctor are told time and again. The Gray Man, it's claimed by those who have seen him, appears most often just before an ocean storm or hurricane.

This area is occupied by immigrants and descendants of immigrants from Jamaica. You'll see them operating roadside stands at which you can buy hand-crafted baskets. This is one of the few places in the United States where voodoo is still practiced; and many of the natives will not, for fear of reprisals by voodoo witches, even discuss the matter. Yet, they do admit it's practiced reverently and enthusiastically in this area.

**Chitlin Strut**

The town of Salley has the unique claim of being the "Chitlin Capital of the World," and thus far it's gone unchallenged. Each year, the people of Salley reaffirm that claim by holding one of the biggest celebrations in all the Southeast—the Chitlin Strut.

It all began in the fall of 1966 when the mayor found the town in too dire financial stress to buy new Christmas decorations. It was then he decided to take the suggestion of some friends and launch the tradition. Each year, the first Saturday after Thanksgiving, the Chitlin Strut becomes a way of life in Salley. For those who need enlightenment on the subject, "chitlins" is a derivation of "chitterlings," or more simply, hog intestines. Chitlin lovers like them either boiled or batter fried; they consider the dish a delicacy. Attendance at the annual affair proves it. More than a ton of chitlins is prepared at each chitlin strut and there usually are no leftovers. Other activities include a parade, the selection of a Miss Chitlin beauty queen, an auction sale, street dances and special exhibits. A country and western music show is also held. Salley is located on SC 39, southwest of Columbia.

**Arthur Middleton's Birthday**

Not far from Charleston each year, a distinguished celebration is held in honor of Arthur Middleton's birthday. It comes each June 24, at Middleton Place Gardens and Plantation. For this was the birthplace of Middleton, one of the signers of the Declaration of Independence. Chamber music is heard throughout the day, and there are art exhibits and eighteenth-century lawn games.

In 1971, Middleton Place was formally dedicated as a registered National Historic Landmark, open to the public year-round. Once limited in tourist appeal to the brief spring season, Middleton Place Gardens now is a popular year-round attraction. The stableyards have been restored; and animals, artifacts and farm implements are assembled there to depict the agricultural activities and day-to-day life of the eighteenth- and nineteenth-century plantation community. Located on high terrain along the banks of the Ashley River, the property has never been out of the Middleton family since it was settled in the latter part of the seventeenth century. Long famous for the elaborate landscaped terraces, butterfly lakes, majestic Middleton oak and endless plantings of azaleas and camellias, the plantation today offers visitors the opportunity to try their hands at milking a cow, driving a team of mules or gathering eggs. Middleton Place Gardens and Plantation is located northwest of Charleston on SC 61.

## Hell Hole Swamp Festival

Each May in the hamlet of Jamestown, the Al Capone Moonshine Era is revived during Hell Hole Swamp Festival Days. There are stories that, during prohibition, moonshine made in this particular area sold at a premium price in New York City. There are some who'll tell you that Hell Hole Swamp was Al Capone's southern headquarters. The swamp, located in the Francis Marion National Forest between Moncks Corner and Georgetown, was long an area of moonshine operations.

Visitors to the festival will have the opportunity to see how a moonshine still operates. A feature event is the Bootlegger and Revenuer Chase, employing old model automobiles. The festival also includes tours of the French Santee and Hell Hole Swamp, visiting Revolutionary War battle sites and the plantation of former Governor McNair. In the evening is a beauty queen contest. Other attractions include a Hell Hole Swamp parade, chainsaw log-cutting contests, horseshoe pitching, sack races, checker playing contests, tug of war, wagon rides, a flea market, a reptile exhibit and a display of native wild boar. A contest to determine who can tell the tallest tale of Hell Hole Swamp is also a popular featured attraction. Jamestown is located on U.S. 17A.

## Scottish Games

A touch of the Highlands comes to the Middleton Place Gardens near Charleston each summer with the reenactment of the Scottish Fair and Highland Games. Participants from several southeastern states compete in dancing and bagpiping contests and in several rugged athletic events. Included in the latter are heavyweight Highland wrestling, hammer throwing, sheaf tossing competitions (a burlap bag filled with hay, tossed with a pitchfork over a crowbar) and the caber toss. A caber is an 18-foot, 100-pound pole or beam. Scottish souvenirs and food, including mutton pie, are sold at booths in the area. The event normally is held in late September.

## Lancing Tournament

The annual lancing tournament is an event right out of the days of King Arthur; but, here, the knights wear no armor. The lances are real enough, but instead of charging one another on horseback, these "knights" try to pick off three small white rings suspended from an arch.

The event is held at Middleton Place with riders from all parts of South Carolina competing. To make a perfect score, the rings, ranging in size from ¾ to 1½ inches, must be plucked from their suspension clip and remain on the

The annual Middleton Place Lancing Tournament at Charleston, South Carolina.

end of the lance. The winner gets to place a crown on the lady of his choice.

The star attraction of this unusual sporting event is playing the game of musical chairs on horseback. It's played like the traditional game except the contestants begin each round on horseback. The riders in the tournament form a circle around a group of chairs. When the music stops, they dismount and scramble for a chair. One chair is removed each time, always leaving one chair less than the number of riders. It's a rugged game on horseback and sometimes leaves the participants in an embarrassing position. The event traditionally is held in mid to late October.

## Sacred Art

At Bob Jones University at Greenville is one of the most elaborate displays of sacred art in the South. The university, an interdenominational school on Wade Hampton Boulevard, has a museum of sacred art containing European paintings from the thirteenth through the fourteenth century. Among them are works by Titian, Tintoretto, Veronese, Rubens and Van Dyck. The collection is effectively displayed in a series of magnificent rooms, including two Gothic chambers. A diorama depicts Biblical household scenes and trees and herbs mentioned in the Bible. To get to Greenville, take I-85 or U.S. 29.

## Raylrode Daze Festival

In 1838, the town of Branchville gained prominence by becoming the first railroad junction in the world. Since that time, three United States presidents— William McKinley, William H. Taft and Teddy Roosevelt—were honored guests in the dining room of the Branchville Railroad Station. That dining room today is one of the showplaces of the festival, and meals are still served there.

The townspeople have restored the dining area, resplendent in "gay nineties" atmosphere with red interior, draperies, dining facilities, and honky-tonk piano. The entire town dresses in gay nineties costumes and in railroad dress to commemorate the days when railroad was a way of life in Branchville.

An outstanding feature of the festival is the arrival of the full-scale replica of the *Best Friend,* which was the first steam locomotive to pull a train in regular service in America. The train travels from Charleston to Branchville and gives rides to children all day on Saturday during the festival. A gunfight is staged between Filthy McDirty and his gang of desperados and the local lawmen at the junction. Later there's a hanging party for the captured outlaws. The Branchville Shrine and Museum has historic railroad pieces on display. Other activities include a costume judging contest, children's games and a community sing at the hobo jungle. Branchville is located on U.S. 21, south of Columbia.

The *Best Friend* on display at the Branchville Raylrode Daze Festival at Branchville, South Carolina.

## Pigeon Plant

At Sumter is the Palmetto Pigeon Plant, the largest of its kind in the world. Founded by Attorney Wendell M. Levi, the plant markets 100,000 squabs a year and you can visit their pens. However, don't try to talk; the pigeons' cooings are much louder than you can overcome. Levi is the author of a book on pigeons which is also on display at the Pigeon Plant. The plant is located on U.S. 76 and SC 378.

For additional information, contact the Division of Travel and Tourism, Department of Parks, Recreation and Tourism, 2712 Middleburg Drive, Columbia, South Carolina 29202.

# South Dakota

## A Mountain Monument, a Sea of Buffalo and a Corn Palace

**Crazy Horse**  Since 1948, Korczak Ziolkowski has been whittling away at a giant project in South Dakota's Black Hills. The result, when finished, will be one of the world's most outstanding and unique monuments to the Indian or to mankind—a colossal statue of Chief Crazy Horse of the Sioux.

From the top of the mountain that is to become the Crazy Horse monument, one can see four states—South Dakota, Nebraska, Wyoming and Montana. The mountain carving will be 563-feet tall and 641-feet long. The arm of Crazy Horse extends 263 feet, and the feather atop his head rises upward a total of 44 feet.

The rock which Ziolkowski blasts from the mountain is now being utilized by the U.S. Army Corps of Engineers; they figure by the time the monument has been finished, there'll be enough rock to pave a highway from the nearby town of Custer all the way to Washington, D.C.

But that's not all Ziolkowski plans to do to immortalize the Indian. At the

One of the largest buffalo herds in the nation occupies Custer State Park, South Dakota.

Wild burrows panhandle at Custer State Park, South Dakota.

base of the mountain, he plans to build an Indian culture center, complete with university, hospital, airfield and museum. He prefers to do all this single-handedly; although upon several occasions he's been offered help by the federal government. The late President John F. Kennedy personally came to see him and to talk about federal aid, but Ziolkowski would not hear of it. The Herculean task is to remain his own. He charges a fee at the Visitor's Center which he built at the base of the mountain; he uses the money to finance his project, ultimately to cost more than $5 million. The Indian Center will cost another $50 million. Crazy Horse is located 5 miles north of Custer on U.S. 16.

**Needles Highway**

In the Black Hills near Custer State Park is one of the nation's most remarkable roads; they call it the Needles Highway. Only 14 miles long, it took workmen 2 years to carve the highway from the rugged South Dakota wilderness. The road wends precariously along sheer precipices, pigtails its way up and down steep grades and takes the motorist around sharp bends. You suddenly come face to face with a tunnel in the mountain which you're sure is too small for your vehicle. It's one lane and you can see the other end only if you swing your automobile to the extreme opposite side of the road just before entering. Consequently, you're asked to sound your horn frequently along the Needles Highway. Many of the tunnels have only inches to spare on each side of your vehicle. At one point, you pass the Cathedral Spires, a field of needle-like formations towering a hundred feet above the forest. At another point is a granite tower with a slit in the top—the needle's eye. The Needles Highway is located off SD 36 at the edge of Custer State Park.

**Buffalo Jeep Rides**

In Custer State Park, you will see one of the largest buffalo herds in the nation. Although buffaloes can be dangerous to anyone walking, jeep rides are offered through the vast black herds. They give adequate protection and, at the same time, allow one to get within arm's reach. Custer State Park is located north of Hot Springs, on U.S. 385 and SD 87.

## America's Moonscape

In southwestern South Dakota is one of the world's most picturesque moonscapes. They call it the Badlands National Monument, but it resembles the mountains and craters of the moon more than it does anything on Earth. Out of the flanks of the prairie, wind and rain, freezes and thaws have carved a world of sharp ridges, steep-walled canyons, gullies, pyramids and knobs. And it's eternally and constantly changing. A feature found in the Badlands today may be literally gone tomorrow, should there be one of the infrequent cloudbursts during the night.

The landscape supports little life, and the water it receives sometimes comes in torrential storms that do little but tear away at its soft surface. Nature trails slice their way into the innards of the Badlands, giving one the opportunity to inspect at close range the erosion processes that have occurred here for centuries. With a little imagination, you could be an astronaut walking over the lunar surface. The Badlands are located on U.S. Alternate 16 just off U.S. 16 and U.S. 14.

## Deadwood— The One-Street Town

Deadwood is a one-street town with its main thoroughfare running down the narrow Deadwood Gulch, with side streets being little more than alleys up the mountain. At Deadwood, however, you'll find several worthwhile attractions. It's the place where Wild Bill Hickok and Calamity Jane are buried, in Mount Moriah Cemetery. At the Old Town Hall, life-size wax figures typify the early pioneer life in these parts with figures of early explorers, miners and gunmen. If you'd like to visit a retired gold mine, you may do so at the Broken Boot gold mine just one mile west of town on U.S. 14A. It no longer produces gold, but that matters little to visitors who tour its tunnels. Deadwood is located on U.S. 14A.

## Wounded Knee

At Wounded Knee on the Pine Ridge Indian Reservation, a National Historic Site has been established featuring a museum and the mass burial grave of Chief Big Foot and the 146 Sioux Indians who fell victims of the U.S. Seventh Cavalry. In the museum is a collection of articles, books and pictures that played a part in the development of culture in North America. Wounded Knee is located in the southwestern part of the state just off U.S. 18.

## Rosebud Indian Reservation

Along the Little White River is the Rosebud Indian Reservation covering some 60,000 acres and offering a variety of recreational opportunities such as water skiing, camping, boating and horseback riding. Inhabited by a portion of the Sioux tribe, the reservation also features, at the town of Rosebud, a craft show which produces beadwork, handicrafts and paintings, all by local Indian artists. The Craft Shop is open June 1 to September 1, 7 days a week.

Eight miles from Rosebud at Saint Francis is the Museum of the Sioux Indians, which features narratives and displays of Indian items and relics from the Battle of the Little Big Horn. During the summer months, roping demonstrations are given during the evenings near Ghost Hawk Campground. On summer weekends, ceremonial Indian dances are held at various Indian communities on the reservation, most of them open to the public. The next to the last weekend in August, Indian dance competitions are held at the Rosebud Reservation Fair. Rosebud is located just south of U.S. 18, which runs through the reservation.

The world's only Corn Palace at Mitchell, South Dakota.

**Corn Palace**

South Dakota's most unusual building is unquestionably the Corn Palace in Mitchell. Both the exterior and interior walls are partially covered with corn, arranged in designs and outlined with grasses and grains. Annual redecoration of the building requires about 3,000 bushels of various shades of natural-colored corn and grasses. Traditionally during the last week of September, the annual Corn Palace Festival is held here; and all summer long, Indian performances, dances and ceremonies are the featured attractions. The Corn Palace is located on 6th and Main Streets in Mitchell, which is on I-90.

**World's Largest Pheasant**

The Dakotas are pheasant country and at Huron near Memorial Park, the bird has been honored with a steel and fiberglass statue 40-feet tall, which is billed as the world's largest pheasant. The statue is located on U.S. 14.

**Other Points of Interest**

The Wall Drugstore in Wall has been declared the world's most unusual establishment of its kind.

The Federal Fish Hatchery and Aquarium, Yankton, features a live exhibit of the paddlefish found only in two spots in the world—in the Missouri River and the Yangtze River in China.

The Pettigrew Museum at Sioux Falls features an excellent collection of Sioux Indian arts and crafts, including a Council Tipi made of buffalo hides.

For additional information, contact the Travel Section, Highway Communications Division, Department of Highways, Pierre, South Dakota 57501.

# Tennessee

## A Mysterious Lake, a Railroad Legend and a Hotel Catering to Ducks

### Reelfoot — America's Largest Earthquake Lake

This mysterious lake was named after a Chickasaw Indian chief, Reelfoot. It was formed by the ravages of this country's greatest recorded earthquake. Located in the midst of west Tennessee's backwoods, it bears an aura of mystery, borne partially from legends and folktales more than a century old.

Yet Reelfoot Lake possesses a rare and exotic beauty which many claim is supreme throughout the South, if not the nation. Not much is left to remind one of the turbulence erupting from the bowels of the earth early one December morning in 1811. The tremors were centered at New Madrid, Missouri, on the west side of the Mississippi River not many miles from Reelfoot. The river, according to many accounts, actually ran backwards for several hours following the quake.

Today, this lake covers 14,500 acres and is a paradise for fishermen and ornithologists. A campground and state park are located on the south shore and there's a national wildlife refuge nearby. Over 240 species of water and land fowl and numerous small wild animals can be seen. Cypress trees grow throughout the lake and along its shores. Crappie, largemouth bass and bream provide the greatest fishery here. Also of interest is the Reelfoot boat, made at Samburg on the shores of the lake by native craftsmen. It's so designed the rower can sit looking forward as he uses hinged oars to propel himself about the lake. It's also a more stable boat for use in the rough waves which sometimes are created by surface winds. Reelfoot is located on TN 21 and TN 22 near Tiptonville.

### Country Music Hall of Fame

In Nashville, known across the country as the home of country music, is the Country Music Hall of Fame. Whether you like country music or not, you'll find the memorabilia and displays here to your liking. Here the history of country music in the United States is told.

The Hall of Fame includes an artists' gallery where you see pictures of country music artists and hear their most famous songs. Many of the instruments played by country music stars are on display, and in one great hall are the all-time greats of country and western music. As you stand in front of each display, you will see a lifelike portrait of each artist fused into an attractive panel above the bronze Hall of Fame plaque, a plaque that tells of each man's contributions to the world of country music and the basic facts of his life. Honored here are such stars as Jimmy Rogers, Hank Williams, Tex Ritter and Roy Acuff. To see Nashville's Grand Ole Opry is one thing, but here at the Hall of Fame is an education and an adventure in sight and sound you'll never forget.

The Hall of Fame is located on Division Street in the music section of

America's largest earthquake lake, Reelfoot Lake, Tennessee.

Nashville. Also, you might check with the Nashville Chamber of Commerce for the possibility of visiting recording sessions of some of your favorite country and western stars. Soundproof studios with glass walls allow visitors to watch many of the recording sessions.

At Jackson, you can visit the home of Casey Jones. In 1900, he died at the throttle of "Old 382" in an ill-fated train ride. His cottage has been converted into a museum relating the glorious days of steam on the rails. It contains old pictures and prints of early American railroads, old railroad passes, historic timetables, early dining car menus, telegraph instruments, railroad money, lanterns, steam whistles, old railroad ballads and other memorabilia. The home of Casey Jones was made a museum after the National Trust of Historic Preservation, custodian of American shrines, encouraged the city of Jackson to preserve it.

In 1950, a postage stamp was issued to honor the railroad engineers of

**Legendary Railroader**

America, and Casey Jones was selected as the engineer most worthy to represent this calling. Many Americans assume Casey Jones was merely a legendary figure, but a visit to his home and museum brings the great engineer into proper perspective. He was 6 feet, 4 inches tall, one of four brothers, each of whom was a crack railroad engineer. He was what railroaders called a high-rolling engineer. He was married in Jackson and, following the world-shaking head-on collision on the Illinois Central at Vaughan, Mississippi, on April 30, 1900, was buried at Mount Calvary Cemetery on the edge of Jackson. You can visit his grave today and see on display the colorful "six-eight Wheeler" steam locomotive that is part of the legend of Casey Jones. The museum is located on Chester Street in Jackson, just off U.S. 45.

## Teapot Museum

At Trenton is one of the most unusual attractions to be found in the Volunteer State—a collection of teapots gathered throughout the world and presented to Trenton by Dr. Frederick Freed of New York. The collection of porcelain *veilleuse-theieres* (night-light teapots) is exhibited in the Peabody High School Auditorium daily, admission free. Included in the display are rare pieces collected over more than a quarter of a century in such places as France, Belgium, Holland, Germany, Spain, Portugal, Switzerland, Italy, Greece, Turkey, Africa, Egypt, Thailand, Singapore, Hong Kong and Indochina. Most of the items were obtained from antique dealers and some from families who had possessed them for generations.

The collection has now grown to more than 350 teapots. Dr. Freed is a native of Trenton, thus the gift to the city. Most of the items in the collection are ornate and of excellent workmanship and, in many instances, the tops are fitted so ingeniously that the piece would not be recognized as a teapot. One

The Country Music Hall of Fame and Museum, Nashville, Tennessee.

such example is executed in the form of a woman who wears a flaring cape and skirt. A slight turn separates her shoulders and head and, as if by magic, she is suddenly a teapot. Trenton is located on U.S. 45W in west central Tennessee.

At Shelbyville in south central Tennessee, the Tennessee Walking Horse Celebration is held annually. Normally scheduled in late August, the celebration includes show ring performances of some of the greatest Tennessee walker bloodlines, including the crowning of outstanding horses. A beauty queen is chosen to reign over the event, but the horses are the real kings and queens and rarely will you see a finer collection. Shelbyville is located in the midst of Tennessee walking horse country and you might like to shunpike the countryside past some of the horse farms. Shelbyville is located on U.S. 231.

**Tennessee Walking Horse Celebration**

In southeastern Tennessee's mountains is Oak Ridge, once a top-secret area in America. Today, it's open to the public with guided tours, demonstrations and exhibits at the American Museum of Atomic Energy on Jefferson Circle. Conducted by the U.S. Atomic Energy Commission, the tours provided are educational. Tracking atomic particles and what happens when metal becomes radioactive are vividly demonstrated for you. Oak Ridge is located off U.S. 11, north of Chattanooga.

**Birthplace of the Bomb**

At the Sheraton-Peabody in Memphis, there's an exquisite penthouse, but it's not for people. For more than four decades, it's been reserved exclusively for the mallard family, a group of web-footed guests who spend their days holding court at the fountain in the hotel lobby. As they preen and paddle in the running water of the fountain, they reign like royalty before admirers of all ages who spend hours watching them. The lobby exhibit continues until 3 P.M. when the mallards end the reception with a formal departure. The hotel's loudspeakers herald the hour with fanfare; and then, in a ceremony that has made them famous, the mallards parade from the fountain along a red carpet to the waiting elevator that will carry them to their rooftop retreat. So outstanding and impressive is this ritual that many local residents as well as out-of-town visitors come to the hotel to watch it. The hotel is located in the downtown section of Memphis.

**Hotel for Ducks**

A little known attraction is Tennessee's Lost Sea, a 4½-acre underground lake located in Craighead Caverns between Knoxville and Chattanooga. The underground lake, according to geologists, may date back nearly 300 million years. The underground sea was discovered in 1913 by a small boy when he crawled through a crevice about a yard wide. Tours are offered of the cave and the Lost Sea, which is open to the public year-round. It's located near the town of Sweetwater on U.S. 11.

**Tennessee's Lost Sea**

On the Capitol grounds in Nashville stands the statue of Army Sergeant Alvin York, a Tennessean who was the most decorated soldier of World War I. York died only a few years ago, a legend within his own lifetime.

**Sergeant Alvin York**

At Cosby each spring, a tribute is held to the foulest plant in the United States—the ramp. Known as the sweetest-tasting, vilest-smelling plant to be found anywhere, it's held in high esteem because many believe it to have medicinal values, particularly as a spring tonic. Besides the gathering and cooking

**Ramp Festival**

of ramps, the festival includes a homecoming for natives of Cosby with picnics, mountain music and other festivities. It is traditionally held the last Sunday in April. Cosby is located on TN 325, off I-40.

For additional information, contact the Division of Tourist Information and Promotion, Department of Conservation, 2611 West End Avenue, Nashville, Tennessee 37203.

# Texas

## A Watermelon Thump, a Unique Zoo and a 4,000-Acre Sandpile

**Zoo for Near-Extinct Animals**

At Brownsville on the Rio Grande is a Noah's Ark for animals and wildlife facing extinction. The zoo, made possible through a philanthropic act by Mrs. Gladys Porter, was designed and built as a permanent survival and breeding center for species of animals that otherwise would be lost to future generations.

The zoo has the only Jentink's duiker, a species of small African antelope,

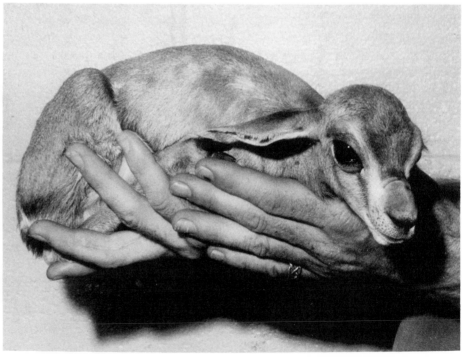

This tiny Speke's gazelle, the smallest gazelle in the world, was recently born in the Gladys Porter Zoo in Brownsville, Texas. *(Courtesy of Gladys Porter Zoo)*

in captivity. The duiker, first seen in West Africa in 1900, was not seen again until 50 years later and is considered one of the rarest animals on earth. The zoo also has Siberian tigers of which fewer than 50 are known to exist. Other endangered species in the zoo include the gaur from southeast Asia (world's largest wild cattle), the pileated gibbon ape of Cambodia, the pigmy hippopotamus from Africa and the mu-lu deer from China.

The $5 million zoo was a gift of the Earl C. Sams Foundations, named after Mrs. Porter's late father who was an associate of department store czar J. C. Penney. The zoo has no bars or cages on its 265-acres. The animals are restrained by water moats and imitation rock-cliff barriers, all resembling the creature's natural habitat. Shatterproof glass viewing windows protect them from spectators. Considered one of the most unusual and humane zoos in the entire continent, it's hoped this will become a model for other such zoos throughout North America.

**Padre Island**

For treasure hunters, beachcombers and self-styled amusement seekers, nature created Padre Island off the southernmost coast of Texas. It's a pristine island that runs for miles, stretching from Port Isabel past Corpus Christi, a magnificent white strip of sand that, with few exceptions, remains as wild and primitive as it was the day America was first discovered by white man.

The island's basic attractions are surf, sand and sun; all its activities are connected with those basic elements. There's excellent fishing from the shore; and if shell collecting is your game, Padre Island compares with Sanibel in Florida as one of the nation's top shelling areas. Offshore on the Gulf side are numerous old shipwrecks from the days of Spanish galleons. Scuba diving for treasure is not allowed, but beachcombers may collect certain items along the shore (no artifacts of archeological, historical or scientific importance may be removed from the island).

Much of the island today is being preserved as a national seashore by the Department of Interior, but the north and south ends are being developed. South Padre Island was cut off from the mainland until 1954 when Cameron County built the Queen Isabella Causeway. All of Padre Island once was a stomping ground for marauding pirates and a graveyard for many a shrimp-boat—and larger craft—swept ashore by vicious winds and currents. You may discover many diverse and grotesque shapes of driftwood, a window frame from a wrecked shrimper's wheelhouse, colorful glass floats or remnants of nets from Portuguese fishing fleets. Exploring Padre Island on foot is a unique and rewarding experience.

**Convict Cowboys' Rodeo**

The Texas Prison Rodeo has been called "The Dang'est Show on Earth," and it may well be. It began back in 1931 as a project to raise the esprit de corps of the inmates. For the first show, there was no rehearsal or practice; the next year, there was one practice period. As word began to spread, more and more spectators came to watch. No one dreamed the number would ever exceed 100,000, but that milestone has long since been surpassed. The stock is rented from outside the prison. From the very first event, "The Mad Scramble," which is referred to as the most dangerous event in rodeo circles, to "The Wild Chariot Race" which closes the show, there's never a dull moment. For there's something in common between the rough recklessness of the convict riders and the unbroken spirits and untamed tempers of the stock. The results are explosive. Huntsville is located off I-45 in east Texas.

Bronc riding at the Huntsville Prison Rodeo, Huntsville, Texas. *(Courtesy of Texas Highway Department)*

## Houston's Livestock Trail

Riders and wagon trains from all over Texas come to officially open the annual Houston Livestock Show and Rodeo. More than 8,000 riders participate in a dozen major trail rides to the city, some of them extending more than 200 miles. This celebration marks the kickoff of one of the Lone Star State's most noteworthy events.

Normally held in February, for at least 10 days, the show itself can hardly compare to the trail rides. The longest is the Old Spanish Trail Ride at 201 miles; while the oldest is the Salt Grass Trail which begins 90 miles from Houston in Brenham and follows the route of one of the great cattle trails. Trucks and cars set up advance camps for the rides, which last several days, and provide food for riders and horses. On the last camp night, riders from all the trails converge on Houston's Memorial Park on the outskirts of the city. More than 15,000 spectators and friends swell the camp and line the roadways to watch the wagon trains and trail riders end their long trek to Houston. Even in this modern age, it's a sight reminiscent of the pioneer days of Texas and the West.

Another such trail ride is held from Bandera to the San Antonio Livestock Exposition and Rodeo. This one is only 65 miles long, however, and departs from the Longhorn Steakhouse in Bandera, the dude ranch town. Trail riders on the 4-day event participate in various activities, including a western parade on the day following their arrival in San Antonio. For those without mounts, horses can be rented from the Twin Elm Ranch in Bandera. Feed and care of the horse is included in the price, and food for riders is available at all trail stops. Bandera is located on TX 16, northwest of San Antonio.

**Cowboy Capitol Trail Ride**

Spitting a tiny watermelon seed at a distant target is one of the most challenging events of the annual Luling Watermelon Thump. But that's only part of the fun, for contestants also are awarded prizes for spitting a watermelon seed the farthest. The Watermelon Thump car rally tests the skills of participants in driving, following directions and watermelon stealing techniques. There's also a watermelon eating contest to test the stomachs of the contestants. A Texas-size melon auction is held followed by the Drug Store Farmers Auction. The melons of this auction are grown in home gardens or flower beds. Other events include street square-dancing, an old-time fiddler's contest, a parade, beauty queen contest and a carnival for the kiddies. Luling lies just north of I-10, 57 miles east of San Antonio.

**Watermelon Thump**

Any town can hold a horseshoe pitching contest, but where else in the world would you expect a "muleshoe" pitching contest except in Muleshoe, Texas. Because there are no others, this one is known as the world championship match, traditionally held on the Fourth of July. Separate divisions are provided for men, women and children. Muleshoe is located on U.S. 84, northwest of Lubbock.

**Muleshoe Pitching Contest**

Not far from Odessa is a 4,000-acre sandpile which Texans are hoping to preserve by erecting a state park around it. With dunes reaching as high as 70 feet, the Texas sandhills provide a landscape similar to that of the Sahara Desert. Here you can wiggle your toes in the sand, climb to the top of a dune, ride a dune buggy in a roller-coaster, helter-skelter assault on the peaks and valleys or visit the Sandhill Museum. The latter is an attractive modern building fronted by scrub brush. Permanent exhibits help you understand the Sandhills. Because the wind constantly shifts the sand—and the winds almost constantly blow—you may find Indian artifacts, some buried treasure or even bones of ancient mastodons preserved for over thousands of years. The sandhills area is located along U.S. 80.

**Texas-size Sandpile**

If you have access to an inflatable raft, a very unique experience is a float trip down a section of the Rio Grande through Boquillas, Mariscal and Santa Elena canyons. Rafts and guided float trips are available from Glen Pepper, Villa de la Mina, Box 47, Terlingua, 79852. It is recommended that a party unfamiliar with the river take along a guide, but you may go alone if you choose. Before launching your craft, be sure that you contact a National Park Service ranger and let him know how long you plan to be gone.

During low water, the river is fairly safe for those who have had any experience in boating or rafting, and common sense should ensure an enjoyable and

**Raft Floating the Rio Grande**

safe voyage. The entire trip can be done in 2 days, and you can get to Mariscal in one day. One word of caution, however: all camera equipment should be insured and/or stored in a watertight container.

Best known of the Big Bend National Park canyons is Santa Elena, whose pictorial eloquence and easy accessibility have made it one of the most frequently photographed attractions of the Southwest.

## Dominos Anyone?

Each year, the State Championship Domino Tournament is held at Hallettsville. Sponsored by the Knights of Columbus, the tournament often attracts more than 150 players and is open to anyone for a small entry fee. The competition runs only one day, with awards being presented late in the evening. Hallettsville is located on U.S. 90A, east of San Antonio.

## Rattlesnake Roundup

While most people think only of cattle roundups, one of a different kind is held annually at Sweetwater. Sponsored by the Jaycees, this event draws thousands of visitors to watch the hunt, taste rattlesnake steaks and experience a snake dance. Close to 10,000 pounds of rattlesnake are caught each year in this hunt, which is billed as the world's largest. Some individual hunters catch in excess of a thousand pounds of rattler. Guided tours are provided for spectators and photographers. Sweetwater is located west of Abilene on I-20.

## Slingshot Matches

If you'd like to witness a "shoot-em-out with slingshots," attend the World Championship Slingshot Matches at Carrizo Springs. There are junior and senior divisions in competition. Slingshot stocks can be made of any material, but official ammunition is supplied by the contest committee. The event lasts 2 days and normally is held in early June. Carrizo Springs is located on U.S. 83, north of Laredo.

## Texas Canoe Race

One of the world's richest and most unusual canoe races is held annually from San Marcos to Seadrift on the Gulf of Mexico. It is billed as the toughest canoe race in the United States. With more than $5,000 in cash prizes, the race comprises 413 miles of paddling. Normally held in June, the start of the race is in the San Marcos city park and the end-of-the-race festival is held there the following weekend.

Other activities of the festival include turtle chasing, canoe jousting, frog jumping and other aquatic sports. Spectators can follow the racing teams through Luling, Gonzales, Cureo and Victoria to its conclusion at Seadrift. San Marcos is located halfway between Austin and San Antonio on I-35.

## Chili Cook-Off

At a west Texas ghost town named Terlingua, the World Championship Chili Cook-Off is held annually. On a Saturday in November, the annual cook-off draws several thousand people to watch, eat chili and enjoy the festivities. Events are nonscheduled and unpredictable; and accommodations are hard to come by if you don't camp out. Terlingua is located on Ranch Road 170, just outside of Big Bend National Park.

## The Indians and Big Thicket

In southeast Texas, along one edge of the Alabama-Coushatta Reservation, is a great swamp called the Big Thicket. At the Indian village, you may take a scenic tour on a 1½-mile hike through forest so impenetrable you'll think you're in an African jungle. From the trail, you can see and perhaps identify more than 100 kinds of indigenous trees and plants. In the area, too, are quicksand bogs, but the trail does not lead near them. The Indian reservation is on U.S. 190, just 14 miles east of Livingston, reached via U.S. 59, north of Houston.

On the fourth Sunday of each October at Harlingen is held the annual Confederate Air Force Show, a flying museum of World War II aircraft of all types. For those who remember the traumatic years from 1939 to 1945, a visit to Rebel Field at Harlingen is a dramatic and emotional experience. In one short step, you are drawn back in time and you are smack in the middle of a memorable era in aviation history and America's struggle for freedom and peace.

The annual Confederate Air Force Show at Harlingen, Texas.

The museum houses memorabilia from all branches of the U.S. Armed Forces as well as those of the enemy in World War II. More than 700 flying Colonels make up the Confederate Air Force, and many of them fly the planes during the annual show. Unlike many collections of World War II aircraft, the Ghost Squadron of the Confederate Air Force is capable of taking to the air. The Colonels stage several major air shows away from their home base each year. You'll see and be allowed to touch such famous planes as the P-38, P-51, P-40, B-29, B-25 Mitchell, a B-17 Flying Fortress, the SB2C Helldiver and the Spitfire. The attraction is open daily year-round. Harlingen is located on U.S. 77, northeast of Brownsville in the Rio Grande Valley.

For additional information, contact the Texas Tourist Development Agency, P.O. Box 12008, Capitol Station, Austin, Texas 78711.

# Utah

### A Dinosaur Department Store, a Mine Train Tour and a
### Devil's Slide

**Dinosaur Department Store**

Want to buy a *Stegosaurus, Brontosaurus* or *Allosaurus?* If so, contact the University of Utah's "Dinosaur Department Store." In this unusual enterprise, scientists recover dinosaur bones, assemble them into full skeletons, number, disassemble and ship them to institutions around the world. Recipients of the skeletons reassemble them guided by the detailed plans supplied by the university. They pay for their unusual merchandise by making a financial contribution to the university. Contributions range from $2,000 to $10,000, depending on the amount of original bone included in the specimen.

Under its cooperative dinosaur program, the university has been sponsoring digs at the Cleveland-Lloyd "Dinosaur Graveyard" in central Utah since 1960. More than 10,000 bones have been unearthed. You can watch the reconstruction and digging activity by checking with the Public Relations Department of the University in Salt Lake City.

**Dinosaurland**

Up the road from the developed campground at Split Mountain is another opportunity to learn about dinosaurs. They call it Dinosaurland. The Dinosaur National Monument Visitors' Center is the portal to a prehistoric world of monstrous reptiles. This modern facility is built over the "working face" of a dinosaur bone quarry where you can watch the progress of archaeologists chipping away to expose the bones at the quarry. If you'd care to continue your dinosaur adventures, you may see at Vernal's Field House of Natural History, a full-scale skeletal reconstruction of a large herbivorous *Diplodocus.*

**Moab Jeep Safari**

In the heart of Utah's Canyonlands area is one of the most rugged and impressive adventures of Eastertide—the annual Moab Jeep Safari. Approximately a half dozen trails are available to safari participants and each may choose his own. Maps are issued; consultations and orientations are offered. Lunches are airdropped to the jeep safari members. The only requirements for the safari include registration and a four-wheel-drive vehicle. The safari is a limited spectator event, although many hundreds of people gather at Moab's business district to watch the safari groups leave. If you have access to a four-wheel-drive vehicle and would like to see some of the most spectacular back country in all America, this is a unique adventure. To get to Moab, take U.S. 160 to the Colorado River.

**Friendship Cruise**

Here's another adventure for which you must supply your own vehicle. This is the Green River Friendship Cruise, and you'll need your own boat. If you have an outboard or outboard-inboard available, you'll find the grand tour through some of nature's most awesome wonderlands—Canyonland Country—worth every effort. As you meander down the Green River and up the mighty Colorado, you'll see the faces of sheer red rock cliffs exposed to more than 280 million years. An overnight campout, with a big steak dinner and combo music, is staged at Anderson Bottom. The cruise includes 183 miles of scenic vistas, natural monuments and colorful country. The Friendship Cruise begins at Green River and ends at Moab. To get to Green River, take I-70, U.S. 6 or U.S. 50.

**Mine Train**

At Park City, you can ride a mine train through the Spiro Tunnel to the Mine Museum. The 20-minute ride in the enclosed train cars takes you to the hoist station of the west end shaft of the Silver King Mine, 1,350 feet underground. Roundtrip on the train and the visit to the museum take about 90 minutes. In the museum, the only one of its kind in the world, you'll see actual mining equipment used in the Silver King, including drills, ore cars, surveying equipment, pumps and hoists. Wax figures of miners at work vividly reconstruct what underground mining was like in this area. Park City is located on U.S. 40.

**Devil's Slide**

A memorable landmark in Utah's rugged country is the Devil's Slide, an unusual limestone formation. Consisting of two parallel reefs 20 feet apart and 40 feet high, the reef is located 9 miles east of Morgan City. As you travel along I-80 N, you can easily see this remarkable bit of terrain. Since the early 1800s, many legends associated with this natural formation have been recorded. The best tale of all gave it its name and helped establish it as one of the West's most unusual wonders.

**Driving the Golden Spike**

At Promontory Summit in Utah on May 10, 1869, the Union Pacific met the Central Pacific Railroad to complete the nation's first transcontinental railroad. Promontory Summit is now a National Historic Site where, during the summer

The Visitor's Center at the Dinosaur National Monument, Utah. *(Courtesy of Utah Travel Council)*

Driving the Golden Spike at Promontory Summit in Utah. *(Courtesy of Utah Travel Council)*

months every hour from 9 A.M. to 4 P.M., there's a reenactment of the ceremony of driving the golden spike. Two replica 4-4-0 engines sitting face-to-face are located at the site. Promontory Summit is located 35 miles west of Brigham City via UT 83. It's open daily 9 A.M. to 5 P.M., October to April; 9 A.M. to 8 P.M., May to September.

**Coral Pink Sand Dunes** Northwest of Kanab on U.S. 89A is a cutoff road leading to Coral Pink Sand Dunes. This area of large windswept dunes of red sand is a barren wilderness, largely undeveloped. Travelers should inquire at Kanab for directions and road conditions. The area is approximately 20 miles northwest of Kanab.

**Bishop's Warehouse** One of Salt Lake City's most unique attractions is the Bishop's Warehouse, a mammoth building located on Welfare Square. It's practically a city within itself and houses many industries. Here, volunteer workers assort, can and process fruits, pasteurize and pack dairy products, weave, make clothing, repair and construct furniture and conduct a combination grocery and department store. No cash registers are to be found here, however, and there's no exchange of money. After careful investigation, supplies are given to deserving families. The system, a kind of Mormon welfare, is explained by a movie shown to visitors before they enter the warehouse. Free bus transportation is offered from the Main Gate at Temple Square to the warehouse.

For additional information, contact the Utah Travel Council, Council Hall, State Capitol, Salt Lake City, Utah 84114.

# Vermont

Quaint Villages, a Sculpture Highway and
Championship Shovel Races

Antiquated
Brookfield

If you yearn for back country roads, a picturesque floating bridge over a scenic lake, fields and forests converging on a New England village that has retained its old-time charm and pace of life, then you'll enjoy Brookfield. You can still see youngsters ride their ponies to the village store and post office and tie them to the old hitching posts. Families can bring their own mounts or ride the horses from a rental stable.

Near the center of town, you'll find the Brookfield Public Library, the oldest in the state, founded in 1791. The floating bridge was built in 1812, its span extending 320 feet over Sunrise Lake, also known as Colt's Pond. At the east side of the bridge, an old mill by a waterfall has been converted into the Fork Shop Restaurant. There are benches throughout the town for you to rest, to ponder town life as it might have been a hundred years ago and still remains today in Brookfield. The stagecoach from Boston to Montreal once passed this way; and as you look down the street, you half expect it to come rumbling through again. Located close to the geographic center of the state, Brookfield can be reached via I-89.

Sculpture Highway

This highway began with the fertile imagination of sculptor Paul Aschenbach who has a profound philosophy that art should not be confined to stuffy museums. His plan was carried out along the Sculpture Highway which threads its way north along I-89 and I-91 from the Massachusetts line through the Connecticut River Valley and north to the Canadian border.

As you follow the 200-mile route, you can drive into any one of the 17 different rest areas and find yourself face-to-face with huge chunks of concrete and Vermont marble hewn into magnificent abstract sculptures. They're the work of 22 artists brought to Vermont from various foreign countries to fashion the art along the Sculpture Highway out of native materials. The works belong to the respective artists who have them on loan to the display. They've been there since the summer of 1971, and many of the artists have voiced the desire to leave them permanently. After all, there's no better way, they feel, to display their art than along Vermont's Sculpture Highway.

Shovel Races

Ever try sliding down a snow-packed hill on a shovel? It's the way many youngsters in rural America learned to sled. Each year at the Killington Ski Area in Killington, Vermont, is held the World Shovel Championship Races, a reenactment of the old days. All contestants are from the ski area staff, but the event is open to spectators. The event is held on Chute Trail on Snowdon

Mountain. Entrants ride a coal-type shovel straight downhill for ½ mile through bumps and drop-offs. The one posting the fastest time is declared the winner. Sometimes speeds of 40 to 50 miles per hour are reached; and if you think an upset is fun at those speeds, it's a good thing you're watching and not participating. The races are traditionally held on the last Friday in March. Killington is located on VT 100 and U.S. 4, east of Rutland.

## Fly Fishing School

Most beginners use a rod as if they were swatting flies instead of casting rods. Though the fish are safe from such reckless people, other people aren't. That's one reason the Orvis Co., makers of fly rods and other sporting gear, set up a fly fishing school at their rod manufacturing plant at Manchester. Some 700 students attend the school each year to learn how to handle a fly rod safely, efficiently and expertly enough to catch fish. A single course lasts only a weekend, but there are seventeen offered each summer, beginning in May. Tuition, room and board run more than $100; however, as a spectator, you may also find the school of interest. Manchester is located on U.S. 7 in the southwestern part of the state.

## Route of the Round Barns

Along a section of rich Vermont farmland between Craftsbury Common and the Canadian border is the route of the round barns. Built at the turn of the century, many have since fallen in ruins, but others remain. Begin your search for round barns on VT 14. A handsome one is located north of Albany on the way to Irasburg. Turn west on VT 58 toward Lowell to see two more in a charming open-field setting. The barns are large and quite practical. Cows and other farm animals all face toward the center where the hay, grain or silage can be easily served. As you drive toward Lowell, you will see others; and if you're particularly interested in the construction features of round barns, almost any landowner will welcome the opportunity to show you inside and point out their advantages. Some of these round barns are at least three stories tall and as picturesque and as unique as any building you'll see in the Green Mountain State.

## Granite Quarries

As you watch workmen carve away in gigantic pits, slicing rocks as old as time itself, you realize the granite quarries are a very special place. To rockhounds and quarry lovers, Vermont's granite quarries are a mecca. From the Green Mountains comes some of the world's finest granite... and visitors are welcome from June through October.

The Rock of Ages Quarry and the Wells-Lamson Quarry in Barre offer guided tours, free of admission. Free specimens selected by professional eyes are available for the taking, as are free postcards with free postage if mailed at either quarry. As you stand on the rim of the immense 350-foot Rock of Ages Quarry, you are bound to be impressed by the rasp and clank of heavy machinery, the difficulty in prying loose immensely heavy chunks of granite and the dogged industriousness of the workers, scurrying like miniature figures. This quarry alone covers more than 20 acres.

Much of the granite in cemeteries across America was quarried here in Vermont. Barre, the center of granite quarry activity, is located just off I-89.

## Old Timers' Skiing and Jack Jump Revival Derby

At Bromley Ski Resort each March, the Old Timers Skiing and Jack Jump Revival Derby, one of Vermont's most unusual events, is held. The competition includes a variety of old-time New England winter sport activities. The feature event is the Wild Boar Classic, a race on jack jumps. Competitors in the race usually consist mostly of lift crews from ski areas of New England.

One of the numerous granite quarries in Vermont.

The term "jack jump" comes from the days when homemade conveyances were used by lumberjacks to ride out from the logging camps in winter. Back then it was a barrel stave with a post and seat nailed to it. Today, it has a sawed off wooden ski as the base.

Other events during this March weekend consist of a slalom race with old-time ski equipment and clothing, a pancake eating contest, a snowshoe race and shovel races, the latter similar to those held at Killington. Manchester Center is located on U.S. 7, in southwestern Vermont.

The annual Jack Jump Competition at Bromley Ski Resort, Vermont.

## Dowsers Den

When autumn descends upon the colorful hills of Vermont, the dowsers gather for their annual convention at the little town of Danville. This 3-day weekend represents one of the most unique gatherings in North America.

Using forked branches of certain trees (willow usually is preferred), the dowser claims he can locate underground streams of water at virtually any spot in the world. At Danville, interested persons from many states and Canada as well as Puerto Rico gather to learn more about promoting the use of dowsing.

More than 500 gather for the workshop seminars, during which map dowsing and information dowsing are demonstrated and taught. Danville is located on U.S. 2.

For additional information, contact Promotion and Travel, Vermont Agency of Development and Community Affairs, 61 Elm Street, Montpelier, Vermont 05602.

# Virginia

Wild Ponies, a Psychic Library and the Great Dismal Swamp

**Tangier Island**

In the midst of Chesapeake Bay is a colorful little island where the speech of many of the residents is still highly seasoned with an Old English accent. Most of Tangier is a fishing community where the way of life is peaceful and rustic. The island has an airport but no automobiles or streets. Its main thoroughfare is an asphalt lane about 8-feet wide.

Settled in the 1680s by a fishing family from Cornwall, England, this unique place of fewer than 1,000 inhabitants is totally dependent on the harvest of oysters, clams, crabs and fish. Store-bought goods are brought by plane or boat from Crisfield, Maryland, 14 miles away on the eastern shore. There's also a once-a-day mail boat which serves the island, and one may obtain passage aboard it. The docks around the island are usually crowded, however, with the activities of the watermen of the Chesapeake. Tour boats are operated to and from the island out of Reedville, Virginia, which can be reached via U.S. 360.

**Assateague Pony Swim**

Uninhabited Assateague Island, across a narrow channel from Chincoteague, Virginia, is a National Seashore and the site of an annual wild pony roundup by the Volunteer Fire Department of Chincoteague. Each July, the cowboy firemen stage a roundup that compares with many of the events of the Old West.

The ponies are descendants of Spanish ponies shipwrecked during the days of ocean-sailing galleons. The firemen-cowboys attempt to catch mares with young colts—colts old enough for weaning. Each year, many of the young colts are sold at auctions as a means of keeping the herd in check. The roundup occurs out of sight on Assateague Island, but the ponies are brought to a point directly across from the town of Chincoteague where a crowd gathers to watch. Boats fill the channel, except in the small area left open for the horses. At low tide, when the currents are least strong, the cowboys force the ponies to swim the narrow channel to Chincoteague. They're then driven down the main thoroughfare to the city park where they're impounded until the auction on the following day. It's a gala event and an unusual bit of Americana. To reach Chincoteague, take VA 175, east off U.S. 13.

The annual pony swim and roundup at Chincoteague Island, Virginia. *(Courtesy of Virginia State Travel Service)*

**Wildlife Tour**

Assateague National Seashore is also the home of several species of wildlife other than wild ponies. Along miles and miles of primitive beach, dunes and marshes are many species of shorebird, waterfowl and even the small Japanese sika deer. There also are red fox, raccoon, muskrat, cottontail rabbit and otter. Assateague is home or a stopping place for nearly half of America's 600 species of birds. Daily interpretative tours are offered via jeep-towed enclosed trailer, giving visitors some insight into the habitat provided for those creatures of the wild kingdom. The Chincoteague National Wildlife Refuge here offers a drive-yourself tour through the refuge and a refuge-operated boat tour around the lower end of the island. For further details, check with the Chincoteague Chamber of Commerce.

**Great Dismal Swamp**

In the 1880s, Thomas Moore wrote poetry about the Great Dismal Swamp. Today, people are still intrigued by its subtle beauty. There is an ever-present aura of mystery about the swamp, forbidding areas of dank darkness amid giant stands of bald cypress trees. Stretching for more than 100 square miles over a vast portion of tidewater Virginia and North Carolina, the Great Dismal was once the hideout of numerous pirates who ventured into its dense abodes to partake of the "root beer" colored water, then bacteria-free and believed by some to have medicinal qualities.

In 1973, a large section of the Great Dismal was declared a national wildlife area under the Department of Interior. Except for a few canals which have been cut into its midst and Lake Drummond, which lies secluded in the depths of the swamp, no roadways are provided. The jungles are thick and marshy; and wildlife within the swamp includes rattlesnake, copperhead, bear, deer, wolves, bobcat and wild turkey. Old swamp rats—and there are only a few of them left—tell many a tale of witches, firebirds, wood demons and other mythical creatures of the Great Dismal. Tours by air are offered out of Suffolk, and tours by boat are offered from Chesapeake. For additional information on the boat excursions, contact Dismal Swamp Boat Tours, Inc., 4300 S. George Washington, Chesapeake, Virginia 23322. The swamp is located just south of Portsmouth.

## Edgar Cayce— The Psychic

Many contend Edgar Cayce was unquestionably the most improbable psychic who ever lived. He was often reluctant and accepted no pay and yet was dedicated to what he called his work. Born in Hopkinsville, Kentucky, Cayce was never educated; yet while in his trances twice each day, he was able to diagnose illnesses and use medical terms he could not otherwise pronounce. He later moved to Virginia Beach where he established a hospital, and it was there he worked until his death in 1945.

Today, in the Edgar Cayce Hospital at Virginia Beach are the headquarters of the Association for Research and Enlightenment, Inc., an organization dedicated to the dissemination of information on the Cayce readings. To help in this work, the readings have been indexed and are open to the public, along with other pertinent material filed in the Association's library. The library contains one of the country's largest collection of books, magazines and papers on psychic research. The Association also works to provide private doctors with all types of information as they explore, in private practice and in clinical study, concepts brought out by Cayce's readings. The library and headquarters are open 9 A.M. to 5 P.M. daily.

## Virginia's Mole Tunnel

Created thousands of centuries ago, this natural tunnel appears to have been made by some prehistoric giant mole. Through the tunnel, which is 850 feet long and as high as a 10-story building, runs a stream and a railroad track. The area is now a state park which also features a wide chasm of steep stone walls, surmounted by several pinnacles or "chimneys." Open Memorial Day through Labor Day, access is about 2 miles north of Clinchport via U.S. 23, U.S. 58 and U.S. 421, then ½ mile north on a two-lane paved highway.

For additional information, contact the Virginia State Travel Service, 911 E. Broad Street, Richmond, Virginia 23219.

The Great Dismal Swamp just south of Portsmouth, Virginia. *(Courtesy of Norfolk News Service)*

The Canyon of the Apes near Mount St. Helens in southwestern Washington. *(Courtesy of Washington Department of Commerce and Economic Development)*

# Washington

Canyon of the Apes, Seattle's Underground and
Wolf Preserve

**Canyon of the Apes**     Near Mount Saint Helens in southwestern Washington is a unique area known as the Land of the Apes. It's a wild and rugged land, heavily forested and beautiful. Near the southern end of the Plains of Abraham is a narrow deep crevice, a window, that leads into Ape Canyon. Somewhere in the deep confines of this canyon, there supposedly lives a colony of Sasquatch, sometimes referred to as Big Foot. In fact, the entire Mount Saint Helens area is claimed to be inhabited by these large, hairy, ape-like creatures. They're seldom seen and to date not one has been captured.

Indians for generations have talked of the Sasquatch, but generally their stories were considered more legend that fact. That is until, in 1924, a group of miners working on the east side of Mount Saint Helens returned to their homes in Longview with stories of being attacked by mysterious apemen. It seems that, while in their cabin during the previous night, huge creatures at least 7-feet tall and covered with long black hair showered them with huge boulders. The next morning, they encountered the creatures again and shot at them. One of the members of the Big Foot clan was believed slain, but was shot so close to the rim of Ape Canyon that he reportedly tumbled into the ravine. The men were too frightened and it was too far around the trail to get into the canyon to investigate further. They fled to their homes and never again went back to their mine, not even to collect their equipment.

Searching parties were immediately mobilized from the Longview area to scour the mountains and seek out these apemen. They were never found, but they did find the cabin wrecked by huge boulders, boulders too large and too heavy to be tossed by ordinary men. To this day, there are expeditions looking for Sasquatch. For since that day in 1924, numerous reports of sightings have been made, but always under obscure circumstances and seldom with substantial evidence.

If you care to visit Ape Canyon, it can be reached by taking a trail from Timberline Campground in the Gifford Pinchot National Forest on Mount Saint Helens' north side. Follow Timberline Trail #240 over Windy Pass to Pine Creek Trail #234. Then follow Trail #234 south for 2 miles and there you will see the legendary land of Sasquatch—and perhaps a real Sasquatch to go with it. To get to Mount Saint Helens (there's a lodge there), take WA 504, east of I-5.

## Omak Stampede and Suicide Race

One of the toughest horse races in the nation is held each year at Omak. The Omak Stampede is a fast-paced rodeo, held the second week in August and climaxed by the "suicide race." All entrants plunge down a cliff and across the Okanogan River on horseback, then race across a finish line inside a crowd-packed arena. Walt Disney's movie, "Run Appaloosa, Run!", featured the Omak Stampede and Suicide Race. So tough is the race that many of the horses reach the arena without riders; some of the riders must be pulled from the river by boat rescue crews and others must be taken to the local hospital for treatment.

Nonetheless, the suicide race continues to be the main feature of the 3-day Omak Stampede and is one of America's most colorful events. On the Stampede grounds is an Indian village with more than 70 tepees where visitors go to watch stick games (a form of Indian gambling) and Indian dances. While the skin drums pulse, colorful beaded and feathered Indian dancers sway in circles to perform for spectators. The activity and excitement goes far into the night. Omak is located on U.S. 97 in north central Washington.

## Home for Lobos

Back in the 1920s, the few remaining lobos or buffalo wolves which still roamed the southwestern states were marked for destruction by government trappers and wolf hunters. But today there's a preserve for the lobo wolf at Gardiner. Operated by Jack and Marjorie Lynch, the 40-acre facility provides a protected preserve for more than 50 wolves, including several litters of puppies. While most of the wolves at Loboland are Lobos, there are six other subspecies, including a big-footed tundra wolf and a pair of small Mexican wolves. Some of the wolves here are as friendly as your pet dog; others are wary and keep mostly out of sight. Loboland is open from 10 A.M. until dusk daily, with conducted tours on weekends. Loboland is located on U.S. 101, just 28 miles east of Port Angeles.

**Dry Falls**  Dry Falls is one of Washington's greatest natural phenomena. At one time during the melting of the glaciers, this falls was the size of five Niagaras in width and 2½ times its height. A 50-foot wall of water dropped 400 feet over a double crescent 3 miles wide. Above it was carved a canyon 50 miles long and 1 to 5 miles wide, including two cataracts greater than any the world has ever known.

Today, the water is gone, the falls are dry, leaving only the mute evidence

The annual Omak Stampede, one of the toughest races in the nation, in north central Washington.

of the awesome forces of nature. Within Sun Lakes State Park are camping facilities as well as boating, swimming, fishing, hiking and horseback riding. Dry Falls and Sun Lakes State Park are located in eastern Washington just off U.S. 2 at Coulee City.

**Forest Giants**

The heaviest rainfall consistently year after year has created this nation's only rain forest in Olympia National Park on the Olympia Peninsula west of Port Angeles. Sitka spruce and red cedar grow as high as 25-story buildings here, and a tour through the area leaves one astounded by the size of these magnificent trees. Shunpike the area around Queets and around Lake Quinault. You can see the forests by automobile, and the Hoh River Forest features a visitor center and self-guided trails. All of these areas are just off U.S. 101.

**Subterranean Seattle**

For a change of pace, you might tour Seattle's underground. When much of this city's central business district was destroyed by fire in the late nineteenth century, businessmen were in a hurry to rebuild. So the city raised the street level, leaving the ground floor of each abandoned building underground. Visitors find this unique tour one of the most fascinating the city has to offer.

**America's Stonehenge**

On a cliff overlooking the Columbia River near Maryhill is a replica of the Stonehenge in Wiltshire, England, which is more than 4,000 years old. Consisting of two circles and two ovals with an altar stone in the center, it was erected by Samuel Hill as a World War I memorial. The outer circle has 30 upright stones 16-feet high and the inner circle consists of 40 stones 9-feet high. The ovals include five pairs of trilithons (two upright stones carrying a third across the top) rising gradually to a height of 28 feet. The center altar stone is 18-feet long. Maryhill is located on WA 14, 95 miles east of Vancouver, near the junction with U.S. 97.

**International Plowing Matches**

The International Plowing Match is held annually at Lynden the first or second Saturday in April. Prizes are awarded for the oldest and youngest contestants as well as for the participant who can plow the straightest furrow. The various classes include large draft horses, shetland ponies and mules. Most of the forty or so contestants come from Washington and Canada. Lynden is one of the few places, outside of Amish and Hutterite communities, where large draft horses are still used for field work. One dairyman uses them to pull his milk delivery wagons which he says keeps them in shape between parade appearances and horse shows. Lynden is just off WA 539, near the Canadian border. Turn off I-5 at Bellingham.

**River Rat Race**

Down the Methow River from Winthrop to Twisp each year, one of the nation's most unusual races is held. The crafts include rubber rafts, canoes, inner tubes and anything that floats, all pitted one against the other. Normally held over Labor Day weekend, the race normally draws up to 100 contestants and spectators line the banks of the stream. Twisp is headquarters for the race, located just off the North Cascades Highway and WA 20 in north central Washington.

**Space Flight**

Unless you're an astronaut, you may never set foot on the moon; but in Seattle, at the Pacific Science Center, you can peer into a lunar crater, sit in the driver's seat of a Gemini capsule and view the earth as it looks from the windows of a spaceship. The major component part of the Science Center is the Spacearium, a circular, windowless room featuring a dome 78 feet in diameter. A cubicle in the center of the room houses two mammoth projectors which throw a film across the entire dome. So when the films are shown of the space missions, it's as if you are there in the spacecraft with the astronauts. James Backstrom, director of the Center, says he doesn't want this to be a museum, but an experience for families who are interested in science and outer space.

## Intertribal Indian Days

The Northwest Intertribal Club's Indian Encampment is held each August near Redmond. Open to the public, this event provides an opportunity to see the ceremonies of Blackfoot, Blood, Cherokee, Kickapoo, Kiowa, Osage, Pawnee, SacFox and Sioux—Plains Indians who have moved west.

The club was founded in the Seattle-Everett area for social contact and preservation of the Plains Indians' culture and heritage. At their 3-day celebration, you'll see Indian games including lacrosse, Indian sign-language prayers and a drum pageant that goes back hundreds of years into Indian history and culture. A camp crier announces each day's events in native tongues. The event also includes a grand parade and Indian dancing contests as well as displays of handicrafts. The encampment is held at Marymoor County Park, closeby to Redmond, which is on WA 522.

For additional information, contact the Tourist Promotion Division, Department of Commerce and Economic Development, General Administration Building, Olympia, Washington 95801.

# West Virginia

Unique Golden Trout, a Sternwheel Boat Race and a Swiss Community

## A Bit of Switzerland

Deep within the mountains of West Virginia lies the community of Helvetia, reminiscent of Switzerland. Founded in 1869 by Swiss immigrants, Helvetia has carefully preserved its Swiss traditions and heritage. Although you can visit Helvetia at any time of year, you'll see it best during the annual fair traditionally held at the end of summer.

Helvetia Swiss folk dancers highlight the activities; you may sample homemade cheese and Swiss food and watch artists or craftsmen at work. If you listen carefully, you may hear a touch of Romansch, still spoken among some of the old-timers. The fair also features a clothesline art show, an archery contest, pottery making and spinning and weaving. Best of all is the warm hospitality of the people and a prevailing atmosphere bred only by the community's remoteness from the rest of the world. It's a community untainted by progress.

Located on a winding, rugged mountain road, Helvetia is not easy to reach. The best route is U.S. 219 from Elkins to Mill Creek; then follow the signs to Helvetia. The scenery along the way is superb.

A most unusual golden trout—a hybrid rainbow that to this day has somewhat baffled scientists—was born at Petersburg in the Potomac Highlands. You can see this species by the thousands at the Petersburg hatchery where it was first discovered and at nearby Spring Run. The ponds and hatcheries are open to the public 8 A.M. to 5 P.M., 7 days a week. You can get an educational tour of how trout—both super rainbows and golden—are reared for stocking the streams of the Mountain State. The golden trout are considered among the most beautiful fish in the world and are highly prized.

### Golden Trout of West Virginia

If you care to fish, there are several streams within a 50-mile radius of Petersburg; but you must first purchase a low-cost fishing license. Trout season is open year-round. The two hatcheries are located a short distance from Petersburg, which can be reached via U.S. 220 or WV 42, south off U.S. 50.

The Green Bank Radio Astronomy Observatory is located in a broad valley entirely surrounded by mountains. It appears like something from outer space; but the giant ears are actually listening antennae. The men working in the buildings are dedicated to the study of sounds in space. "We listen to the music of the stars," one of them said.

### Ears for Space

Of course, among the functions of this facility is the monitoring of space

Green Bank National Radio Astronomy Observatory at Green Bank, West Virginia. *(Courtesy of Commerce Photography)*

for possible radio transmissions from other planets or other galaxies. The area is aptly sprinkled with giant rotating cup-shaped antennae that would dwarf many of the buildings in West Virginia's largest cities. Conducted tours are available from mid-June through Labor Day. Green Bank is located on WV 28, off U.S. 250.

**Sternwheeler Boat Race**

The nostalgia of the annual Sternwheel Regatta takes one back to the days when riverboats were an integral part of America's way of life. Old sternwheelers from several states compete in two heats of the race before a grand cham-

The annual Sternwheel Regatta on the Kanawha River in Charleston, West Virginia. *(Courtesy of West Virginia Department of Commerce)*

pionship competition determines the prize-winner. Only a few genuine old-time sternwheelers are left in the entire nation, but a great many of them are found within this general area. Eight or more usually compete in the race. A number of these boats are still used in river traffic by the companies that own them; however, the majority have been taken out of commercial service and converted into pleasure craft. The race course covers a 2-mile section of the Kanawha River between the South Side and Kanawha City bridges in Charleston, the state's capital.

**Dolly Sods**

One of the most unique areas in all West Virginia is a high mountain plateau known as Dolly Sods. It's a slice of Canada—a boulder-strewn, sparsely vegetated plateau on which the winds are so wicked that most of the limbs grow on only one side of the scrub trees. A primitive campground is located here, and the area has several hiking trails maintained by the U.S. Forest Service. Most unique is the flora growth which includes wild cranberries and gooseberries and a variety of wildflower species. Each spring a wildflower pilgrimage is held at Blackwater Falls State Park and features trips to Dolly Sods. Each autumn, usually in early September, the annual Hawk Count is held. Over Bear Rocks on the northern end of the plateau, thousands of migrating hawks pass here on their southern migratory route. The Brooks Bird Club of West Virginia is instrumental in the hawk count and in trapping and banding some of them. The count is open to the public, however, For the exact date, check with the U.S. Forest Service, Monongahela National Forest, Elkins, West Virginia. Dolly Sods is located off WV 28, west of Petersburg. Check at the Forest Ranger Station at Petersburg for a map and literature.

**Beckley's Exhibition Mine**

At Beckley's city-owned coal mine, visitors are offered a tour of a working coal mine. Located in New River City Park, visitors are taken through 1,300 feet of underground passageways aboard a mine train pulled by a battery-powered engine. During the tour, a coal miner demonstrates the use of a hand auger in preparing to shoot coal as it was done in "pick and shovel days." You'll be briefed on the history of coal mining in the Mountain State in general. Beckley Exhibition Mine explains a great deal about this most unusual way of life—that of a coal miner. The mine is open May through September, 10 A.M. to 6 P.M. daily. Beckley is located just off the West Virginia Turnpike, south of Charleston.

Visitors tour the Beckley Exhibition Mine, Beckley, West Virginia. *(Courtesy of West Virginia Department of Commerce)*

**Hatfields and McCoys**

Logan, in the coal-mining country of West Virginia, is the center of the great Hatfield-McCoy feud. Today, you'll find little evidence of the notorious violence; it's as peaceful as any sleepy little mountain town.

The Hatfield Cemetery is the most concrete evidence that the great feud ever occurred. On a lonely slope at Sarah Ann, a few miles out of Logan, you can visit the grave of Devil Anse, leader of the Hatfield clan. Ironically, Devil Anse died in bed of natural causes at the ripe old age of 82. Inscribed on his headstone are the names of all his children, including Jonse, who aggravated the feud when he ran off with Rosanna McCoy. If you are interested, you'll have to find the cemetery yourself; for people around Logan would just as soon forget the famous feud.

A few of the Hatfields are still living in this part of the state, and occasionally you'll even run across the name McCoy. Logan is located on U.S. 119, southeast of Charleston.

**Jousting Tournaments**

The center for jousting activities in the Mountain State is around Moorefield in the South Branch of the Potomac Valley; although you may find jousting events in several locations throughout the state. For details on this most unusual sporting event, a carry-over from the days of King Arthur's Knights of the Round Table, check with the State Travel Development Division.

For additional information, contact the Travel Development Division, Department of Commerce, 1900 Washington Street, E., Charleston, West Virginia 25305.

# Wisconsin

## Clowns, Lumberjacks and an Orphanage for Wildlife

**Holiday Folk Fair**

Hundreds of ethnic groups gather each November in the Milwaukee area to stage the Holiday Folk Fair. These are not jet setters, but immigrants who build their own houses, raise their own meat and make their own strudels. The food served at the Fair's sidewalk cafes comes from the tables of thirty-four countries. The costumes come from village greens of at least twenty-five countries.

Their pride of heritage compels the forty-five participating ethnic groups to display Spanish castanets, streamers flying from Polish crowns of flowers, Indian drums, shoes with Greek pompons or Serbian turned-up toes. The result is a carnival of diverse heritage, all brought together at this Holiday Folk Fair. German bands, Polish folk dancers and Norwegian blonds give the event a special flavor. The cultural exhibits may portray a Danish candlemaking shop, a Norwegian fisherman's shack, a Far Eastern bazaar or an old English pub. The groups select a beauty queen—Miss Holiday Folk Fair. The event is cosponsored each year by the International Institute and the Pabst Brewing Company of Milwaukee. A visit to the Holiday Folk Fair will help you understand the heritage that makes up America.

**Wilhelm Tell**

A 3-day Labor Day Festival is held annually at New Glarus. It's highlighted by the Wilhelm Tell drama, a delightful episode for all ages. The drama, while not as professional as a Broadway production, qualifies as an exceptional human

Goats and dogs lend an old-world atmosphere to the Wilhelm Tell Festival, New Glarus, Wisconsin.

interest story simply because it involves almost all the people in this small Swiss village. The drama is staged three times, twice in English and once in German.

The festival includes more than the drama, of course; it features continuous live music, dancing, yodeling, flag-throwing events and a large outdoor art show, as well as gourmet European-style dining. Many of the buildings in this town have the appearance of Swiss chalets, especially the Swiss Village Museum and the Chalet of the Golden Fleece. New Glarus is located on WI 69 in southern Wisconsin.

## Cheese Country

The center of the dairying and cheese industry in Wisconsin is Monroe, county seat of Green County. This area probably fits your expectation of Wisconsin. Cheese Days, a biennial celebration, is held in Monroe, just 2 weeks following Labor Day. Monroe can be reached by taking WI 11, west of Beloit.

## Baraboo and the Ringling Brothers

In May of 1884, five boys named Ringling started a circus in the backyard of the Baraboo Jailhouse; they established a heritage for the town which has never ceased to add to its popularity. The Ringling Brothers Circus came to be known as the "Greatest Show on Earth." Today, merged with Barnum and Bailey, it remains one of the two great American circuses still on the road.

The Ringling Brothers long ago ceased to call Baraboo home, but the town has capitalized on its circus heritage. Each year on July 4, Baraboo holds an old-time circus parade in Milwaukee which draws thousands of spectators from around the country. Some 500 horses pull the old wagons in teams of 12 to 40. There are lions, tigers and elephants in the parade.

At Baraboo, there's a big museum called the Circus World Museum which is one of the most educational and attractive sights in the state. The museum is housed in buildings once used by the Ringling Brothers Circus as winter quarters. From mid-May to mid-September, the museum is open daily; and a real one-ring show is staged in a round tent-like building—a professional performance of top quality. In the museum are many colorful old circus wagons, and a train of flatcars is loaded and unloaded with circus wagons twice a day in a 40-minute show. Youngsters will find the display of John Zweifel's animated miniature circus, with more than 25,000 accurately scaled pieces, particularly interesting. Baraboo is located 10 miles south of Wisconsin Dells on U.S. 12.

## Hayward Lumberjacks

Perhaps no other town in America has ever been more known for its logging days than Hayward. Each year, to celebrate that rip-roaring heritage, Hayward holds the Lumberjack World Championships. The 3-day competition, pitting the best lumberjack skills in the nation against one another, usually is held in July at the Lumberjack Bowl on Lake Hayward.

It's a worldwide show with Australian wood choppers battling America's best; Canadian log rollers also compete against Americans. More than $10,000 in prize money is usually awarded. There are two types of chopping events: "standing cut" and the "underhand." In both events, white pine logs 14 inches in diameter are used. The hand-saw competitions called "bucking" are held for both individual and 2-man teams. There's also tree-topping and speed-climbing events. In the topping, the lumberjack scampers up a 100-foot pole and whacks a slice off the top with a handsaw. For the speed-climbing, they race to the top of the pole.

Other events include canoe jousting and log rolling. In both cases, the object is to knock the other fellow out of his canoe or roll him off the log into the water. While the competitors take matters quite seriously, it's a lot of fun for everybody and is one of America's most colorful festival events. Hayward is located in the northwestern part of the state on U.S. 63.

## Old Hayward

A Hayward businessman, Tony Wise, collected a number of vintage buildings and logging equipment, moved it outside of Hayward and formed a village called Old Hayward. The village includes an historic Hayward hotel, the old railroad station, a logging museum and lumberjack cook shanty. The cook shanty is considered the most popular part of the exhibition, for here you are entitled to all you can eat, lumberjack style, at a very modest price. The village also has an Indian village, an old steam passenger train and an excursion boat.

## Animal Orphanage

At Three Lakes, there is a swanky resort which is the home of one of the state's greatest private game preserves. The resort is called Northernaire; the man behind the game preserve is resort operator Carl Marty, who has also established an orphanage for wildlife. When conservation officers find a young fawn whose mother has been killed on the highway, they often take it to Marty; and people from across the nation send him motherless wild animals.

Marty may sleep with a baby mink to keep it warm or he may have a dozen little beaver in his bedroom. Fawns drink from a bottle on the lawn of the resort and are fed by employees of Northernaire. Marty has had just about every kind of wild animal native to North America in his orphanage over a period of years. Marty also has established a private wildlife preserve containing many hundreds of acres. Northernaire is located near Three Lakes, which is on U.S. 45, south of Eagle River.

## Trees for Tomorrow Camp

At Eagle River, there is a camp where you can learn all about today's forests, how they are harvested and replanted. Many groups of school children go to hear lectures; while frequent seminars are held for those who are engaged in conservation and lumbering. The Trees for Tomorrow Camp is sponsored by several paper mills and power companies.

The home of the Hodag is at the northern Wisconsin town of Rhinelander. In fact, you can see this awesome creature at the Logging Museum there. The Hodag is generally known to be the fiercest, most frightening monster ever to set claws upon Earth. The Hodag made his appearance in 1896 when Gene Shepard, a Rhinelander pioneer and timber cruiser, snapped its picture just before the beast sprang at him from a white pine log. The hairy monster was 7-feet long and at least 30-inches tall. Copies of the photograph are in the museum and can be seen today. The creature's backbone bristled with a dozen gleaming white horns and wicked-looking tusks hung menacingly from its jaws. The claws on its short muscular legs were razorsharp. A party of brave lumberjacks led by Shepard later cáptured the monster in a cave by putting it to sleep with a chloroform-soaked sponge tied to the end of a 30-foot bamboo pole.

 It all seemed pretty convincing until the people of Rhinelander became suspicious and confronted Shepard, who later admitted the whole matter was a hoax. The Hodag was made of wood and ox hides, and its armor of horns once belonged to various bulls. The vicious claws were bent steel rods. The Hodag did become a local legend and today is the symbol of the city. Rhinelander is located on U.S. 8 and U.S. 45.

At Spooner, there is a monument dedicated to the wood sculptor Joe Barta, who spent much of his life carving the story of Christ in life-size figures. Today, the carvings are on display at the Spooner Woodcarver's Museum; many of them are astounding feats of ingenuity. For example, the Last Supper

**Home of the Hodag**

**Spooner Woodcarver's Museum**

Fawns drink from a bottle and nipple at Carl Marty's Wild Animal Orphanage, Northernaire, Wisconsin.

is carved in wood with exact life-size figures that took Barta 4 years to consummate. In so doing, he used more than 2,500 pieces of sugar pine and Ponderosa pine. Other massive religious scenes Barta carved include the Crucifixion, Daniel and the Lions' Den, Garden of Eden, the Nativity, Escape into Egypt, the Good Shepherd and the Resurrection.

During one stage of his life, Barta spent most of his free time carving miniatures; and many of them are on display at the museum, including a nude ballet dancer, a litter of suckling pigs, monkeys doing the jitterbug, an elephant strutting with a cane, ostriches, kangaroos, dinosaurs, water buffalo, twenty-two varieties of dogs and an exciting group of galloping horses. Spooner is located on U.S. 53 in the northwestern part of Wisconsin.

For additional information, contact the Department of Natural Resources, State Division of Tourism, Box 450, Madison, Wisconsin 53701.

# Wyoming

## A Mountain Climbing School, Fast Rivers and Wagons West

**Mountain Climbing School**

There is a school in the Grand Tetons that'll teach you to climb a mountain safely. Each summer, hundreds upon hundreds of students graduate from the Exum Mountain Climbing School, center of mountaineering in the United States. Some of those who enroll have been rescued from the peaks and cliffs of the Grand Tetons, but most of those who enter finish on their own power. It's a rugged school, one that builds character as well as wits needed to climb a mountain. Hardly anyone who enters comes away without a great experience and an education.

Glenn Exum, who founded the school, is one of the nation's pioneer mountain climbers and has scaled the Grand Teton as well as other peaks in the Teton Range. Most beginners who take the one-day course find the climbing school a delightful challenge and one that any child over 12 can handle. The school, open from the second week in June until the second week in September, is operated out of Moose, located within the Grand Teton National Park.

**Yellowstone Canoe Trail**

Wyoming has many canoe streams, but there's only one in Yellowstone National Park—the Lewis River, between Lewis and Shoshone lakes. Here is an experience any nature-lover definitely should not miss—a colorful stream, pristine and infinitely beautiful. Many little islands dot the stream; its water is clear and pure enough to drink. In the deeper holes, cutthroat and brown trout are lurking. Along the banks of the stream, particularly early in the morning and late at evening, you may see moose, elk, grizzly and black bears as well as numerous birds.

The quietness of the canoe allows one to come into close proximity of

Students learn to climb at the Exum Mountain Climbing School in the Grand Teton National Park, Wyoming.

such wildlife without disturbing it or frightening it away. Campsites are plentiful along the route as well as at Shoshone Lake, one of the most primitive lakes in the state. You may go for several days without seeing another person, and if you do, it'll only be another canoeing party.

Few people take the canoe trip in Yellowstone for several reasons. First, many are afraid of marauding grizzlies in the back country. Secondly, the Park Service does not promote the trips and you'll only learn about them by asking. Thirdly, no canoe rentals are available closer than West Yellowstone. If you can arrange to have a canoe and supplies available and feel you can find a safe place (and there are islands which are less likely to have bears than the mainland area), you'll find one of the greatest canoe experiences to be found anywhere. The fishing is often good enough for you to replenish your food supply from the stream or lake. For information, check with the Ranger Station at West Thumb or with the chamber of commerce in West Yellowstone.

A canoe trail on the Lewis River in Yellowstone National Park, Wyoming.

**Biking the Great Circle Route**

Another unique way to see Yellowstone National Park is by bicycle, a considerably better way, in this writer's opinion, than in the family car. By bicycling the great circle route in Yellowstone, you become better acquainted with the park and its wild inhabitants than you could ever hope to do otherwise. It's best to arrange for pickup and delivery transportation at the beginning and end of each day for you and your party so you don't have to sleep in unauthorized camping areas. Bicycling solves the problem of parking, and you can see wildlife and sights you would very likely miss if you were traveling by car. By exercising common sense and common courtesy, you'll have no difficulty getting along with the bears. They're too busy panhandling automobile clients to pay any attention to bicycle riders. One should plan about 3 days for the great circle tour; however, it can be done in less time.

Old Trail Town

One of the most interesting trail towns in America, known as Old Trail Town, is located at the mouth of the Shoshone River Canyon on the west edge of Cody. Although there's no sign directing one here, no flashing lights, no shiny paint, no curio shops—not even a hamburger stand—Old Town is an off-the-beaten-path tourist attraction. It was assembled by a gent named Robert Edgar, and all he asks in return for your visit to Old Trail Town is a signature in his guest book and, hopefully, a comment about his work.

With meagre savings from what he could earn at odd jobs, Edgar has accumulated items for his village from all over Wyoming. He obtained a log cabin from the Sunlight Basin north of Cody, trucked it to his 6-acre plot of land, refurbished it and moved into it the following spring. This was the beginning of the Old Trail Town project. "I saw that historical material was disappearing faster than the archaeological material," Edgar says. Mr. Edgar attended Northwest College and later served as a member of an archaeological team working at the Buffalo Bill Historical Center near Cody. He and his wife began looking around for buildings to save. Some of them required little effort to gain possession; in some cases, he traded one of his paintings for them. He picked up an 1890 stagecoach station on Clarks Fork of the Yellowstone River; a miner's cabin from Meeteetse on the Greybull River; plus a blacksmith shop and a trapper's cabin from the same area southwest of Cody. An 1880 cabin built by Charles Carter, first man to bring cattle into the area, was recovered on Carter Creek south of Cody. An 1895 dance hall came from Clarks Fork; an 1883 trading post from Cottonwood Creek; an 1890 store building from Burlington; the 1897 log home of Cody's first mayor, Frank Houx, who later became governor, from nearby. Edgar has all of these plus a saloon and other buildings at his Old Trail Town. He makes his living painting; but in summer, he spends a lot of time repairing and fixing up his Old Town. Tourists are welcome at any time of year; you'll find Old Trail Town just north of U.S. 14, U.S. 16 and U.S. 20, west of Cody at the mouth of the colorful Shoshone River Canyon.

Wagons West

When you're up in a sleek jet flying at close to 600 miles per hour, have you ever wondered what it was actually like traveling across country via prairie schooner? At Afton, Wyoming, you can experience that feeling when you embark upon an adventure called Wagons West. This is an authentic replica of a pioneer wagon train as used by early settlers and pioneers. To provide for your safety, all wagons, patterned after the famous Conestoga wagon, are pulled by gentle teams of horses or mules and are driven by local ranchers or cowpokes.

You can plan the trip for as many days as you'd like, but whatever you decide probably won't be enough. For the trip goes through colorful Grand Teton country; and the flavor is so rustic, you'll soon find yourself unwinding from the pressures of today's world. The trains are brought to a halt early in

A trip through Grand Teton country by pioneer wagon can be arranged through Wagons West, Afton, Wyoming.

the evening to allow you time to explore the area, hunt for exotic wildflowers or search for wildlife. There's time for hiking, fishing, riding or relaxation before dinner. Meals are prepared family style from a chuckwagon; and after dinner, a cowboy sings and strums the guitar around the campfire. Square dancing and authentic Indian dances are featured, too. Guests may sleep in a tepee, under the stars or in the wagon. Pickup and delivery point for the trip is at Jackson. The season begins in June and continues through August. For further information, just write to Wagons West, RFD, Afton, Wyoming.

## Wild Horse Lands

In Wyoming's Red Desert, wild herds of mustangs roam today no differently than they did a hundred years ago. You might wonder what's so unusual about this, but until you've watched a wild stallion and his pack of mares and you've felt your heart leap with excitement at the very sight of these magnificent animals, you could not begin to understand. Several hundred wild mustangs roam this area in small bands, with the largest concentration some 50 miles northeast of Rock Springs. Many local residents will be able to direct you to closer herds.

To get to the main area, drive 45 miles east of Rock Springs on I-80 to Table Rock, then take the road going north. Within half an hour, you'll probably see the mustangs. Be sure to take binoculars, for the mustangs are often wary and the very sight of dust from your automobile is enough to spook them into the next county.

If you like to rough it, to get off the beaten path and enjoy solitude, you'll like the Red Desert. It's not unbearably hot, but it is arid and sparsely populated. A four-wheel-drive vehicle isn't necessary here, and the average traveler can see the wild horses without fear of being stranded. Farther north along the Montana border, one can see undisturbed mustangs in the Pryor Mountain Wild Horse Refuge or in the McCullough Peak area. More than 150 wild horses roam this 31,000-acre refuge, and about 50 still range near the protective canyons of McCullough Peak. The town of Lovell is nearest the Pryor Mountain refuge, while Cody is only 20 miles from the McCullough Peak herds.

**Brinton Ranch**

If you have never visited a working ranch, you can do so at the Quarter Circle A Ranch at Big Horn. Open daily, free of admission, the Bradford Brinton Memorial Ranch is an educational exhibit of a gentleman's working ranch. Among the things you'll see is the spacious, 20-room main ranch house with its antique furnishings; monogrammed linens, handmade quilts and exquisite table settings; an outstanding collection of western paintings and sculpture by such well known artists as Charlie Russell, Fred Remington, Frank Tenney Johnson, Hans Kleiber, Edward Borein and Winhold Reiss; an extensive display of Indian arts and crafts; and a collection of trophies from world-wide hunting trips made by the late Bradford Brinton, owner of the ranch.

Outside the ranch house are the buildings which comprise the working ranch, stables, a blacksmith shop, saddle houses, bunkhouse and servant quarters, an enormous horse barn and carriage barns. Supported by the Northern Trust Company in Chicago, the ranch visit is an opportune experience to see what was once known as the Old West. The ranch is located just off WY 1703, south of Big Horn.

**KOA's Diamond Ranch**

Another working ranch, but with a resort flavor, is located at Chugwater, north of Cheyenne. The 72,000-acre ranch is the location for a Kampgrounds of America camping area and affords guests a variety of activities including rockhounding, swimming in an Olympic-size pool, hiking, horseback riding and some of the greatest western gourmet food in all Wyoming. You can also watch the cowhands work the cattle, harvest hay and mend fences. The restaurant, equivalent to the best you'd find in New York City, is located in a renovated stallion barn. Cabins are available for those who do not wish to camp; and there's fishing with guide service in the lakes and streams on the ranch. The ranch is located off I-25.

**Other Points of Interest**

The South Pass City, an 1867 gold mining town that later became a ghost town, is now being restored by several agencies including the U.S. Department of Interior. It is located in central Wyoming near Atlantic City.

The Bird-Woman Grave, grave of the Indian maiden, Sacajawea, who guided the Lewis and Clark Expedition west, is located in the Shoshone Cemetery near Fort Washakie.

For additional information, contact the Wyoming Travel Commission, 2320 Capitol Avenue, Cheyenne, Wyoming 82001.